THE LIMITS OF FAMILY INFLUENCE:
GENES, EXPERIENCE, AND BEHAVIOR

THE LIMITS
OF FAMILY INFLUENCE

Genes, Experience, and Behavior

DAVID C. ROWE

THE GUILFORD PRESS
New York   London

© 1994 The Guilford Press
A Division of Guilford Publications, Inc.
72 Spring Street, New York, NY 10012

Printed in the United States of America

This book is printed on acid-free paper.

Last digit is print number: 9 8 7 6 5 4 3 2 1

Library of Congress Cataloging-in-Publication Data

Rowe, David C.
    The limits of family influence : genes, experience, and behavior /
by David C. Rowe.
      p. cm.
    Includes bibliographical references and index.
    ISBN 0-89862-132-1 (hard) — ISBN 0-89862-148-8 (pbk.)
    1. Nature and nurture. 2. Behavior genetics. 3. Socialization.
I. Title.
BF341.R68 1993
155.7—dc 20
                                 93-21876
                                   CIP

ACKNOWLEDGMENTS

This book represents the contributions of many people. I gratefully thank Sandra Scarr, David Reiss, and John Loehlin for reviewing the manuscript and making suggestions for its improvement. Joseph L. Rodgers and Irwin Waldman also read the manuscript and made helpful recommendations. I thank Bill Gulley, who transformed my crude drawings into clear and understandable figures. Finally, I thank my wife, Carol Bender, for her patience while I worked on this book and for her careful reading of its chapters. The ideas advocated and the positions taken here are solely my own, and I must take responsibility if any errors remain in the published book.

CONTENTS

INTRODUCTION

Most people believe that different rearing experiences have something to do with differences in the way children turn out. Parents who want bright children are told to read to them, and encouraged to take them to a library rather than to a roller-skating rink. Parents are warned to be affectionate, lest a child become worried and anxious; in the parlance of socialization science, the child may develop feelings of "low self-esteem." Parents are held to blame, or hold themselves to blame, when a child develops a psychological disorder such as schizophrenia. In our cultural beliefs, the idea that family experiences mold a child's life course is strongly endorsed—that is, "As the twig is bent, the tree grows." A social scientist opposing this cultural belief would be dismissed as uninformed and possibly dangerous. In response, many people would recount stories from their own lives. Social scientists would mention the massive research literature showing influences of rearing on behavioral development. Nonetheless, many societies once accepted a flat earth; both experts and cultural beliefs, on some occasions, may be wrong.

This book is about socialization science, which is the empirical effort to understand how children acquire traits from their families and cultures. It proposes the radical theme that one part of this process—broad differences in family environments, except for those that are neglectful, abusive, or without opportunity—may exert little influence on personality development over the life course. The book holds that the environmental variables most often named in socialization science (e.g., social class, parental warmth, and one- vs. two-parent households) may be devoid of causal influence on such child outcomes as intelligence, personality, and psychopathology. The major evidence supporting this thesis originates in behavior genetic studies, some old, others completed since the end of World War II. This book seeks to inform socialization science with what behavior genetic studies can teach us about environmental influence.

The Nature–Nurture Debate

In science, good experimental design is paramount. A well-designed experimental study would vary important variables systematically. Suppose a scientist were to study the effects of both a drug and psychological therapy on depression. He or she would design a study with at least four groups: (1) drug and therapy together, (2) therapy alone, (3) drug alone, and (4) no treatment. Other groups might be added, such as a placebo drug group, but the four groups listed would be essential. If the scientist were to design a study with just two groups, drug and psychological therapy together compared with no treatment, and then to conclude, "Look, psychological therapy works!" because the treated group improved, the research would be dismissed. Even if the scientist completed 10 similar demonstrations, skepticism would remain. After all, might not the treatment effect be attributable to the drug rather than the therapy, if the scientist looked *only* at their combined effects?

Yet just this blatant error exists throughout many studies of socialization. The workhorse of socialization studies is the family study research design, in which associations are sought between family environmental variation and developmental outcomes in children. According to this research, families that provide more intellectual stimulation have (on average) brighter children; families that are affectionate and provide supervision have (on average) less delinquent children.

In all these family studies, however, the research design is flawed. As in the hypothetical scientist's experimental study described above, in the family research design something has been left unaccounted for: namely, variation in genes that parents and children share. In psychological traits, genes may be one source of parent–child resemblance; they also may be one source of variation in family environments. Which is it that influences a child, heredity or family environment? To discover an answer, social scientists must separate the relative influence of genetic and environmental variation, using appropriate behavior genetic research designs. Asking for this effort is not being extremist or advocating genetic determinism; it is just asking for well-designed studies of environmental influence.

To some social scientists, though, the influences of "nature" and "nurture" are deemed inseparable. No organism could develop, this argument goes, without the workings of both nature and nurture, so that they appear as intertwined as threads in a cloth. Or, in Harvard psychologist Jerome Kagan's (1984) beguiling metaphor, they are like water transforming from liquid to ice: The formation of ice crystals cannot be apportioned partly to the inherent properties of water and partly to the external change of temperature. In *The Nature of the Child*, Kagan disparaged attempts to separate nature and nurture as profoundly misguided: "Some social scientists have accepted the unprofitable and misleading dichotomy between biology and experience, in part, because they inherited statistical models that assume that influences due to endogenous forces can be separated from those due to exogenous ones" (p. 10).[1]

Kagan's freezing metaphor may apply to water, but it is untrue of nature and nurture, because understanding the growth and development of a single individual has been confused with understanding the origin of different traits in a population (Plomin, 1986, p. 7). Mary Lou Retton did not grow into an Olympic champion gymnast either without eating her Wheaties or without her DNA. Nonetheless, among the millions of well-fed Americans, we know that *variation* in most physical traits (such as height and weight) is attributable to DNA variation. We regularly observe parent–child resemblance in physical traits, and as verified in twin and adoption studies, this family similarity results from family members' genes (Grilo & Pogue-Geile, 1991). Height and weight are not behaviors, of course. But the principal question remains the same for both physical and behavioral traits: "What influences variation in a population more strongly, genetic or environmental variation?"

Problems with Socialization Science

Although this book emphasizes the separation of genetic and environmental influences, it is also concerned with the separation of the environmental influences themselves. This latter separation can say something about "how" environmental influences operate. Some environmental influences are tied to the family unit; they can be described as "shared" by different family members, operating to make them alike in different behavioral traits. Other environmental influences touch each individual in some unique way; we call them "nonshared" environmental influences.

As defined above, shared environmental influences operate to make the members of a family (i.e., siblings, parents and children) alike. On the basis of this definition, the operation of shared influences becomes a *hypothesis* for personality resemblance in families. If we find that schizophrenic parents are more likely to have schizophrenic children than other parents, or shy parents are more likely to have shy children, or intellectually bright parents are more likely to have bright children, this hypothesis of shared family environmental influence is likely to be invoked. This book's thesis is that shared environmental influences do not create the many observed behavioral similarities in families. Thus they cannot explain why children have such different developmental outcomes (i.e., variation in normal or pathological traits among families). In this way, the influence of family environments on children's behavior has been overestimated, and is actually more limited than many people would believe.

Shared influences correspond to many specific environmental variables mentioned as developmental explanations for children's traits. Any rearing behavior that is relatively uniform for all siblings in a family, but different for children in other families, qualifies as a possible shared influence. Such family characteristics as the level of intellectual stimulation in a home, parents' emotional expressiveness, their disciplining styles (to the extent that these are alike for siblings), parental beliefs about politics and religion, family structure (e.g., whether parents are divorced or married), parental use of legal and illegal drugs, and many other rearing variables all generally operate on children as shared influences. That is, siblings are more equally exposed to them than would be children raised in different families, who thereby are exposed to different family environments. These preferred variables of socialization science are themselves called into question by the book's thesis that shared family environments have little effect on developmental outcomes.

Nonetheless, not all family enviornmental influences are "shared" by family members. For example, parents may favor one child over a brother or sister—a kind of parental favoritism that may spark rivalry among siblings. Therefore, not all parental treatments can be equated theoretically with a notion of "shared" family environmental influences as defined here. The book's thesis (i.e., limited shared influences) is not, then, a disproof of *all* effects of parental behaviors on children's development—because nonshared treatment effects may exist even if shared rearing effects do not.

In Chapter 5, possible nonshared effects of child rearing are considered in greater detail. Although research on nonshared parental treatments is fairly new, I do not believe that it will upset this book's basic thesis that family rearing effects (and other family-tied environmental influences) are, on the whole, limited in their effects on children's developmental outcomes. Nonshared environmental influences constitute an entire class of environmental effects; as such, they include many influences that are not tied to particular parental behaviors—all the way from accidents of embryological development that make nervous systems different (even for identical twins) to vicissitudes of experience that are somehow unique, depending on who is affected, when, and by how much. Along with siblings' genetic differences, these other forms of nonshared environment, rather than specific parental treatments, may explain why siblings are so different from one another in behavior.

The nature–nurture debate, then, may end on a discordant note. Social scientists can accept both environmental and genetic influences as important in behavioral development; no one today advocates either complete biological or environmental determinism. Still, socialization science may miss entirely which experiences are influential for personality development, and in many cases these may be experiences we cannot grasp to change our children's lives.

This book gives evidence for this conclusion and explores its many implications. The weaknesses of socialization science constitute the topic of Chapter 1. Chapter 2 provides the technical "know-how" for interpreting behavior genetic studies. The absence of family-tied environmental influences on personality and psychopathology is discussed in Chapter 3. Chapter 4 looks critically at human intelligence. Chapter 5, "Uniting Nature and Nurture," argues that the measures we label as environmental (including such central ones as social class) may hide genetic variation. Chapter 5 also covers the subtle issue of nonshared parental treatments. The next chapter deals with one kind of group difference rather than with individual differences, covering the lack of rearing influence on behavioral sex differences. In Chapter 7, the book moves beyond empirical evidence to speculation, considering why variation in family environment has so little effect on personality development.

The main conclusion is that socialization science has placed too heavy an emphasis on the family as a bearer of culture. Human learning capacities and biological reproduction enable two modes of trait transmission—one through cognition and social learning, and another through genetic heredity. But the former mode, learning via cognition and imitation, is an extremely general and robust one because people can acquire information from many sources. One source, experiences in the family, may diminish in importance as exposure to other sources increases. Nothing said here reduces the importance of the cultural (but nonfamilial) transmission of beliefs, technologies, social practices, and those behavioral elements that blend into traits. But before we arrive at this more differentiated view of cultural and genetic influence, we need to examine how simple assumptions about family influences may fail. This is the task of Chapter 1.

Note

[1]At the same time, in his recent writings, Kagan has been deeply appreciative of inherited behavioral tendencies: "Temperament has become the preferred name for the variety of initial, inherited profiles that develop into different envelopes of psychological outcomes. An infant's temperament renders some outcomes very likely, some moderately likely, and some unlikely—although not impossible—depending on experience" (Kagan & Snidman, 1991, p. 856).

References

Grilo, C. M., & Pogue-Geile, M. F. (1991). The nature of environmental influences on weight and obesity: A behavior genetic analysis. *Psychological Bulletin, 110,* 520–537.

Kagan, J. (1984). *The nature of the child.* New York: Basic Books.

Kagan, J., & Snidman, N. (1991). Temperamental factors in human development. *American Psychologist, 46,* 856–862.

Plomin, R. (1986). *Development, genetics, and psychology.* Hillsdale, NJ: Erlbaum.

CHAPTER 1

THE PRIMACY OF CHILD REARING IN SOCIALIZATION THEORY

Not long ago, an investigative TV team brought its hidden cameras into a day care center. Inside, they found all manner of neglect, even abuse, of the children placed there; incredibly, one young boy had been left to play alone with matches near a gas stove. Although only a small minority of day care centers have hurt children, a third party's concern for a child is almost never as deep as a parent's— whose love forms the bedrock of the family, the world's most enduring social institution. We know that parents will sacrifice more for their children than anyone else will. I accept it as virtually axiomatic that a parent's presence and concern is essential for a child's physical and emotional security.

The focal issue in this book is, instead, whether different rearing experiences shape differences in children's traits. The term "trait" refers broadly to enduring characteristics—intellectual characteristics, such as reading achievement and IQ; personality characteristics, such as sociability and anxiety; serious mental illnesses, such as schizophrenia; and finally, social attitudes and beliefs. I share with other behavior geneticists (Scarr, 1992) the position that parents in most working- to professional-class families may have little influence on what traits their children will eventually develop as adults. Moreover, I seriously doubt that good child-rearing practices can greatly reduce an undesirable trait's prevalence, whether it be low IQ, criminality, or any other trait of social concern.

To see the very real limits of parental influence, one need only be reminded of how remarkably different siblings are, even though they grow up together. In her book *Life Lines*, the late movie actress Jill Ireland wrote about her heartbreak over her adopted son, Jason, who was

7

a drug addict as a young adult. He was diferent from her in character even as an infant. Ireland wrote:

> From the very beginning there was always a different energy emanating from him [Jason], one as unlike mine as chalk to cheese. His energy blew with an almost Eastern heat and sensuality, an energy that demanded instant gratification and satisfaction. He needed all my attention, something I gave with pleasure and love. (1989, p. 13)

As an adolescent, when her son Valentine was caught sneaking out of the house at night, he accepted responsibility and stopped breaking house rules. Jason, in contrast, left home for days at a time without telling his parents his whereabouts. Perhaps a socialization theorist would try to find some way in which Ireland was inept in her treatment of Jason, or think that Jason was somehow set apart as the family scapegoat. Yet I see in her book a deep concern for Jason, and Ireland made strenuous efforts on his behalf. So why was Jason so different?

Contrary to what Ireland had been disingenuously told at the time of Jason's adoption, he was not the biological child of an architect (a married man leading a conservative life) and an unwed mother. Instead, Jason's biological father had been a heroin abuser, and his mother had been hospitalized several times for psychiatric reasons. Ireland herself became convinced that the "lifeline" explaining how different Jason was from her biological children lay in the DNA of his natural parents.[1] This anecdote, or any other, raises but does not settle the issue of relative rearing and genetic effects; hence our need to turn to the science of child care. This chapter is the story of the weaknesses of socialization science. We know less about child-rearing effects than we think we do.

Parental Treatment Effects in Socialization Theories

The scientific justification for child-rearing influence spans three major theoretical perspectives: Freudian theory, early behaviorism, and social learning theory. All three perspectives emphasized the family context and parental treatments in their explanations for children's developmental outcomes. Freudian theory and Watsonian behaviorism, in particular, focused on early treatment experiences in infancy and childhood. Social learning theory has examined more the possible influence of parental treatments on older children and adolescents. Despite the widespread influence of these theories, both in the past and at present, they each contain empirical and theoretical shortcomings in the insistence on parental treatment as the major shaper of personality and intellectual development.

Freudian Theory

In its most influential period from the 1920s to the 1950s, Freudian theory inspired both practical advice to parents and many research efforts by social scientists. Freudian ideas were widely interpreted to imply a primacy of early (infantile) experience for later personality development (Lomax, Kagan, & Rosenkrantz, 1978). Freud had described several psychosexual stages of development in which experience (combined with constitutional dispositions) molded personality development. The earliest stages involved breast feeding (oral stage) and toilet training (anal stage). Insensitive parenting in the oral period could lead to later anxiety disorders; similarly, inappropriate toilet training—mainly, forcing a child to control bowel movements at too early an age—could lead later to anxiety problems, or even to obsessional–compulsive personality traits. To avoid "traumatic" treatments that could result, in their view, in later psychiatric illnesses, the popularizers of Freud's theory advocated a relatively permissive regimen of child rearing.

Although Freudian theory was a major cultural influence, many social scientists never accepted it even during its heyday. Its internal contradictions, complex logic, and lack of readily observable variables kept strict Freudianism outside the realm of most empirical investigations. Freud's use of inaccurate 19th-century biological concepts, such as Haeckel's dictum that ontogeny (the life of a single individual) repeats phylogeny (the history of a species), also discouraged its use by 20th-century social scientists. Moreover, many social scientists distrusted Freud's empirical evidence because his conclusions about children were based mainly on retrospective inferences drawn from what adult patients had revealed in psychoanalytic therapy. Clinical data are more private and singular than behavioral data collected according to the scientific canons of replicability and observability. Freudian theory thus made inroads into the science of child development without ever dominating it.

Empirical research after World War II also brought central claims of Freud (or at least his interpreters) into question (Lomax et al., 1978). The primacy of early experience lost credence against findings such as the observations of Guatemalan infants by Kagan and his colleagues (Kagan & Klein, 1973; Kagan, Kearsley, & Zelazo, 1978). As infants, these children were raised without much social or physical stimulation; their parents did not play with them, and their movements were restricted. Yet, despite a lack of parental attention to them as infants, by age 10 years the Guatemalan village children exhibited normal behavioral traits, and in most ways they were indistinguishable from children of similar age in Boston suburbs. Case histories of recovery from early emotional and physical traumas also weakened arguments for the primacy of early experience (Clarke & Clarke, 1976). Similarly, the strong claim about the importance of the mother as the sole figure for a child's attachment was also weakened by empirical observations. For example, the children of the *kibbutzim* in Israel made adequate social and intellectual progress, despite their multiple attachments and a lack of exclusive contact with their biological mothers (Lomax et al., 1978).

There is no need to belittle Freudian theory to see that *as a basis for a science of child development*, it is limited. At present, socialization science is not turning to literal forms of Freudian theory for explanation of psychiatric disorders or children's personality outcomes. Social science has moved in other directions.

Early Behaviorism

Tremendous enthusiasm for environmental effects arose in early behaviorism. In place of psychoanalytic clinical insight, behaviorism offered objective procedures—classical and, later, operant conditioning—to change observable behaviors. John Watson was at the forefront of the behaviorist movement that reacted against the subjective and mentalistic psychology prominent in his day. Watson wrote both for the general public and for the scientific audience. His advice that parents not hug or kiss a child may seem harsh by modern standards, but it reflected his concern that the levers of reward and punishment be applied systematically, and that care be taken not to spoil a child.

Watson proclaimed the environmentalist credo when he wrote in 1924:

> Give me a dozen healthy infants, well-formed, and my own specified world to bring them up in and I'll guarantee to take any one at random and train him to become any type of specialist I might select—doctor, lawyer, artist,

merchant-chief, and, yes, even beggar-man and thief, regardless of his talents, penchants, tendencies, abilities, vocations, and race of his ancestors. I am going beyond my facts and I admit it, but so have the advocates of the contrary and they have been doing it for many thousands of years. Please note that when this experiment is made I am to be allowed to specify the way the children are to be brought up and the type of world they have to live in. (Watson, 1924/1970, p. 104)

In fact, the evidentiary basis for Watson's extraordinary statement was slim. His primary, and subsequently most frequently cited, demonstration of the power of conditioning to mold traits was a case study of a single infant, Albert (Watson & Rayner, 1920). The experiment, carried out some time in the winter of 1919–1920 (Samelson, 1980), involved classically conditioning Albert to fear a laboratory rat (hardly equivalent to producing a scholar or a criminal). Presentation of the rat was paired repeatedly with a noise stimulus from the striking together of two metal bars. According to Watson's report, after several conditioning trials Albert came to fear the rat when it was presented alone.

This demonstration—which even today is discussed in many social science textbooks—became hugely popular in spite of its evident weakness. The experimental procedures were sloppy; the baby's thumb had to be removed from his mouth during conditioning trials (Samelson, 1980). Watson himself never replicated the experiment. And, according to Hilgard and Marquis's (1940) authoritative work on conditioning, Watson's simple chaining concept of conditioned responses failed when applied to the prediction of complex habits.

A persisting weakness in general conditioning approaches to socialization is the avoidance of biological concepts. Watson advocated the use of animals in research, but paid no heed to the *continuity* of humans with other animals; he thus took no account of the possibility that biological instincts present in kin species might be present in humans as well (Degler, 1991). Animals were to be used because their behavior was overt (and thus countable and measurable), and also because animal studies avoided the nasty concept of consciousness, which the behaviorists sought to excise from social science. An arbitrary program of conditioning, they believed, should be able to produce any trait in any organism.

Since Watson's early behaviorism, research on conditioning has belied the independence of learning from instinct. Two students of the famous psychologist B. F. Skinner, the Brelands (Breland & Breland, 1961), provided a humorous demonstration of the limits of conditioning. They trained animals for circus acts using rigorous principles of operant conditioning, but despite their best efforts, trained animals often reverted to instinctive behavior patterns. For example, a pig, trained to carry a wooden coin to a "piggy bank" in return for a food reward, started rooting the ground in pig-typical food-searching movements; the rooting became so exhaustive and time-consuming as to ruin the act. In another classic study, the University of Wisconsin psychologist Harry Harlow (1971) demonstrated that monkeys preferred an artificial mother made out of cloth over one made out of wire with a bottle on it. They would go to the food-bearing "mother" when hungry, but they returned to the cloth "mother" for as much time as possible, and also retreated to it in response to fear. In the wild, monkeys cling to their mothers' soft fur in a species-typical protective response.

Sometimes biological dispositions aid classical conditioning. Garcia and Koelling (1966) discovered that rats would learn to associate a taste with a poison-induced sickness, but would not learn to associate the same taste with electric shock. As they anthropomorphized, "The hypothesis of the sick rat, as for many of us under similar circumstances, would be, 'It must have been something I ate'" (p. 124). The notion of biology-independent learning processes thus appears flawed.

Social Learning Theory

Social learning theory is a much more flexible and catholic approach to socialization than Watsonian behaviorism. Without either abandoning basic learning concepts or some elements of Freudian theory, social learning theory broadened the concept of socialization to emphasize humans' strong cognitive capacities.

Albert Bandura (1971) invigorated the theory of socialization with the powerful concept of "modeling," also called "imitation learning." His undeniable observation was that children can acquire many behaviors simply by watching others perform them. This learning process is inherently cognitive: Attention to a model and subsequent encoding of the model's behavior in memory are the crucial elements determining the extent of learning. For a child, attention to a parental model is dependent on whether the relationship of the parent and child is emotionally close and satisfying. It also depends on the power and control available to a parent, as more powerful models are preferred to ones with less power.

Bandura noted the independence of learning and performance. Behaviors were thought to be learned through observation, without requiring a pairing of the behavior with a reward. In one of Bandura's (1965) imitation of aggression experiments, children who watched an adult model kick and hit an inflated, adult-size Bobo the Clown toy were later able to reproduce the model's actions when playing with a similar toy. Children who did not spontaneously reproduce the acts, though, could be prompted to do so with a bribe of fruit juices. They also had learned the behavior, but had not displayed it for lack of any incentive to do so. Thus Bandura reasoned that observational learning should generally occur independently of reward, but that what is learned should be repeated only when incentive conditions are right. A concept of reward was believed to be essential to understanding socialization, because rewards and punishments should decide which of the many behaviors that a child has acquired will be performed. Bandura also noted that performance can depend on rewards to others (called "vicarious rewards"), as well as on rewards directly received.

Some social learning theorists also borrowed from Freudian theory. Early behaviorism had been very molecular in its approach, with each behavior having a separate history of shaping reward and punishment. In contrast, character traits seemed broader and more enduring than such a molecular approach would imply. The Freudian concept of "internalization" was used to resolve this dilemma. In this view, particular behaviors, after sufficient observational learning and reward, become ingrained as a behavior repertoire that continues despite temporary changes in reward conditions. More recent statements of social learning theory refer to cognitions such as "expectancies," which are lasting beliefs about the relation of behavior and reward outcomes. Because these cognitions do not change readily, they are "internalized" aspects of personality that loosen the control over behavior of daily reward and punishment.

Family Primacy?

Many elements of social learning theory seem to place primacy on socialization in the family. Parents seem clearly to be behavioral models. The aggressive parent who yells and hits a disobedient child models the use of violence as a solution to family conflicts. A parent who smokes or who drinks hard liquor models substance use. The social learning conditions for strong influence effects are also thought to exist in the family context because parents exhibit the kinds of power and control that make models attractive, and, moreover, because children who love their parents should be receptive to their teachings. For these reasons, social learning theorists regard broad child-rearing styles, such as parental emotional acceptance versus rejection, as crucial for understanding the socialization process. In general, parents should be using their leverage over the child to shape socially desirable behaviors. The process of imitation nonetheless means that children may acquire parents' negative behaviors, despite the parents' wishes that they do not. Thus social learning processes should generally make children similar to their parents in behavior—clearly in the case when parents model socially desirable behaviors that they wish to see also in their children, but also in the case when parents display undesirable behaviors that are nevertheless effective within the family or in the broader society.

Although the family would appear to be a primary agent of personality development, the very universality of the social learning process raises a warning flag. If children readily learn by observation, then any person—another child, a teacher, a friend of the family—is also a potential source of influence. If vicarious rewards are used to evaluate a behavior's potential consequences, why should a child restrict his or her attention to those rewards received by siblings and parents? Later in this book, I argue that an understanding of cultural transmission processes reveals that parents may *not* be a child's primary behavioral models.

For now, let us consider the principal evidence supporting this conclusion: studies of biological children in two-parent families. These studies seem to provide a strong reason for social learning theorists to adopt a family-centered theory of socialization—namely, the ubiquitous parent–child similarity observed for behavioral traits, and the consistent correlation of rearing experiences with behavioral outcomes in children. There are literally thousands of studies verifying these kinds of "socialization" processes, so that on the surface, the evidence for the social learning model of parental effects would seem unassailable.

Research on Rearing and Child Outcomes in Biological Two-Parent Families

My purpose is not to review the whole literature on socialization. I have instead picked a few studies that serve to illustrate the data in which scientists place some faith.

Although extremes of child rearing have been examined in the empirical literature (Widom, 1989), in most studies of normal personality traits the families were comfortably middle-class and not criminally neglectful toward their children, and the children's traits fell well within the normal range. The child-rearing practices examined marked nuances within a range of normal concern and care for children.

Even in this slight range of child outcome and variation in child-rearing style, significant associations have been found between the two. One illustration comes from a frequently cited study by Baumrind (1967). In this study, the 32 children were enrolled in a university child study center. The parents were middle-class and well educated. None of the children were reported to have serious behavioral or psychological problems, and their mean IQ of 123 made them brighter on the average than about 94% of American children.

On the basis of behavior observations by child center staff members and psychologists, the children were divided into groups. In group I, the children were zestful, self-reliant, and explorative, the kind of well-adjusted kids any teacher would like; in group II, they were more unhappy and socially isolated; and in group III, they were more impulsive and immature. Parents of children in each group were then compared on a variety of measures involving observations of each parent with his or her child in a laboratory playroom and in the home.

For each group of children, different rearing experiences predominated. Group I's parents were both controlling and nurturant—a child-rearing style later labeled "authoritative." The authoritative parents mixed high maturity demands reasonably imposed on children of a particular age with love and affection. The parents of groups II and III were more like one another than they were like group I parents; in particular, they were lower in communication and affection. Group II parents used more control and less nurturance than group III parents (an authoritarian pattern, whereas group III parents used more nurturance and less control than group II parents (a permissive pattern). Remember, though, that none of these parents were likely to be child abusers, and none of the children were likely to be grossly pathological.

Studies of extreme populations show similar findings—imperfect statistical associations between a pattern of child care and children's outcomes. Widom's (1989) investigation of child abuse provides an example. In a matched case–control design, childhood victims of physical abuse and neglect were matched for age, sex, race, and class with children born at the same hospital at the same time, some 20 years ago. Widom wondered whether children who were themselves victims of abuse and neglect would be more prone to later violent and criminal behavior—a cycle in which "violence breeds violence." Widom vigorously searched state, local, and federal records for these children's adolescent and adult outcomes. And indeed, abused and neglected children had a higher prevalence of behavior problems: 26% of the abused versus 17% of the controls had juvenile delinquency records, and 29% of the abused, versus 21% of the controls had adult criminal records. Thus a child who had been neglected or abused had about 1.4–1.5 times the risk of a control child for antisocial outcomes. The outcomes were more dramatic, and potentially more important for society, then the personality differences manifested by Baumrind's (1967) children. Note, though, that about 70% of abused and neglected children failed to repeat the "cycle of violence" in their own lives.

Literally hundreds of studies have been conducted in the search for associations between intellectual experiences in the home and children's IQ and academic achievement. Like Baumrind's (1967) study, the great majority have examined data on biological families. These studies have given rise to "social class" as the nearly universal environmental explanation for behavioral differences among people who differ in income or occupational status. Although its historical roots can be traced, this explanation is so pervasive and influential in socialization science today that it is not commonly tied to a particular theorist or a single notable investigation. "Social class," as an explanation of behavior, is as much a part of the *Zeitgeist* as heredity was at the turn of the century. In a later chapter of this book, a classic study by Christopher Jencks (1972) provides a starting point for investigating the role of genetic inheritance in accounting for social class differences.

In the field of criminology, a classic investigation, begun in the 1920s, was the Cambridge–Somerville Youth Study of adolescent boys (McCord, 1991). Counselors made home observations, which were used later to evaluate the child-rearing styles of both mothers and fathers. Criminal records were collected on the men when they were 45–53 years old. Child rearing was associated with adult criminal behavior. At the extremes, fairly large differences emerged between boys who had experienced good and poor child rearing. In the best families, just 11% of the retraced youths had adult criminal records; in the worst, three times as many (34%). As McCord concluded, "Competent mothers seem to insulate a child against criminogenic influences even in deteriorated neighborhoods (p. 411)." And she wrote of incompetent fathers "who undermine their wives, who fight with the family, and who are aggressive and provide models of antisocial behavior" (p. 412). Fathers' behavior had an apparently stronger association with adult outcomes than did mothers' behavior.

Many forms of serious psychopathology are known to run in families. The risk of schizophrenia is about 1% in the general population, but 13% to the child of a schizophrenic parent; this we know on the basis of numerous Western European studies from 1920 to 1987 (Gottesman, 1991, p. 96). The risk of manic–depressive psychosis is about 0.5% in the general population (Tsuang & Faraone, 1990), but about 10 times greater to the child of a manic–depressive parent.

In an example of how psychoanalysts have historically have envisioned the etiology of psychopathology, the burden of responsibility for schizophrenia was placed on mothers: The schizophrenia-causing mother was thought to be overly restrictive and to engender dependency. In response, it was believed, a child would withdraw by becoming isolated from the family and friendless. Another influential theory of schizophrenia focused on communication problems between parents and children. To present an overly simple version of this "double-bind" theory, "Catch-22" messages from the parent, in which verbal messages contradicted nonverbal communications, were believed to produce disordered thought and emotion in a child. A double-binding parent might nonverbally elicit a loving hug from a child and then say, "Don't touch me," contradicting her own request for affection. In this double-binding explanation of schizophrenia, parental behavior reproduced schizophrenic-like behaviors in a milder form—so an influence of parental treatments would seem a natural inference.

Research on Authoritarianism

In the 1950s, Else Frenkel-Brunswik, a refugee from the violence of Nazi Germany, teamed up with three colleagues to investigate the determinants of anti-Semitism (Adorno, Frenkel-Brunswik, Levinson, & Sanford, 1950). Their study took place in California and included over 2,000 respondents, including, in addition to the "white rats" of personality studies (i.e., college students), public school teachers, nurses, labor union members, and prison inmates. The authors administered questionnaires on anti-Semitism, ethnocentrism, and political conservatism, and found that they all correlated positively with authoritarian personality (as assessed via the F or Fascism scale). Thus they felt confident in concluding that at the root of social prejudice is the personality disposition they called "authoritarianism," a trait tendency to adhere rigidly to authority and to reject democratic values—a core of personality that finds expression in disparate social prejudices. Authoritarian individuals expressed these attitudes in personal interviews (Brown, 1965):

> Concerning Negroes: "They're very closely linked with the jungle. They're built for it." Concerning Jews: "Most all of them Jews talk about sex mostly, or beatin' a guy out of his money . . ." Concerning parents: "[They] always tried to teach me the right thing; being in prison is not my folks' fault." Concerning the determinants of human behavior: "If I ever did anything wrong, it was the Latin in me." (p. 495)

The authors of *The Authoritarian Personality* (Adorno et al., 1950) concluded that this trait and its (sometimes abhorrent) correlates arise because of child rearing. They thought that parents who are unsure of their own social status will adopt strict and punitive discipline styles. In their interviews with authoritarian and nonauthoritarian individuals, they confirmed the existence of stricter discipline and greater demands for conformity in the former's generally lower-class households. A psychoanalytic process was invoked to explain the transformation of punitive discipline into prejudice: Child victims of harsh and unreasonable discipline dare not direct their anger and frustration back at the disciplining parents, who have the power to hurt them further. The children's anger and frustration are instead displaced onto safer social targets (any minority group or foreigners will do), thus relieving the unpleasant emotions resulting from the psychological conflict of normal desires with harsh discipline. And the social approval of prejudiced parents may be earned at the same time.

In an explanation more consistent with current socialization theory than one based on Freudian psychoanalysis, social class differences can be invoked to explain the development of authoritarian beliefs. According to Brown (1965), instead of these beliefs' being products of intrapsychic conflict, lower-class status can lead to anxiety and insecurity because of actual competition among ethnic minorities, poor whites, and immigrants for jobs and social prestige. Authoritarian beliefs would then be ways of dealing with real threats to status and income. Certainly, the degree of authoritarianism increased greatly among Adorna et al.'s (1950) subjects as years of schooling declined: The least authoritarian persons averaged 14 years of education; the most, only 11 years. The authoritarians' admired heroes were Douglas MacArthur, Charles Lindbergh, and Henry Ford; the unprejudiced named Pushkin, Beethoven, Voltaire, and Freud. The second list would be more likely to be learned through exposure to a college education. Yet, for the reasons discussed next, neither explanation of authoritarianism may be correct. In a later chapter, I discuss adoption data on the authoritarian trait.

Limitations of Socialization Studies

Not all studies of socialization share in the weaknesses of the examples just mentioned. Intervention studies employing control groups (ideally, randomized ones) can demonstrate child-rearing effects. Although such studies are few in number, they suggest that giving parents advice on child rearing can help some parents reduce the severity of problem behavior in children (Patterson, 1974; Patterson, Chamberlain, & Reid, 1982). Studies of socialization also excel at describing in detail the psychological processes underlying behavior. Consider Dodge and Coie's (1987) elegant demonstration that aggressive children tend to assume that others want to hurt them, when there is little real threat to justify their attributions, or Coie and Kupersmidt's (1983) demonstration that rejected children recreate their poor social statuses in new groups. Longitudinal studies can be methodologically stronger than cross-sectional ones, but even studies of children at two or more time points fail to avoid all weaknesses of single-time-point studies: Genetic influences can be dynamic and change over time, just as environmental ones do.

What is wrong with the collection of socialization studies described above? It is that they do not provide a shred of evidence about rearing experiences, because they have failed to eliminate the influence of genes.

Imagine that the National Institutes of Health were to hire someone to investigate the effects of two drugs with different active ingredients on childhood hyperactivity. Imagine further that our intrepid scientist were to find some hyperactive children and divide them into two groups—one group to receive *both* pills (drug A and drug B), and the other group to receive two placebo pills that tasted and looked like those containing real medication. Imagine that, lo and behold, the experiment worked: The hyperactive children calmed down and performed better in school. Would our intrepid scientist then approach the executives of a pharmaceutical firm and ask them to market drug A? Would the National Institutes of Health renew the grant?

The pharmaceutical firm's executives would turn the offer down. How could they be sure that the true active ingredient was the one in drug A, not drug B? Moreover, the National Institutes of Health would drop the grant like a hot potato at the next funding cycle. How could this scientist have irresponsibly forgotten to administer different amounts of pill A at fixed levels of pill B, and different amounts of pill B at fixed levels of pill A, as well as the matched amounts? Such an abuse of science would be punished in an experimental study.

Somehow, this exact flaw is constantly excused in studies of socialization. Studies that show some degree of behavioral resemblance *in biological families*, or some degree of relationship between a child-rearing style and a child outcome *in biological families*, are consistently interpreted as though they automatically say something about socialization. They do not. Ten studies with a poor research design (i.e., one that confounds genes and environmental effects) do not tell us more than one. Like the experimental example, biological family studies confound one influence, family environment (drug A), with another, the genes shared by parent and child (drug B). If social scientists conclude some effect from such a research design, they must implicitly assume that heredity lacks any agency.

Parent–child resemblances for matching behaviors can be explained most easily through genetics. Genes possessed by the parent determine the parent's behavior via their organizing effects on the central nervous system. Some of the same genes—or, rather, copies of them—are possessed by the children and may produce the same traits in them.

But genetic effects also cloud the interpretation of child-rearing styles and child outcomes. The problem here is one of "spurious causality." Consider first that a child-rearing style is merely a behavior on the part of a parent. Even physical aspects of the home relate back to parental choices (e.g., of neighborhood, or of whether to buy an encyclopedia or use the disposable income for something else). If child rearing is a trait construct—more akin to a personality trait than to environmental influences independent of human origin—then genes can influence variation in child-rearing styles. And then copies of these same genes may produce a trait in a child that co-occurs with the particular rearing style, just because the gene effect in the parent is what social scientists call a child-rearing style and the gene effect in the child is what they call a personality trait. In the terms a statistician would use, the association of child-rearing style and children's traits can be "spurious" (noncausal). We know, for example, that the rooster's crowing does not cause the sun to rise; similarly, the conjunction of rearing style and behavior does not prove that one caused the other. A parent may hold the belief that reading to a child makes the child smarter, but this is merely evidence of association. In McCord's (1991) and Baumrind's (1967) studies of rearing styles *in biological families*, and in many studies of intergenerational mobility *in biological families*, just this kind of confounding has occurred. Socialization theories may be on stronger grounds when they predict differences among family members—but even here genetics may be confounded with family environment, because (except for identical twins) biological family members also differ genetically.

Another problem is "self-selection" or "niche picking" (Scarr & McCartney, 1983). That is, people self-selected into groups may differ genetically as well as environmentally. In Widom's (1989) work, a comparison was made across two groups of biological families. In one set, there was an abusive or neglectful parent; in the other, there was no legal record of abuse (some control parents may have abused or neglected their children, but this effect would have worked against finding the differences that Widom reported). The groups were equated for age, sex, race, and parental social class, but they were intentionally different in child abuse histories. This comparison assumed no relevant genetic differences between groups. Yet such differences may exist, and they may contribute to the "cycle of violence." Unless we can be assured that the parents did not differ in heritable traits relevant to crime and delinquency, we cannot be assured that the family environmental interpretation of Widom's findings is the correct one.

Any time people select themselves into social categories, genetic and environmental variation may be confounded. Self-selection processes permeate societies as people move through them to find geographic locations and social roles most suited to their genetic dispositions. A clear example is the high prevalence of men with a homosexual orientation in San Francisco. No one thinks that something in the Bay Area water transforms heterosexual men into homosexual men. We recognize that the life of a homosexual man in Every Small Town, USA, is probably more oppressive and intolerant than one in San Francisco; we are not surprised that many homosexuals move from America's small towns into larger, more accepting communities like San Francisco's. If genes dispose individuals toward homosexuality (Bailey & Pillard, 1991; Bailey, Pillard, Neale, & Agyei, 1993), then they will be more prevalent in San Francisco than in Every Small Town, USA, because people migrate from small towns to the big city. These genes, and not the social environment of San Francisco, will partly account for its population's characteristics.

A third pitfall is that of child effects (Lytton, 1990). It is easy to see that parental treatments may respond to, as well as cause, a child's characteristics. The parent of a highly active son would be unwise to keep him cooped up indoors all day; the parent of a very shy daughter would not want to push her into a role in a school play; an active child's parent may have to be more assertive in discipline than the parent of a lethargic child. Child effects do not automatically correspond directly to genetic effects, just as they are not automatically linked to socialization processes. The two explanations are certainly compatible, because parents may be reacting to inborn traits. On the other hand, any environmental source of a child's trait could have the same net effect: The child's characteristics drive the parental response.

In *The Broken Cord*, Dorris (1989) describes adopting a Native American child with fetal alcohol syndrome, a child whose nervous system was damaged in his mother's womb. Before the syndrome was recognized, Dorris spent years of quiet frustration trying to understand why his adopted son, Adam, performed so poorly in school, and trying to find compensatory academic help. Like many people, he was quick to blame social biases in IQ testing for his son's failure:

> I all but dismissed the [IQ test] results. . . . I noted that the WISC [Wechsler Intelligence Scale for Children] was "in significant part culture biased" in favor of "mainstream America"—as if Adam, the son of a Dartmouth professor, living in Cornish, New Hampshire, came from some exotic society. While allowing that, at age ten, such terms as "alike/different," "older/younger" were confusing to Adam, I brought all my anthropological mumbo jumbo into play in denying the accuracy of his scores. (1989, p. 112)

Reluctantly, Dorris later came to admit that the WISC test scores had been right. Although Adam continued to pass from grade level to grade level, "the further on paper Adam got ahead, the further he fell behind" (1989, p. 113).

Where Does Environmental Influence Start and Stop?

On long sailing voyages, fruits or fruit juices were carried and eaten or drunk regularly to prevent scurvy, a dietary deficiency of ascorbic acid that results first in loosening of teeth and bleeding gums, and ultimately in death. The disease was checked in 1795, when the British govern-ment began issuing a regular dose of lime juice to sailors in the Royal Navy. Beyond dietary minimums, however, there is no solid proof that megavitamin doses will either delay aging or improve fitness (Nobel Prize winner Linus Pauling thinks that they can cure the common cold, but the scientific community is skeptical). Over a wide range of ascorbic acid levels, then, the health effects are essentially equivalent: Eating one orange a day is as good at preventing scurvy as eating five oranges a day.

Family environments also exist over a wide range, both physically (in terms of housing, food quality, and community safety) and emotion-ally (in terms of emotional closeness and supervision of the child, as opposed to the most hideous acts of parental abuse and neglect). One could clearly imagine that some family environments are similar to nor-mal nutrient levels—people vary greatly in their environmental expo-sures, but all exposures within a wide range are functionally equivalent in their effects on psychological functioning (Scarr & Weinberg, 1978)—and that more extreme environments may produce consequences as harmful to the psyche as scurvy is to the body.

Our conclusions about environmental effects, then, may depend on the range of environments considered. To some scholars, the very exist-ence of this problem shows the futility of attempting to compare genetic and environmental effects quantitatively. The psychologist Lytton (1990) concluded that child effects predominate in the causation of conduct disorder (fighting and serious opposition to parental discipline). In a critical reply to Lytton published in the same journal issue, Dodge (1990) answered skeptically: "This conclusion [that child effects predominate] is unfortunate because it follows from a question that need no longer be asked in this field" (p. 698). Dodge continued:

> The relative strength of effects can vary greatly depending on the sample, variance of measures, and the pattern of distribution of scores. In a popu-lation in which environmental variation is great (such as an urban area in which poverty and wealth coexist), environmental effects might overwhelm child effects. In cases in which environment variation is relatively small (such as when a society has provided at least adequately for all of its mem-bers), child effects might appear larger than the environmental effects. (1990, p. 698)

Dodge's reply to Lytton is, of course, correct, but his proposed solution of abandoning quantitative estimates is practically and theoreti-cally bankrupt. A politician may want to know whether changing the environment in a working-class home earning $31,000 1990 dollars per year to be more like that in an upper-middle-class home will make a difference in child outcome. Some 40% of the U.S. population is working-class, so if changes from working-class to middle-class family environments make a big difference, then many children could potentially be saved from social failures. If only children in deep poverty are affected by environmental change, this is important too. In this case, though, far fewer children could potentially benefit from the intervention, because children in severe poverty constitute only a small fraction of all children. Moreover, once these gains were realized, no further gains would be forthcoming. The point is that to know the family environmental effect for any environmental context, one must make numerical estimates that control for the influence of genes. Admittedly, behavior geneticists have been remiss in not exploring more fully how estimates of heritability and environmentability vary with social context; however, analytic methods exist for this purpose, and they can be applied to address how genetic influences on conduct disorder vary with social class (see Rowe & Waldman, 1993). The views (1) that heritabilities are *necessarily* nongeneralizable, and (2) that population-specific estimates have no policy relevance, are both mistaken.

The social learning processes of modeling and imitation should work as well in a restricted environmental range as in a broad one. There is nothing in social learning theory to say that *only* children in poverty learn by imitating their parents, but that rich ones somehow learn in some other way. I have chosen Baumrind's (1967) study earlier to illustrate precisely this point: that the families in many socialization studies have been middle-class—that this research has focused on bright and eager children free of the pains of poverty. If social learning does not work for middle-class children, this is important to know—and socialization science must answer why. Socialization science should also explain where along the threshold of family environments socialization effects begin and end. And if these effects are rare over a broad range, then our current theories must be abandoned and replaced with better ones.

Socialization science should ideally produce information about the whole range of environmental contexts. Yet information about environments to which reasonable numbers of children are exposed would seem more important than information on tiny numbers at great extremes. Furthermore, information from many animal and human case studies does not seem particularly relevant, because these examples represent very rare events. In a best-selling sociology textbook (Bassis, Gelles, Levine, & Calhoun, 1991), the necessity of socialization was demonstrated with two case histories of extreme child abuse reported by Davis (1940, 1947)—children who had been raised in nearly total isolation during their first 6 years of life. Both children were placed in foster care after they were discovered. Of the two cases, one girl never recovered fully and died young; the other child eventually made a complete recovery. That nearly "feral" children have at least initial social and emotional problems is not a surprise. The *National Enquirer* notwithstanding, the number of such severely abused children produced in Western industrialized societies is very small. We should not turn to their case histories for answers about socialization in more typical contexts.

Although animal studies produce remarkable effects, their relevance to human socialization science is also unclear. Cats raised in complete darkness have trouble seeing—but what child is so raised? The Wisconsin psychologist Harry Harlow and his colleagues conducted a classic study of rhesus monkeys raised in their cages in an isolation as complete and sterile as solitary confinement, with no contact with their own kind (the separation was initially effected to reduce the chance of disease transmission in the monkey colony, and was only later used as a scientific method). The isolation-reared monkeys were extremely fearful of other monkeys and had confused sexual responses later (Harlow & Novak, 1973). Total isolation rearing, without sight or sound of any living thing, belongs in league with the most severe child abuse; in modern industrialized societies, anything like it happens very, very rarely.

In any case, the exact lesson to be drawn from Harlow's study is unclear, because Harlow later discovered that the severe effects of isolation rearing could be reversed. The monkeys were placed with younger monkeys who had been reared normally. Although fearful, the isolation-reared monkeys allowed the younger ones to approach and play with them. Sometimes an isolation-reared monkey was paired with just one normal monkey; at other times, a form of "group therapy" was tried, in which two isolation-reared monkeys were placed together with two normal ones. In isolation-reared monkeys so treated, normal social play and sexual behavior were restored to the degree that "experienced primatologists seldom differentiate between the normal and isolate monkeys during sessions involving social contacts and interchanges including vigorous play" (Harlow & Novak, 1973, p. 469). That species-typical behaviors return even when disrupted by severe experiences is a chink in the armor of socialization theory.

Socialization science needs to know what the limits of family influence are. The existence of flaws in past socialization research does not imply that socialization processes cannot be properly researched. Some studies of socialization have been attuned to the necessity to control for inheritance of trait-determining genes. A study of schizophrenia has sought family environmental influences on adoptees instead of biological children (Tienari et al., 1991). A study of nonshared environmental processes combines the expertise of behavior geneticists and environmentally oriented researchers: It involves sampling twins, full siblings, half-siblings, and unrelated siblings (stepsiblings), with the latter two groups coming from families formed after previous divorce (Reiss et al., in press). There are many similar opportunities for behavior geneticists and enviornmentally oriented researchers to combine their areas of expertise. These efforts should lead to changes in theories of socialization that reflects the extent and limits of family influence; they should also lead to future theories of behavioral development that integrate knowledge about genetic and environmental influences of all kinds.

In later chapters, attention is paid to who was sampled in various studies as a way toward establishing the environmental context for a given conclusion. In behavior genetic studies, the range is often broader than Baumrind's (1967) sample of middle-class professional families. Many twin and adoption studies include good numbers of children in working-class families—the sons and daughters of electricians, factory workers, truck drivers, and the like. The range represented in Widom's (1989) study is broader still. Most behavior genetic studies probably underrepresent victims of child physical or sexual abuse, or children in rural or urban poverty; unfortunately, these cases are not so rare that socialization science can afford to ignore them. The claims advanced in this book are mainly limited to working-class to professional-class contexts.

In the next chapter, I discuss identifying the influences of rearing while avoiding the pitfalls of genetic confounds. The importance of this endeavor cannot be overemphasized. Much socialization science is based on studies that make no attempt to separate nature and nurture; much socialization science may thus be misleading in direction and emphasis, if not just plain wrong. Chapter 2 introduces basic biological and genetic concepts, so that the reader may learn these methods and be able to make independent judgments of the evidence.

Note

[1]Sadly, Jason later committed suicide. This example is not meant to imply that most adoptions turn out poorly; most infant adoptions turn out well for both the infant adoptees and the families.

References

Adorno, T. W., Frenkel-Brunswik, E., Levinson, D. J., & Sanford, R. N. (1950). *The authoritarian personality*. New York: Harper.

Bailey, J. M., & Pillard, R. C. (1991). A genetic study of male sexual orientation. *Archives of General Psychiatry, 48*, 1089–1096.

Bailey, J. M., Pillard, R. C., Neale, M. C., & Agyei, Y. (1993). Heritable factors influence sexual orientation in women. *Archives of General Psychiatry, 50*, 217–223.

Bassis, M. S., Gelles, R. J., Levine, A., & Calhoun, C. (1991). *Sociology: An introduction*. New York: McGraw-Hill.

Bandura, A. (1965). Influence of models reinforcement on the acquisition of imitative responses. *Journal of Personality and Social Psychology, 1*, 589–595.

Bandura, A. (1971). *Social learning theory*. Morristown, NJ: General Learning Press.

Baumrind, D. (1967). Child care practices anteceding three patterns of preschool behavior. *Genetic Psychology Monographs, 75*, 43–88.

Breland, K., & Breland, M. (1961). The misbehavior of organisms. *American Psychologist, 16*, 681–684.

Brown, R. (1965). *Social psychology*. New York: Free Press.

Clarke, A. M., & Clarke, A. D. B. (1976). *Early experience: Myth and evidence*. New York: Free Press.

Coie, J. D., & Kupersmidt, J. B. (1983). A behavioral analysis of emerging social status in boys' groups. *Child Development, 54*, 1400–1416.

Davis, K. (1940). Extreme social isolation of a child. *American Journal of Sociology, 45*, 554–564.

Davis, K. (1947). Final note on a case of extreme isolation. *American Journal of Sociology, 52*, 432–437.

Degler, C. N. (1991). *In search of human nature: The decline and revival of Darwinism in American social thought*. New York: Oxford University Press.

Dodge, K. A. (1990). Nature versus nurture in childhood conduct disorder: It is time to ask a different question. *Developmental Psychology, 26*, 698–701.

Dodge, K. A., & Coie, J. D. (1987). Social-information processing factors in reactive and proactive aggression in children's peer groups. *Journal of Personality and Social Psychology, 53*, 1146–1158.

Dorris, M. (1989). *The broken cord*. New York: Harper Perennial.

Garcia, J., & Koelling, R. A. (1966). The relation of cue to consequence in avoidance learning. *Psychonomic Science, 4*, 123–124.

Gottesman, I. I. (1991). *Schizophrenia genesis: The origins of madness*. New York: W. H. Freeman.

Harlow, H. F. (1971). *Learning to love*. San Francisco: Albion.

Harlow, H. F., & Novak, M. A. (1973). Psychopathological perspectives. *Perspectives in Biology and Medicine, 16*, 461–478.

Hilgard, E. R., & Marquis, D. G. (1940). *Conditioning and learning*. New York: Appleton-Century.

Ireland, J. (1989). *Life lines*. New York: Warner Books.

Jencks, C. (1972). *Inequality: A reassessment of the effect of family and schooling in America.* New York: Basic Books.

Kagan, J., Kearsley, R. B., & Zelazo, P. R. (1978). *Infancy: Its place in human development.* Cambridge, MA: Harvard University Press.

Kagan, J., & Klein, R. E. (1973). Cross-cultural perspectives on early development. *American Psychologist, 28,* 947–961.

Lomax, E. M. R., Kagan, J., & Rosenkrantz, B. G. (1978). *Science and patterns of child care.* San Francisco: W. H. Freeman.

Lytton, H. (1990). Child and parent effects in boys' conduct disorder: A reinterpretation. *Developmental Psychology, 26,* 683–697.

McCord, J. (1991). Family relationships, juvenile delinquency, and adult criminality. *Criminology, 29,* 397–417.

Patterson, G. R. (1974). Intervention for boys with conduct problems: Multiple settings, treatment and criteria. *Journal of Consulting and Clinical Psychology, 43,* 471–481.

Patterson, G. R., Chamberlain, P., & Reid, J. B. (1982). A comparative evaluation of a parent-training program. *Behavior Therapy, 13,* 638–650.

Reiss, D., Plomin, R., Hetherington, M., Howe, G., Rovine, M., Tryon, A., & Stanley, M. (in press). The separate worlds of teenage siblings: An introduction to the study of the nonshared environment. In E. M. Hetherington, D. Reiss, & R. Plomin (Eds.), *Separate social worlds of siblings: Impact of nonshared environment on development.* Hillsdale, NJ: Erlbaum.

Rowe, D. C., & Waldman, W. (1993). The question "how" reconsidered. In R. Plomin & G. McClearn (Eds.), *Nature, nurture, and psychology* (pp. 355–373). Washington, DC: American Psychological Association.

Samelson, F. (1980). J. B. Watson's Little Albert, Cyril Burt's twins, and the need for a critical science. *American Psychologist, 35,* 619–625.

Scarr, S. (1992). Developmental theories for the 1990s: Development and individual differences. *Child Development, 63,* 1–19.

Scarr, S., & McCartney, K. (1983). How people make their own environments: A theory of genotype —> environment effects. *Child Development, 54,* 424–435.

Scarr, S., & Weinberg, R. A. (1978). The influence of "family background" intellectual attainment. *American Sociological Review, 43,* 674–692.

Tienari, P., Kaleva, M., Lahti, I., Laksy, K., Moring, J., Naarala, M., Sorri, A., Wahlberg, K. E., & Wynne, L. (1991). Adoption studies of schizophrenia. In C. Eggers (Ed.), *Schizophrenia and youth: Etiology and therapeutic consequences* (pp. 40–51). Berlin: Springer-Verlag.

Tsuang, M. T., & Faraone, S. V. (1990). *The genetics of mood disorders.* Baltimore: Johns Hopkins University Press.

Watson, J. B. (1970). *Behaviorism* (rev. ed.). New York: Norton. (Original work published in 1924)

Watson, J. B., & Rayner, R. (1920). Conditioned emotional reactions. *Journal of Experimental Psychology, 3,* 1–14.

Widom, C. S. (1989). The cycle of violence. *Science, 244,* 160–166.

CHAPTER 2

SEPARATING NATURE AND NURTURE

I n a *New Yorker* cartoon, a pair of identical twins is shown reunited, sitting in the waiting room of a patent office, with identical Rube Goldberg inventions upon their laps. In actual cases, reunited twins are known for striking coincidences in their lives. Reunited twins Jim Lewis and Jim Springer were separated at 4 weeks of age and met for the first time when they were 39 years old (Chen, 1979). They had first wives named Linda and second wives named Betty; named their sons James Alan and James Allan, respectively; and named their dogs Toy. They worked as part-time deputy sheriffs in two different towns and pursued woodworking as a major hobby. As children, they had both liked math and disliked spelling; as adults, they had similar smoking and drinking habits. Coincidences? Perhaps so, as many boys are poor at spelling and many fathers want their names carried on. On the other hand, in the Minnesota study of twins reared apart, reunited fraternal twin pairs produced few such stories, whereas many examples of amazing similarities came from biographies of reunited identical pairs (Lykken, McGue, Tellegen, & Bouchard, 1992). This chapter reviews research designs for separating the effects of nature and nurture.

Variability

Social science seeks the causes of behavioral variability. Some children learn to read before first grade, others later. Some men and women are homosexual, others heterosexual. Shyness, impulsivity, honesty, and many other character traits vary enormously among individuals. In an early study of famous men, Francis Galton (1869), a pioneer of behavior genetics, sought to understand variability in social accomplishment—that is, in the type of eminence that would today put a person on the cover of *Time* magazine. Of course, some nonvarying traits also exist in humans, such as walking on two legs and possessing a spoken language. Even here, though, a causal understanding will come only from making comparisons that will reveal variability; for instance, in our species' evolution, new genetic combinations led to walking on two legs and to language, because these human traits are missing in "cousin" primate species.

Ideally, to explain variability, a social scientist conducts an experiment manipulating potential causes. In animal studies, scientists have great freedom to manipulate both genetic backgrounds and rearing conditions. We could, for instance, study aggressiveness toward an unfamiliar person in two breeds of dogs: German shepherds and Labrador retrievers. These dog breeds should provide genetic variability, because gene substitutions have produced differences in many physical and behavioral traits. Dogs of both breeds could be reared under two sets of circumstances. In one, rearing would be relatively harsh and cold; for instance, mild physical discipline would be employed. In the other condition, the dogs could be reared by an affectionate trainer who would never use physical punishment. Thus, the experiment would have four groups of dogs: two dog breeds combined with two rearing conditions. In a test encounter with an unfamiliar person, each dog would be rated for number of snarls, barks, and other threats. The term "phenotype" refers to a measurable, expressed outcome of development. In this experiment, the dogs' aggressiveness phenotype could be predicted from the following equation:

Phenotype score (aggression)	=	Genetic score (breed)	+	Rearing score (condition)	+	Other environmental influences	+	Measurement error

This equation apportions dogs' aggressiveness to different causes. The dogs' breed should have an influence—German shepherds should be more aggressive, in general, than Labrador retrievers. So should their rearing conditions: Those dogs raised more harshly, we might predict, should be more aggressive. Other environmental influences should also contribute (e.g., unique incidents in the life of a particular dog, the dog's mood on the test day). Finally, all behavioral measurements would be imperfect; hence the need to include a measurement error term.

Scott and Fuller (1965) conducted actual studies of behavior genetics in dogs that were similar to the example above. For example, cocker spaniels showed much less fear of people than basenji hounds. The authors then formed selective crossbreeds to test for the genetic determination of fear. Crossing cockers with basenjis resulted in offspring with half their genes from a cocker parent and half from a basenji parent. Because the crossbred dogs were raised either by a cocker mother or by a basenji mother, rearing effects were also tested. The maternal rearing environment had no influence on fear, but all the crossbred puppies were as fearful as their basenji parent. From this experiment and other genetic crosses, Scott and Fuller concluded that fearfulness of people may be determined by a dominant gene. The crossbred dogs, all inheriting one copy of this gene from their basenji parent, should always show fearfulness of people.

In human behavior genetics, these ideal experimental designs cannot be implemented. We cannot assign all redheads to one rearing condition and all brunettes to another, for both practical and ethical reasons. Nor can we make planned genetic crosses. So to determine the causes of behavior, a research design must capitalize on "experiments" of nature, in which either environment or heredity is "manipulated" by means of the social and genetic relatedness of pairs of relatives. Adoption affords a nuclear family structure like that of an ordinary family, but without the genetic relatedness of family members. Twins afford two levels of genetic relatedness—100% in monozygotic (MZ; one-egg) twins, and 50% in dizygotic (DZ; two-egg) twins. Uncle–nephew, aunt–niece, and grandparent–grandchild pairs afford a weaker (25%) level of genetic relatedness. If MZ twin brothers or sisters marry nontwin individuals, their children would be *socially* cousins, but *genetically* related at the same level as half-siblings (25%, instead of most cousins' 12.5%). These different relatedness levels occur because closer relatives share more genes affecting a trait than more distant relatives do.

As in the hypothetical dog study proposed above, human behavior genetic studies can apportion children's or adults' phenotypes to different causal influences. An equation expressing the phenotype in terms of underlying causes is as follows:

Phenotype score		Shared environment score		Nonshared environment score		Genetic score		Measurement error
	=		+		+		+	

It is essential to understand each component shown in this equation. Let us start with the two environmental terms—"shared" and "nonshared" environment. The central message of this book is that we can learn much about the family environment by teasing shared and nonshared influences apart.

Environmental Components of Variation

As in the hypothetical dog animal study, shared environment is a "manipulation" of rearing conditions. The dog experiment would have had just two conditions: loving versus harsh discipline. All dogs in the "loving" condition would have been exposed to affectionate rearing; all dogs in the "harsh" condition would have had a cold, discipline-minded trainer. Family environments may also differ greatly. Some families have more resources, in terms of education and income, than others. Families may differ in their emotional climates and in their neighborhood characteristics as well.

Shared Environmental Variation

The shared environment score captures these broad family differences; by definition, composite shared environmental influences act in common on siblings (or on parent and child) to make them alike in their trait phenotypes. Imagine that we could score siblings for all environmental resources that affect their intellectual development equally (e.g., books in the home, parental vocabulary, nutrition). Now consider two families living in different parts of town. One family might have more resources to promote the growth of intelligence than the other. In the first one, children A and B might have a hypothetical shared environment score (when an average family scores 100) of 110. In the other family, on the poorer side of the town, the shared environment score of the two siblings might be just 90. That is, in the second family, this score would be exactly 90 for sibling A and exactly 90 for sibling B. A shared environment score is a *composite*, therefore, of all influences that the two siblings have in common.

In the case of IQ, the total variation is 225 (the standard deviation of IQ scores, 15, is squared). If, say, behavior genetic studies have estimated that shared environmental variation accounts for 30% of this total, the amount of this variation would be estimated at 67.5 (one would multiply .30 × 225). This number represents the *maximum* variation in

IQ attributable to all family rearing conditions that make siblings alike in intelligence. Any measured (shared) rearing condition must explain *less* variation than the composite shared estimate (of which it is a part). For example, if "number of books in the home" correlated .27 with IQ, then it would explain 7% of the variation in IQ ("variance explained" is the correlation coefficient squared). Thus, its part of total IQ variation would be 15.7 (.07 × 225). Other shared rearing influences, such as parental vocabulary or neighborhood schools, must account for the remainder, 51.8 (i.e., 67.5 − 15.7).

Behavior genetic studies can give us a numerical estimate of composite shared rearing influences. The shared rearing estimate is defined as the ratio of shared environmental variation to phenotypic variation, and is given the symbol c^2. In the IQ example, c^2 is .30, a ratio of 67.5/225. This ratio has important policy implications, because it indicates how a phenotype might be changed by altering the rearing conditions of children with poor phenotypes to be like those of children with good ones. The greater the shared rearing estimate, the more change can be expected to follow from changing rearing conditions. Christopher Jencks (1980), writing for an audience of sociologists, has recognized the policy importance of shared rearing estimates (note that in this quotation, a different symbol is used for shared rearing):

> . . . many policy proposals consist, in essence, of providing all families with advantages currently enjoyed by the privileged. If e^2_c [the shared rearing estimate] is initially large for a given phenotype, successful efforts along this line can be expected to substantially reduce the total variance of the relevant phenotype and greatly improve the relative position of the disadvantaged. (p. 734)

Thinking of particular environmental influences, however, we must realize that they do not always make siblings alike. For instance, for siblings close in age, the quality of neighborhood schools is generally a shared rearing influence. But for particular siblings who are some years apart in age, it could be also partly unshared: For example, a school district might not pass a bond issue, so that educational quality would be worse for one sibling than for another. Hence a measured environmental influence might make some contribution to our theoretical estimate of shared rearing influence (i.e., making siblings alike); it might also make some contribution to the estimate of nonshared influence (i.e., making siblings different). To some extent then, shared and nonshared rearing influences may be like the two sides of a coin.

Nonshared/Unshared Environmental Variation

Unshared environmental influences touch each individual in a unique way. By definition, they are uncorrelated across siblings (or parent and child), and so operate to make family members dissimilar in a phenotype. First, all the accidents of embryological development are unshared; they can affect siblings differently, because each child has a different birth history. Even identical twins can have different *in utero* developmental courses (some MZ twins actually compete with each other for maternal nutrients, resulting in the twins' having very dissimilar weights and health statuses at birth). Parental favoritism can be an unshared influence: A sibling receiving more love may develop differently from his or her less favored sibling. Friendship networks can act as another unshared influence. Although some siblings may befriend the same individuals, most often, because of their different ages, they belong to different friendship groups. A special person (e.g., a particularly influential teacher or friend) or an emotionally intense experience (e.g., a very severe illness) can be yet another unshared influence. The list of potential unshared influences is extremely long (see Rowe & Plomin, 1981, for other examples).

Behavior genetic studies may yield a numerical estimate of composite nonshared (synonym: unshared) environmental variation. The nonshared rearing estimate is defined as the ratio of nonshared environmental variation to phenotypic variation, and is given the symbol e^2.

Genetic Variability

A discussion of genetic variability requires terminology that may be unfamiliar. These terms are defined as they appear. A "locus" is the physical location of a gene on a chromosome (e.g., the genetic material). Chromosomes come in pairs; in each pair, one is inherited from one's mother, and the other is inherited from one's father. Therefore, except for those genes located on the sex-determining X and Y chromosomes, a person has two distinct physical copies of each gene (one maternal in origin, the other paternal). In a population, all genes at a locus may be exactly the same in their internal composition. Such a gene is then said to be "monomorphic," meaning that it comes in just one form. If we use the letter D to symbolize this gene, then Joe's genotype would be DD, because he possesses this gene in two copies. Bob's genotype is also DD, as is everyone's in this population. Genes at other "loci" (the plural of locus) may have different internal compositions; that is, they can come in different forms. When this occurs, the gene is said to be "polymorphic." The technical term for different forms of a gene is "alleles." Thus, we may use a capital letter A to represent one allele, and a lowercase letter a to represent another. For this gene, an individual may have any one of three genotypes: AA, Aa, or aa. The term "genotype" refers to a person's exact genetic makeup at a genetic locus.

For instance, in the familiar ABO blood group, three alleles exist: A, O, and B. A child will inherit one allele from the mother and one from the father, yielding the child's blood group. At the ABO locus, one child may inherit the genotype AB, whereas a sibling may inherit AO. The first child has blood type AB; the second has blood type A, because a single O allele does not change blood type. With three alleles, there are six possible blood group genotypes in human populations: blood type A (AA or AO), blood type O (OO), blood type B (BO or BB), and blood type AB (AB).

Such varying alleles may influence trait phenotypes.[1] That is, when they influence a continuous (many-valued) trait (like IQ or height), a substitution of one gene for another will change its value. Suppose that a hypothetical A locus influences young children's activity levels when counted as the "number of fidgets per minute." Table 2.1 provides examples of different types of gene effects for this locus.

A gene locus's effect can be called "additive" when the substitution of one allele for another increases the fidgeting rate linearly. As shown in Table 2.1, if it is assumed that the effects of the A locus are additive,

TABLE 2.1. The Fidgeting Gene Locus: Examples of Different Gene Effects

Type of effects	Fidgets per minute for fidgeting locus genotype:		
	AA	Aa	aa
Additive effects	6	4	2
Dominance effects	6	6	2
Epistasis effects in presence of B locus genotype:			
BB	6	4	2
Bb	6	4	2
bb	2	2	2

children who possess genotype AA fidget an average of six times per minute; those who possess Aa fidget four times per minute; and those who possess aa fidget just twice per minute. In other words, the difference in fidgeting rates between genotypes is always *two* fidgets per minute (i.e., 6 – 4 is 2, and 4 – 2 is also 2), so that a substitution of one allele for another always increases the trait by an equal amount.

Additive gene effects may make biological relatives resemble one another in a trait. The average level of genetic similarity indicates how likely two individuals are to possess the same alleles. The greater the number of alleles matching in two people, the closer their numerical trait scores. In our example, two AA individuals both fidget six times per minute, but AA and aa individuals fidget at different rates. Siblings or parent–child pairs (first-degree relatives) share, on average, 50% of their alleles at different loci affecting a trait; half-siblings and uncle–nephew or aunt–niece pairs (second-degree relatives) share, on average, 25%; and MZ twins, of course, share 100%. Thus, allele substitutions influence a trait so that more closely related biological relatives are more alike in their trait scores.

A statistical measure for similarity is the correlation coefficient. When marriage is approximately random in a population (i.e., spouses are not matched for a particular continuous trait to a greater extent than would happen by chance), then the genetic correlation for first-degree relatives is close to .50; for second-degree relatives, close to .25; and for third-degree relatives (e.g., cousins), close to .125 (see Falconer, 1981, for mathematical derivations; see also Plomin, DeFries, & McClearn, 1990). For MZ twins, it is 1.00. Thus, different groups of genetic relatives can be used to test for additive genetic influence on trait variation.

Other kinds of genetic influence are "nonadditive." These include genetic dominance and epistasis. "Genetic dominance" refers to intra-locus interactions among alleles. As shown in Table 2.1, if it is assumed that the effects of the fidgeting locus are determined by genetic dominance, individuals with genotypes AA and Aa fidget an average of six times per minute, whereas aa individuals fidget at only two times per minute. Somehow, the A and a alleles interact, so that having one of each has the same total effect as having two A alleles.

Another kind of genetic nonadditivity is "epistasis," which refers to interlocus interactions among genes. As shown in Table 2.1, the effects of the fidgeting locus might depend on that of a hypothetical B locus, somewhere else in the genome. When a person possesses genotypes BB or Bb, the fidgeting locus acts just as we would expect: Fidgeting

increases from genotype aa to genotype AA. But in the presence of genotype bb, something unexpected happens: Regardless of the particular
fidgeting locus genotype, the rate of fidgeting is only two times per
minute. With epistatic effects, a trait's numerical value depends on the
whole *configuration* of genes. Only identical twins share all nonadditive
gene effects, because they are the only kind of biological relatives who
possess exactly the same genotypes at all loci.

The "heritability coefficient" summarizes the strength of genetic
influence on trait variation in a particular population. It is defined as
the ratio of genetic variation to phenotypic variation, and is given the
symbol h^2. The more a trait changes as one allele is substituted for
another, the greater trait heritability is. As with shared environmental
variation, heritability can be estimated from behavior genetic research
designs. Heritability is called "narrow-sense" if it just estimates additive
gene effects; it is called "broad-sense" if it estimates all (additive plus
nonadditive) genetic effects.[2]

Heritability will vary from one population to another, depending on
the kinds of genotypes and environmental exposures present. For
instance, the heritability of skin color will be greater in a racially diverse
population than in Sweden. In Sweden, environmental effects will be
greater if we compare Swedes returning from a Mediterranean summer
vacation with those staying home (untanned vs. tanned skin). Nonetheless, heritability coefficients may be generalizable over a range of environmental conditions, and the degree of generalizability can be evaluated empirically.

Research Designs for Separating
Nature and Nurture

Separated-Twins Design

The study of separated twins is the most direct method for estimating a
trait's heritability. Separated MZ twins are reared by different parents,
and hence have different family environments, whereas they possess
identical heredity. Thus the effects of heredity are distributed against a
background of different family environments, and we can infer genetic
influence on a trait from resemblance in separated twins. Data exist from
five studies of separated twins—three quite small studies (Juel-Nielsen,
1980; Newman, Freeman, & Holtzinger, 1937; Shields, 1962) and two

larger, more recent studies (Bouchard, Lykken, McGue, Segal, & Telle-gen, 1990; Pedersen, Plomin, McClearn, & Friberg, 1988). The Swed-ish twin study (Pedersen et al., 1988) is unique because the separated MZ and DZ twins were identified through national records, rather than being recruited through advertisement or word of mouth, and because of a larger sample size (about 200 pairs of twins of each type separated early in life). A sixth study of separated twins, by the British educational psychologist Cyril Burt (1955), has been the center of controversy over possible scientific fraud, and the proper response of most social scien-tists has been to exclude his data from consideration.

In a separated-twins study, the heritability estimate (h^2) is merely the trait correlation for all MZ twin pairs. Thus we can write:

$$r_{MZ} = \frac{\text{Genetic variation}}{\text{Phenotypic variation}} = h^2$$

As noted earlier, this heritability has a special interpretation: It is called "broad-sense" heritability because it reflects the action of all genes. MZ twins share the same pattern of genes at all loci, so that nonaddi-tive gene effects also contribute to their behavioral resemblance in a way they cannot contribute to that of other biological relatives, who do not share the whole pattern of genes relevant to a trait. In the nature–nurture arena, we are particularly interested in the *maximum* possible influence of genes. Indeed, the best guess we could make about the psychologi-cal and physical traits of another person, without interviewing him or her directly, would be based upon characteristics of the person's MZ twin (if one could be found). Nothing we might discover about conditions of rearing, schooling, neighborhood, religion, or schoolyard friends would come close to the usefulness of an MZ twin in providing information about this person's height, weight, eye color, temperament, mental ill-ness, habits, IQ, values, or nearly any other trait.

Any single type of study design is, of course, subject to particular weaknesses; therefore, my emphasis in this book is on the number of different studies using different approaches and converging on similar conclusions. Critics of separated-twins studies mention two weaknesses of this design: (1) lack of total separation of the twins and (2) selective placements.

Because MZ twins are typically separated for a great number of reasons, and because they are sometimes adopted by relatives, their separations are not always as complete as they would be in an ideal (but impractical) experimental study. A trio of ardent critics of separated-twins studies, Lewontin, Rose, and Kamin (1984), mention the stories of separated twins who were not completely separated, such as the following: "Benjamin and Ronald had been 'brought up' in the same fruit-growing village, Ben by his parents, Ron by the grandmother. . . . They were at school together. . . . They have continued to live in the same village" (p. 108). Although it is true that MZ twins reared apart are sometimes not perfect separations, it is also true that first cousins often have similar degrees of contact: They too may live in the same village, in houses not that far apart, with parents who are siblings and socialize together, and with many opportunities to play and visit together. If social contacts can miraculously make people alike, then why do we not find great resemblance in cousins—to say nothing of nontwin siblings, who have even more social contact?

A more scientifically convincing response to this objection is that the timing of separation, the frequency of social contacts, and other contact measures have been included in separated-twins studies as variables themselves. Thomas Bouchard (1983), in his reanalysis of the three older studies of separated twins, found that separation age and degree of contact failed to condition the MZ twins' IQ resemblance. Similar results have been obtained for separation variables in the Swedish (Pedersen et al., 1988) and Minnesota (Bouchard et al., 1990) separated-twins studies: Separated MZ twins who have had later contact have generally not been found to be more alike in either personality or IQ.

Thus, the occasional social contact of "separated" twins may not introduce strong biases. A more serious problem in adoption studies is that of selective placement. Although this was not the case in Jill Ireland's adoption of Jason (see Chapter 1), many adoption agencies do consciously attempt to match the social status of adopting parents with that of the biological parents. In a completely scientific study, adoption agencies would want to match adoptees randomly with adoptive parents— so that (for example) a factory worker would rear a child of a doctor, at least on occasion. The effect of selective placement is most serious for IQ and related traits, because these correlate most highly with years of education and income, which are used to assess social class. If we think that selective placement has occurred, its quantitative strength is the correlation between the trait as measured in the biological parent (usually the unwed mother of the adoptee) and as measured in the adoptive parent. The strength of selective placements varies among adoption studies. In Bouchard et al.'s (1990) study of twins raised apart, the social class of the adoptive fathers of reared-apart twins correlated .27; in the Colorado Adoption Project (Plomin & DeFries, 1985), there was no association of biological and adoptive parents' social class.

Selective placement represents a potential bias for both genetic and environmental interpretations of adoptive studies. It upsets the environmental part of an adoptive design, because the adopted-away children may be raised in homes resembling what their homes would have been like had they stayed with their biological parents. It also upsets the genetic part of the adoptive design: Selective placement may make the genotypes of adoptive children and adoptive parents similar, whereas they would not be if the children were randomly assigned to adoptive families.

Fortunately, selective placement can be handled in behavior genetic studies. When analyzing their data statistically, behavior geneticists can allow for selective placement effects. For a genetic effect to be accepted, it must be greater (quantitatively) than all the adoptee–adoptive parent resemblance that could occur as a result of selective placement. Replication of results across studies with low or high levels of selective placement is another protection against false leads. Finally, because placement selectivity is most strongly oriented toward the IQ trait domain, it is seldom a concern when other traits are investigated.

Nontwin Adoption Designs

In the last 20 years, adoption in the United States has become more diverse. In the traditional adoption process, a child was adopted in early infancy, and records on the biological parent(s) were closed to the adoptive parents. Most children were given up for adoption by unwed mothers, who sometimes left home and lived in church-run homes where they could bear their children while avoiding social stigma and ostracism. Today, a pregnant girl is not a social outcast, and she may decide to keep her baby rather than relinquish the child for adoption. Moreover, abortion is an option for ending an unwanted pregnancy. If a child is relinquished today, the varieties of adoption are much greater: Placements are increasingly made by private attorneys rather than agencies, and it is not uncommon for the adoptive parents to know the biological parent(s). Despite these many changes, the major U.S. adoption studies since World War II have used traditional adoptions. The largest postwar American adoption studies, cited later in this book, are the Minnesota Adolescent Adoption Study (Scarr & Weinberg, 1983); the Minnesota Transracial Adoption Study (Scarr & Weinberg, 1976); the Colorado Adoption Project (Plomin & DeFries, 1985); and the Texas Adoption Project (Horn, Loehlin, & Willerman, 1979).

The adoption study is the most direct means of estimating the shared rearing component of variation. If selective placement is ignored, a trait correlation for unrelated sibling pairs—who may be either different children adopted into a family, or an adoptee and a biological child of the adopting parents—directly estimates shared rearing variation (c^2):

$$r_{\text{unrelated pairs}} = \frac{\text{Shared environmental variation}}{\text{Phenotypic variation}} = c^2$$

The same equation holds for shared rearing influence when the adoptive parent and adoptee are correlated.

Although these comparisons are completely informative for shared environmental effects, it is desirable for an adoption study also to estimate genetic effects. The two main strategies are (1) the "full" adoption design and (2) the "matched" adoption design. In the full adoption design, traits are assessed on the biological parent(s) (usually the mother) who relinquished a child for adoption. The Texas Adoption Project is an example of a study employing this design. The study was initiated when Joseph Horn and his colleagues found a private adoption agency in Texas that routinely gave the unwed mothers IQ and personality tests. With this information, the investigators completed the full adoption design by relocating the adoptees and their adoptive families. In this design, genetic effects are estimable from the trait correlation of the adoptees and their biological parent.

In an alternative design, adoption families can be compared to biological families matched for parental age and social class. In the latter, the correlations contain both rearing and heredity components. For example, the sibling correlation in biological families estimates the following:

$$r_{\text{related pairs}} = \frac{\text{Shared environment}}{\text{Phenotypic variation}} + \tfrac{1}{2} \times \left\{ \frac{\text{Shared heredity}}{\text{Phenotypic variation}} \right\}$$

Given this mathematical expectation, we can find the genetic effect by subtracting the correlation for *unrelated* pairs from that for *related* pairs in the matched families, assuming that the match of the two sets of families was good. The latter can be checked by comparing environmental assessments on the two sets of families for differences in mean levels and variances. Other opportunities may arise when an adoptive family has both a biological child and an adoptee. In these cases, there is no need to match two sets of families, because the comparison can be made solely within the adoptive families in which the two children were reared. Even critics of behavior genetic methods acknowledge that this is a powerful research design. As Lewontin et al. (1984) observe, "There is plenty of room for any genetic effect to display itself in a higher correlation for the biological parent–child pairs" (p. 113).

The main criticism of adoption studies is the possibility that adoptive parents treat adoptees differently from the way that biological parents treat their own children. A hypothesis of differential treatment is worthy of some concern, but it is *post hoc* and nonspecific. After all, treatments may differ, but adoptive parents still use the same rewards, punishments, and examples to influence their children. If this is true, then rearing in adoptive families should show a direct relationship to child outcome (especially in young children, who cannot cognitively appreciate that they are "adopted"), even if the differences in treatment move personality development in a somewhat different direction in adoptive families than in biological ones.

As to a special knowledge of adoption, at least one test of its possible biasing effects yielded no significant findings. If a sense of similarity to a child *makes one similar to that child*, then parents' perceptions of similarity should drive actual similarity. This test was applied by Scarr, Scarf, and Weinberg (1980) in both adoptive and biological families. In the domains of intelligence and temperament, family members were completely inaccurate in guessing whether they were alike or unalike. Because the perceptions of resemblance were such a poor guide to actual resemblance in this case, it is hard to imagine how feelings about similarity might have guided personality development.

Classical Twin Designs

Most twin studies do not involve the rare pairs of twins who were separated and raised apart. Instead, two kinds of reared-together twins (MZ and DZ) are compared. It was only early in the 20th century that the existence of two biologically distinct types of twins was first acknowledged. It was then realized that the number of same-sex DZ twins must equal the number of opposite-sex twins: DZ twins are simply genetic siblings who happen to have shared a pregnancy, and half of all siblings are born boy–girl pairs and the other half are born either boy–boy or girl–girl pairs. By counting the number of twins, and determining how many of these are opposite-sex twins, a researcher can do a simple calculation to find the approximate number of MZ twins. In 1924, an American psychologist, Merriman, and a German dermatologist, Siemans, first proposed using the method of comparing MZ with DZ twins to infer the degree of genetic influence. They discovered that MZ twins' correlation for the size of birthmarks was .40 and that for DZ twins was .20, exactly as one would expect for a trait with purely genetic variation and unshared environmental variation (cited in Rende, Plomin, & Vandenberg, 1990). For birthmarks, doubling the DZ twin correlation reproduces the MZ twin correlation, as expected on the basis of these equations:

$$r_{\text{MZ pairs}} = \frac{\text{Genetic variation}}{\text{Phenotypic variation}} = h^2$$

and

$$r_{\text{DZ pairs}} = \frac{1}{2} \times \left\{ \frac{\text{Genetic variation}}{\text{Phenotypic variation}} \right\} = \frac{1}{2} h^2$$

The remaining variation—the difference between the MZ twin correlation and 1.00—represents the proportion of phenotypic variation that is attributable to unshared environmental sources and measurement error (reliability limitations are also inherent in physical measurements).

Composite shared rearing influences can also enter into this twin design. In a pure case of shared rearing influence, the MZ and DZ twin correlations would be equal because of the twins' common rearing experiences. Thus, the correlations can be expressed as follows:

$$r_{\text{MZ twins}} = r_{\text{DZ twins}} = \frac{\text{Shared environmental variation}}{\text{Phenotypic variation}} = c^2$$

When twin samples are large, a twin study can reveal both genetic variation and composite shared rearing variation. Algebraically, the shared rearing variation can be estimated as $2r_{\text{DZ}} - r_{\text{MZ}}$ and the heritability as $2 \times (r_{\text{MZ}} - r_{\text{DZ}})$.

In one twin study, Coon and Carey (1989) found that for high school musical interest and honors, MZ and DZ twin correlations were nearly equal when both twins had taken music lessons together (because parents had not wanted to arrange them for just one). For instance, MZ twin brothers correlated .71 for musical interest, whereas DZ twin brothers correlated .63. With this pattern, we can infer that about half the variation (as noted above c^2 is twice the DZ correlation – the MZ correlation, or .55) in high school musical interest was attributable to the music lessons and other shared experiences. Coon and Carey's study shows that the twin method can successfully demonstrate composite shared rearing influence.

In another example, twin studies of delinquency have also demonstrated shared environmental influences. In a study of adolescents' deliquent acts (Rowe, 1983), the twin correlations for confessed delinquent acts yielded quite large estimates of shared rearing. The MZ male twin correlation (r_{MZ} = .62) was close to that of DZ male twins (r_{DZ} = .52). From these correlation coefficients, the shared family effect can be inferred to be substantial (c^2 = .42). Similarly, in female twins, the estimated shared environmental effects were also large (c^2 = .26). In the case of official delinquency records, twin similarity can be estimated from twin concordances (i.e., given a delinquent index twin, the probability that the cotwin is also delinquent). From a summary review of twin studies, DiLalla and Gottesman (1989) concluded that shared influences had large effects on adolescent crime, because MZ and DZ twin concordances were close in value: "The weighted concordances across the delinquency studies were 87% for MZ twins and 72% for DZ twins. The high concordance rates for DZ twins, greater than 50%, suggest a fairly large influence of shared family environment" (pp. 341–342).

Although detailed explanations of this shared effect lie outside the scope of this chapter, I interpret it as one of sibling mutual influence. In a study of nontwin siblings' delinquent behavior, the sibling correlation was *conditioned* on the degree of siblings' mutual contact (Rowe & Gulley, 1992). Siblings who liked each other (or who had the same friends) were substantially more alike in their rates of delinquency than those who were emotionally distant (or who belonged to different peer groups). Consider, for example, that the correlation coefficient of delinquency in "close" brothers (r = .63) was about triple that in "distant" brothers (r = .20). From this pattern of correlations, I infer that "close" brothers imitated each other's delinquency (or the delinquent behavior of their mutual friends). Similar findings obtain for twin siblings (Carey, 1992). On the basis of his mathematical models, Carey concluded that sibling mutual influence appears to explain a part of twins' resemblance for officially recorded delinquent acts. From these behavior genetic studies, what is surprising is that for delinquent behavior, a "shared family effect" estimated from twin models may involve *shared sibling influences* rather than, as would be commonly assumed, parental treatments. Nonetheless, in both the musical performance and delinquency examples, the twin method has been shown to identify the component of shared environmental variation successfully.

In contrast to these examples, twin studies typically find an absence of shared environmental influences on behavioral traits (as will be amply documented later in this book). This persistent failure to find shared rearing effects has led to accusations against the method rather than against its message—a natural tendency to blame the messenger for news many do not wish to hear. So Lewontin et al. (1984) have explained the greater behavioral resemblance of MZ than DZ twins in terms of uneven treatments of the two types of twins:

> . . . there are also some obvious environmental reasons to expect higher correlations among MZ than among DZ twins. . . . Because of their striking physical similarity, parents, teachers, and friends tend to treat them very much alike and often even confuse them for one another. MZ twins tend to spend a great deal of time with one another, doing similar things, much more so than is the case with same-sexed DZ twins . . . (p. 115)

Do parental treatments mold twins' traits alike? Or do twins' similar genetic traits provoke a search for similar, mutually reinforcing environmental opportunities? In the tendency of MZ twins to receive similar treatments, or to seek them out, the arrow of causation is certainly bidirectional (Lytton, 1980; Scarr & Carter-Saltzman, 1979).

Moreover, the question is not whether MZ twins receive more similar treatments (they do, and to claim otherwise would be foolish), but whether those treatments influence a particular trait. Some traits may be influenced by MZ twins' similar treatments, and others not. A useful example is the case of dressing twins alike. Three-year-old MZ twins, when dressed alike, seem adorable, and simple observation shows that MZ twins are dressed alike more often than DZ twins. Yet this particular treatment is not likely to mold a trait such as IQ. Intuitively, we know that clothes do not make a person's intelligence, and putting the same T-shirts on siblings does not homogenize variation in their IQs.

Dressing alike, though, may be just one example of a broader range of parental treatment similarities that could affect personality development. If so, those twin pairs whose parents attempt to treat them alike should be more alike in personality and intelligence than those twins given more *laissez-faire* treatment. Just this prediction was tested by the psychologists John Loehlin and Robert Nichols (1976) with 850 twin pairs. They constructed a scale of differential experience including these items: "dressed alike," "played together" (ages 6–12) or "spent time together" (ages 12–18), "same teachers in school," "slept in same room," and "parents tried to treat alike." The scores on these items, and a composite score based on all five items, were correlated with the (absolute) difference in twins' intellectual abilities, personality traits, vocational interests, and interpersonal relationships. Loehlin and Nichols described their findings as follows:

> We will probably not be accused of extravagance if we say that these correlations are not very large. More of them *are* positive than negative (393 to 181, as a matter of fact), but the typical r is not greater than +.05 or +.06. . . . it is clear that the greater similarity of our identical twins' experience in terms of dress, playing together, and so forth cannot plausibly account for more than a very small fraction of their greater observed similarity on the personality and ability variables of our study. (1976, pp. 51–52)

Of course, the typical failure of differential treatments to matter does not mean that Lewontin et al. (1984) are always wrong. Social scientists must be alert to occasions when unequal environmental contexts may affect behavior—for instance, siblings' mutual closeness (see Carey, 1992; Rowe & Gulley, 1992). But for most broad personality and intellectual traits, concern over treatment differences has been misplaced.

People often claim that because identical twins look alike, they act alike. As in other exaggerated criticisms, there may be a few grains of truth in this one. Surely, more MZ than DZ female twins go on a similar number of dates, because their physical beauty is more closely matched. But to extrapolate an occasional effect of physical appearance to all traits is plainly wrong. If IQ or personality could be so easily read in a face, then the 19th-century phrenologists, who looked in the face for signs of "atavism" (large jaws, extreme size of the eye orbits, monkey-like noses, and other "primitive" features) would have earned great scientific dividends from their explanation of criminality.

To appreciate the weakness of this "similarity of appearance" explanation, let us consider physical attractiveness and a trait phenotype, such as self-esteem. Suppose, for example, that attractiveness is correlated .20 with self-esteem for each twin. Now, using the rules of path analysis, one can determine how much appearance may contribute to MZ twins' resemblance in self-esteem. As shown in Figure 2.1, two causal pathways connect MZ twins' self-esteem phenotypes. One of these pathways is through attractiveness. It depends on the correlation of the twins'

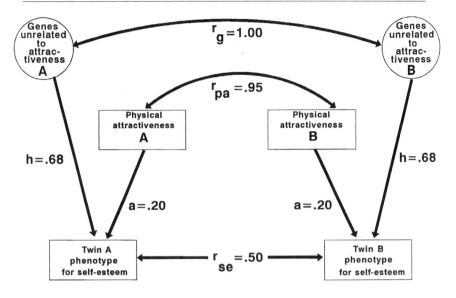

FIGURE 2.1. Physical attractiveness and MZ twins' phenotypic resemblance in self-esteem. a, correlation between attractiveness and self-esteem in each twin; h, correlation between genes unrelated to attractiveness and self-esteem in each twin; r_g, genetic correlation between the twins; r_{pa}, physical attractiveness correlation between the twins; r_{se}, self-esteem correlation between the twins.

physical attractiveness—which, because MZ twins are not *exactly* alike in appearance, is less than 1.00 (in Figure 2.1, this r =.95). It also depends on the correlation of attractiveness and self-esteem for each twin, already given here as .20. Now, to calculate the expected correlation between the twins' phenotypes that is attributable to this causal pathway, one multiplies the path coefficients connecting them (i.e., .20 squared [.20 for twin A × .20 for twin B] is multiplied by .95). This correlation works out to be .038. Genes that are unrelated to attractiveness may also contribute to behavioral resemblance. In Figure 2.1, they are assumed to correlate .68 with the phenotype of self-esteem. The twins' phenotypic correlation attributable to this causal pathway works out to be .462 (when .68 squared is multiplied by the twins' genetic correlation, 1.00). According to path analytic methods, the twins' self-esteem correlation should be the sum of these two pathways; it equals .50. But notice, too, that just a tiny fraction (7.6%) of this association is attributable to the twins' appearance; most of their behavioral similarity results from other genetic influences, the ones *independent* of physical appearance. Because the numerical values chosen for this hypothetical example are conservative ones, its lesson is that appearance similarity should be only a weak determinant of MZ twins' behavioral resemblance.

Empirical data also tend to discount appearance similarity. For instance, MZ twins remain alike in personality, even after their degree of facial attractiveness is statistically controlled for (Rowe, Clapp, & Wallis, 1977). In two twin studies, those twins who were rated as more alike in appearance were not more alike in their personality traits (Matheny, Wilson, & Dolan, 1976; Plomin, Willerman, & Loehlin, 1976).

In summary, merely matching people in physical appearance should have little effect on similarity in their psychological traits, because, whatever greater treatment similarity lookalikes receive, it cannot make them alike in psychological traits if these treatments lack causal influence on the biological functions relevant to broad traits. How alike in personality or musical talent is even the best Elvis Presley lookalike to the King of Rock and Roll? If we gathered 10 Elvis lookalikes together, would they be alike in personality at all? The remarkable similarity of MZ cotwins is attributable to genes' creating matching neurons. Personality and temperament reside in the brain, not in a face.

Model-Fitting Designs

In behavior genetic studies, the state of the art consists of model-fitting research designs, which can combine features of the aforementioned designs (Neale & Cardon, 1992). Model fitting uses equations defining the *expected* correlations for different groups of biological and/or social relatives, so that relatives of many types can be combined into a single study that yields estimates of shared environmental variation and heritability. Figure 2.2 gives a simple example of the model-fitting approach. Each diagram describes a causal process on a phenotype in relatives of a particular social or biological type, and each can be expressed as an equivalent equation according to path-analytic rules. The three diagrams yield equations for MZ twins, related siblings, and unrelated siblings reared together, respectively. Arrows labeled with an "h" mark genetic influence; arrows labeled with a "c" mark shared environmental influence. The circle labeled "u" represents unshared environmental influence.

In this example, $h = .7$ and $c = .4$. The equations in Figure 2.2 thus result in the following expected correlations: MZ twins, $r = .65$; related siblings, $r = .41$; and unrelated siblings reared together, $r = .16$. With actual data, one works in the reverse direction, using the three equations with two unknowns (h and c) to estimate the values of those unknowns. Because there are more equations than unknown values, one also obtains a sense of how well the model fits the data. For instance, if the real correlations were .60, .45, and .11 for MZ twins, related siblings, and unrelated siblings, respectively, the equations would fit well with $h = .7$ and $c = .4$, but *not* perfectly. Discrepancies between expected correlations and obtained ones allow for a statistical test of a model's "goodness of fit."

Figure 2.2's model illustrates several points. First, with model fitting, data from many different behavior genetic studies can be combined in a single analysis to recover estimates of genetic and environmental influence. Second, the more groups that are included, the more vigorously assumptions can be tested. For instance, the simple model shown does not allow for special MZ twin environments, and discrepant values of this correlation could reject the model of Figure 2.2. Third, model fitting can ground our conclusions by means of statistical tests of significance and goodness of fit. The powerful model-fitting approaches, based on statistical procedures, should only follow a direct examination of the observed statistics.

Molecular Genetics and Behavior Genetic Designs

Behavior genetic studies may seek to identify specific genetic and specific environmental influences in the composite estimates of variance components (Plomin, 1990; Loehlin, Horn, & Willerman, 1989; Rowe & Waldman, 1993). Until recently, the possibility of identifying specific genes in composite heritable influences seemed remote; with the advent of molecular genetics, however, cautious optimism has increased in regard to identifying some genes that are relatively more powerful causes of variation in behavioral traits. This section briefly reviews advances in molecular genetics that may lead to biologically grounded behavior genetic research designs.

Specific details of genetic inheritance are known more precisely than ever before. The basic unit of inheritance, a gene, is a stretch of DNA molecule containing a sequence of chemical information. Like a written sentence, it has a meaning for the biological cell as a set of instructions for creating proteins, which are both the structural materi-

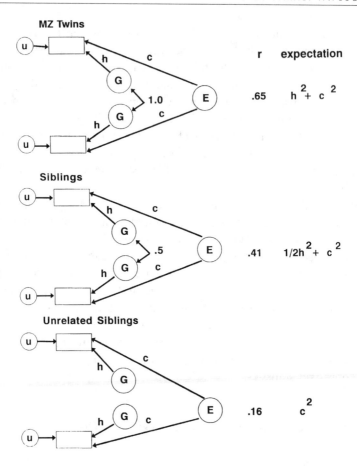

FIGURE 2.2. The phenotypic resemblance of MZ twins, related siblings, and unrelated siblings. G, genotype; E, shared environment. See text for details.

als of all cell components and also the enzymes that regulate the rates of biochemical reactions. The message in a gene is coded much like words in a sentence, except that instead of 26 letters, the alphabet is four letters: the chemical bases adenine (A), thymine (T), guanine (G), and cytosine (C) that physically lie within the double helix of DNA. And each "word" in the gene sentence is just three letters (chemical bases) long.

The genetic code is among the greatest discoveries of 20th-century science. Each three-chemical base word in the gene sentence corresponds to a particular amino acid, the chemical components of proteins, except for three "words" that are like a period at the end of a sentence, marking where a gene ends. For example, the sequence CAT is the amino acid valine; AAT is leucine; and ATT is one "stop" signal that indicates the end of a gene. A typical gene codes for 400 amino acids (or, equivalently, is about 1,200 bases long), when read sequentially from its start to the stop signal.

Estimates of the genetic loci coding for different proteins (or for RNA transcripts) in the human genome vary; a range from 50,000 to 100,000 is currently favored. Even if the genes at two-thirds of these loci were found to be monomorphic, there would be still as many as 33,000 loci that have two or more alleles and that are thus able to contribute to behavioral variability. This is a gigantic domain in which to find genes influencing a particular trait. Robert Plomin (1990) has likened this problem to finding the proverbial "needle in a haystack."

Two general approaches exist for finding the genes affecting a particular trait (viz., the needles) in the background of thousands of irrelevant genes (viz., the haystack): association studies and linkage studies (Plomin, 1990). In an association study, candidate loci with likely physiological relevance to a trait are first identified. Ideally, the alleles at this loci differ in mutational changes that alter the amino acid sequence of the gene product—not in "silent" mutations that may change a gene's "base" sequence without altering the amino acid sequence (e.g., ATC and ACG both code for valine) or in mutations in nonfunctional regions of a gene (i.e., in regions called "introns"). Genotypes at the loci are then scored numerically, and these values are subsequently correlated with variation in the trait. Association is shown if particular genotypes or alleles are more frequent in individuals who express a particular trait.

For example, alcohol dehydrogenase is an enzyme involved in the breakdown of alcohol into nontoxic compounds that are removed from the body (Crabb, Edenberg, Bosron, & Li, 1989). This locus is polymorphic, with a normal allele and a mutant one that is less effective in breaking down compounds derived from alcohol. This mutant gene is also genetically dominant over its normal counterpart. One effect of having the mutant gene is that the faces of affected people tend to flush red after these people drink alcohol. This mutant gene is more common in Asian racial groups than in other populations. In these Asian populations, alcoholics are several times more likely to carry normal alleles than abnormal ones; for instance, only 2.3% of Japanese alcoholics, as opposed to 41% of the general population in Japan, were found to have a genotype with the mutant allele (Crabb et al., 1989). Thus, this single gene exerts a considerable influence on the risk of alcoholism by making drinking less attractive for many individuals.

The other primary approach to identifying single genes is linkage analysis. In linkage studies, both genes and specific traits are followed through a family pedigree. The coincidence of particular genes with a specific phenotype throughout the family pedigree is evidence of genetic linkage. For example, if it were found that schizophrenia usually co-occurred with allele A at a locus affecting schizophrenia, whereas nonschizophenic family members inherited allele a, this would constitute evidence of genetic linkage. Sibling pairs also can be used in linkage studies. At a genetic locus, siblings can share no alleles, one allele, or two alleles—making them like unrelated individuals, like ordinary siblings, or like MZ twins in terms of their genetic relatedness at that locus (and in nearby genome regions). If siblings who share more alleles are also more alike in behavior, this correlation also demonstrates genetic linkage. Unlike candidate genes, linked genes may not be the ones directly influencing a trait phenotype, but may merely represent genetic loci close in physical proximity to the truly influential loci.

Both association and linkage methods are being pursued to locate genes for behavior. Although promising, both methods face considerable obstacles. The association research design suffers from the disadvantage that population histories may be confounded with direct gene effects; for instance, the association of skin color genes with IQ does not mean that the former directly cause intelligence. Linkage studies have a weakness of low statistical power, unless huge samples are used. Because the main conclusions of this book depend on the examination of environmental rather than genetic variation, they can stand independently of the direct identification of genetic loci affecting different behavioral traits. Nonetheless, the identification of these genes will provide an intellectually satisfying closure on the question of genetic influence on behavior, and will open new areas of research.

Environments and Behavior

In this review of genetics, many complexities of both inheritance and environment have been omitted. For instance, I have failed to discuss gene × environment interactions. At some level, the world is undoubtedly a more untidy place than that implied in my very simple description of how genetic and environmental variation combine. Yet, in a surprising number of applications, simple ideas capture enough of trait variation so that more complicated ones are hardly needed, or are a luxury for explaining the final few percentage points of variance.

Behavior genetic methods can be used to estimate the strength of shared family environmental influences, even when the specific mechanisms are unknown. A shared environmental estimate indicates how much changing family environments would change trait phenotypes; if this statistical term accounts for appreciable outcome variation, then changing the family environments of disadvantaged children to be like those of the most advantaged should change developmental outcomes for children. The thesis of this book is that the effects of shared family environments on children's developmental outcomes are limited. The data assembled in the next two chapters show, in particular, that for many personality and intellectual traits, variations in shared family environment have little influence on trait development. A lack of shared environmental influences would weaken, if not falsify, many explanations of behavioral variation tied to the family unit, including standard rearing variables such as the general emotional climate of the home (e.g., warmth vs. coldness), parental discipline patterns, home intellectual stimulation, family structure, and many other family variables. In the next two chapters, the phrase "rearing variation" is used to refer to those aspects of parental treatments that correspond to the theoretical shared environment component of variation, as defined above. This shorthand is used even though this variance component includes, in addition to parental treatments, other environmental effects tied to the family unit (e.g., neighborhood schools).

As discussed above, behavior genetic studies also estimate nonshared (also called unshared) environmental influences that vary within a family—they constitute the world of experience unique to each child. The behavior genetic studies reviewed in the following chapters consistently affirm the effects of different nonshared environmental influences on trait variation; after all, even genetically identical MZ twins are not perfectly concordant for behavioral characteristics. One part of unshared environmental influence may be the effects of parents' differential treatments of their children. Thus, an exclusion of shared environmental influences does not necessarily negate the influence of all family rearing influences. The possible role of differential parental treatments of siblings is considered later in Chapter 5. The next chapter explores evidence regarding shared environmental influences on nonintellectual personality traits and psychopathology.

Notes

[1]The purpose of predicting developmental outcomes from genotypes is sometimes criticized as "genetic determinism." But there is really nothing wrong with a deterministic outlook in the social sciences. After all, reliable prediction of developmental outcomes is an implicit goal in environmentally oriented as well as genetically oriented research.

In general, social scientists have adopted a "probabilistic" view of causation, in which "the values of an independent or causal variable do not determine the specific *outcomes* of a dependent variable but rather the specific (conditional) *probability distributions* with which the values of the outcome variable occur" (Mulaik, 1987, p. 24; emphasis in the original). To apply this to the genotype → phenotype relationship, a particular genotype implies a probability distribution of the relevant phenotypes. In some single-gene diseases, the conditional distribution has low variance, so that a high degree of "determinism" obtains. For instance, all bearers of the dominant gene for Huntington's disease will develop this neurological disorder if they live long enough. Most conditional probability distributions have greater variance. In the case of Down's syndrome (a chromosomal abnormality that causes mental retardation), though the IQ distribution of affected children is definitely far below average, an affected child occasionally possesses normal intelligence.

With these ideas in mind, we can see that whether a developmental outcome is highly "genetically determined" depends both on its heritability and on how it is defined. Thus, the probability of one child of a schizophrenic mother's becoming a schizophrenic adult is about 1 in 10, a weakly determined outcome for a single child. Of the offspring of 1,000 schizophrenic mothers, about 100 will become schizophrenic adults. We may define another outcome as the probability that *at least 40* offspring will become schizophrenic adults. This latter outcome would be more strongly "genetically determined," with a probability close to 1.00, although the fate of any single child would be hard to know in advance.

Better prediction would be obtained if we had genetic tests for the specific genes that lead to schizophrenia. Even so, prediction would be imperfect because these genes do not always express themselves as schizophrenic disease, as shown by the imperfect concordance of MZ twins. If one MZ twin is affected, the probability is about 50% that the other twin is also affected.

[2] A variance component is sometimes expressed in a percentage form to refer to what part of phenotypic variance it explains. For example, if h^2 equals .25, then 25% ($100 \times h^2$) of phenotypic variation is attributable to genetic variation.

References

Bouchard, T. J., Jr. (1983). Do environmental similarities explain the similarity in intelligence of identical twins reared apart? *Intelligence, 7*, 175–184. (Erratum, 397–398.)

Bouchard, T. J., Jr., Lykken, D. T., McGue, M., Segal, N. L., & Tellegen, A. (1990). Sources of human psychological differences: The Minnesota study of twins reared apart. *Science, 250*, 223–228.

Burt, C. (1955). The evidence for the concept of intelligence. *British Journal of Educational Psychology, 25*, 158–177.

Carey, G. (1992). Twin imitation for antisocial behavior: Implications for genetic and family research. *Journal of Abnormal Psychology, 101*, 18–25.

Chen, E. (1979, December 9). Twins reared apart: A living lab. *New York Times Magazine*, pp. 110–124.

Coon, H., & Carey, G. (1989). Genetic and environmental determinants of musical ability in twins. *Behavior Genetics, 19*, 183–193.

Crabb, D. W., Edenberg, H. J., Bosron, W. F., & Li, T. (1989). Genotypes for aldehyde dehydrogenase deficiency and alcohol sensitivity: The inactive ALDH2^2 is dominant. *Journal of Clinical Investigation, 83*, 314–316.

DiLalla, L. F., & Gottesman, I. I. (1989). Heterogeneity of causes for delinquency and criminality: Lifespan perspectives. *Development and Psychopathology, 1*, 339–349.

Falconer, D. S. (1981). *Introduction to quantitative genetics*. London: Longmans, Green.

Galton, F. (1869). *Hereditary genius: An inquiry into its laws and consequences*. London: Macmillan.

Horn, J. M., Loehlin, J. C., & Willerman, L. (1979). Intellectual resemblance among adoptive and biological relatives: The Texas Adoption Project. *Behavior Genetics, 9*, 177–208.

Jencks, C. (1980). Heredity, environment, and public policy reconsidered. *American Sociological Review, 45*, 723–736.

Juel-Nielsen, N. (1980). *Individual and environment: Monozygotic twins reared apart*. New York: Internatioal Universities Press.

Lewontin, R. C., Rose, S., & Kamin, L. J. (1984). *Not in our genes: Biology, ideology, and human nature*. New York: Pantheon.

Loehlin, J. C., Horn, H. M., & Willerman, L. (1989). Modeling IQ change: Evidence from the Texas Adoption Project. *Child Development, 60*, 993–1004.

Loehlin, J. C., & Nichols, R. C. (1976). *Heredity, environment, and personality: A study of 850 sets of twins*. Austin: University of Texas Press.

Lykken, D. T., McGue, M., Tellegen, A., & Bouchard, T. J., Jr. (1992). Emergenesis: Genetic traits that may not run in families. *American Psychologist, 47*, 1565–1577.

Lytton, H. (1980). *Parent–child interaction: The socialization process observed in twin and singleton families*. New York: Plenum Press.

Matheny, A. P., Wilson, R. S., & Dolan, A. B. (1976). Relations between twins' similarity of appearance and behavioral similarity: Testing an assumption. *Behavior Genetics, 6,* 343–351.

Mulaik, S. A. (1987). Toward a conception of causality applicable to experimentation and causal modeling. *Child Development, 58,* 18–32.

Neale, M. C., & Cardon, L. R. (1992). *Methodology for genetic studies of twins and families.* Dordrecht, The Netherlands: Kluwer.

Newman, J., Freeman, F., & Holzinger, K. (1937). *Twins: A study of heredity and environment.* Chicago: University of Chicago Press.

Pedersen, N. L., Plomin, R., McClearn, G. E., & Friberg, L. (1988). Neuroticism, extraversion, and related traits in adult twins reared apart and together. *Journal of Personality and Social Psychology, 55,* 950–957.

Plomin, R. (1990). The role of inheritance in behavior. *Science, 248,* 183–188.

Plomin, R., & DeFries, J. C. (1985). *Origins of individual differences in infancy: The Colorado Adoption Project.* New York: Academic Press.

Plomin, R., DeFries, J. C., & McClearn, G. E. (1990). *Behavioral genetics: A primer* (2nd ed.). New York: W. H. Freeman.

Plomin, R., Willerman, L., & Loehlin, J. C. (1976). Resemblance in appearance and the equal environments assumption in twin studies of personality traits. *Behavior Genetics, 6,* 43–52.

Rende, R. D., Plomin, R., & Vandenberg, S. G. (1990). Who discovered the twin method? *Behavior Genetics, 20,* 277–285.

Rowe, D. C. (1983). Biometrical genetic models of self-reported delinquent behavior: A twin study. *Behavior Genetics, 13,* 473–489.

Rowe, D. C., Clapp, M., & Wallis, J. (1987). Physical attractiveness and the personality resemblance of identical twins. *Behavior Genetics, 17,* 191–201.

Rowe, D. C., & Gulley, B. (1992). Sibling effects on substance use and delinquency. *Criminology, 30,* 217–233.

Rowe, D. C., & Plomin, R. (1981). The importance of nonshared (E_1) environmental influences in behavioral development. *Developmental Psychology, 17,* 517–531.

Rowe, D. C., & Waldman, W. (1993). The question "how" reconsidered. In R. Plomin & G. McClearn (Eds.), *Nature, nurture, and psychology* (pp. 355–373). Washington, DC: American Psychological Association.

Scarr, S., & Carter-Saltzman, L. (1979). Twin method: Defense of a critical assumption. *Behavior Genetics, 9,* 527–542.

Scarr, S., Scarf, E., & Weinberg, R. A. (1980). Perceived and actual similarities in biological and adoptive families: Does perceived similarity bias genetic inferences? *Behavior Genetics, 10,* 445–458.

Scarr, S., & Weinberg, R. A. (1976). IQ test performance of black children adopted by white families. *American Psychologist, 31,* 726–739.

Scarr, S., & Weinberg, R. A. (1983). The Minnesota adoption studies: Genetic differences and malleability. *Child Development, 54,* 260–267.

Scott, J. P., & Fuller, J. L. (1965). *Genetics and the social behavior of the dog.* Chicago: University of Chicago Press.

Shields, J. (1962). *Monozygotic twins brought up apart and brought up together.* London: Oxford University Press.

CHAPTER 3

AS THE TWIG IS BENT?:
FAMILIES AND PERSONALITY

Personality Traits and Their Identification

Traits are the enduring themes of our lives. In Robert McCrae and Paul Costa's summary of longitudinal studies of adults, one of the impressive findings was the consistency of personality over the adult years (McCrae & Costa, 1990). The top scorers on a given trait stayed high; the lowest scorers stayed low. For instance, the least shy members of any group studied remained more sociable than others over the years, and the most painfully shy remained relatively more shy than others. Although at high school reunions we easily slip into our old relationships—and perhaps thus overestimate the endurance of traits—we cannot help being struck by how people who have particular traits manage to maintain them and find social niches compatible with their personality dispositions and interests. In California, the words "personal growth" hold the promise of infinite change and variety, of discarding an old self like an old set of clothes; however, scientific evidence suggests that such recasting of the self is at best an extremely rare event. For those individuals prone to anxiety, panic, or depression, the inability to replace one personality trait with another is an impediment. On the other hand, stability makes us consistent social objects to others. It also allows us gradually to "know ourselves," and thus to find ways to satisfy the many complex requirements of our characters.

This book focuses primarily on traits rather than on specific behaviors, for several reasons. In human culture, technological and social innovation is a constant process, and new devices and behavior patterns are constantly being adopted and abandoned. Not long ago in historical time, buck-naked college students sprinted across campus lawns, asserting their

freedom from social convention in the short-lived fad of "streaking."
Today, college students are now pursuing other (more serious?) endeav-
ors. Who became the streakers was certainly partly a function of individual personality—extraverts were probably more likely to do so than
introverts. In this brief period, streaking was probably a good behavior
to use to diagnose extraversion; conversely, we might have predicted that
extraverts were more likely to streak. Although this behavior has now
virtually ceased to exist on college campuses, extraverts still enliven parties, and introverts still avoid the social limelight. Indeed, there is little
evidence that the distribution of the underlying personality dispositions
has changed appreciably in a single generation, although the particular
behaviors used to express a given disposition may change rapidly. The
greater constancy and breadth of traits are good reasons to focus on their
inheritance, rather than on the transmission of more molecular single
"behaviors" or on the transmission of cultural artifacts. In Chapter 7, I
discuss further the cultural transmission of both traits and specific cultural innovations.

Traits are usually inferred from clusters of behaviors that "hang
together," correlating with one another. Figure 3.1 shows a general model
of sociability. The large circle represents the trait itself, which is presumably a result of nervous system activity. The indicators in boxes on the
right are the behaviors from which its existence has been inferred. The
amount of the disposition to sociability depends on the presence or
absence of these indicator behaviors. A sociable person should attend
parties, talk to strangers in the supermarket, break into discussions at a
business meeting, enjoy entertaining business associates, and so on. If
we could pay a detective to trail people for several weeks, we would find
that sociable people would display more of these behaviors during the
time they were followed than shy people would. In this diagram, the
arrows from the trait point to these behaviors because the trait is con-
ceptualized as *one* cause of each behavior. I do not regard the use of a
trait in a causal explanation as tautological: "When we call someone
'friendly' or 'aggressive' or 'generous,' we are saying something about how
the person behaves (or would behave) in certain kinds of situations *and*
about the functioning of his or her mind" (Funder, 1991, p. 32). For
simplicity, the diagram omits other traits and immediate situational influences that are also causes of a behavior. Certainly, the behavior of breaking into a discussion at a business meeting would have other causes,
including other traits (such as whether the boss was feared) and imme-

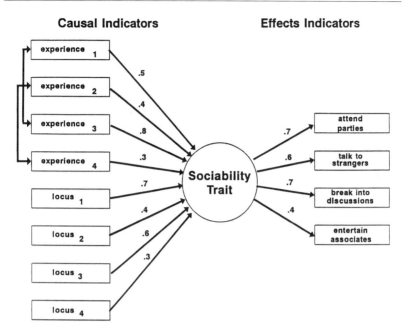

FIGURE 3.1. A model of sociability.

diate situational influences (such as whether the individual cared about the issue under discussion).

Many trait descriptions are the result of a factor-analytic investigation. Factor analysis is a statistical technique of grouping behaviors that occur together and inferring from these groupings the existence of underlying trait dispositions. The technique uses correlation matrices of many variables and reduces them to fewer underlying variables, which are correlated with each observed variable. In a correlation matrix of weight and height measurements—say, of arm length, waist size, shoulder width, head size, and neck size—factor analysis would quickly identify the underlying trait of *body* size. Some variables would correlate more strongly with the underlying body size trait than other variables; for instance, arm length is probably a better indicator than head circumference is.

The use of factor analysis has been attacked by some critics of personality research. In his book *The Mismeasure of Man*, the Harvard biologist Stephen Jay Gould (1981) noted that factor analysis can group indicators that have no underlying source of causality. Thus a single statistical factor could be found among the positive correlations since 1960 of stock market prices, the universe's expansion, the price of gold, and U.S. population size because all grow with time, not because a single cause links these disparate events. In particular, Gould objected to the inference that because behaviors tend to intercorrelate positively, they must imply a trait within the person as something physical and real in the brain. He asserted: "Factorists have often fallen prey to a temptation for *reification*—for awarding *physical meaning* to all strong principal components" (p. 250; emphasis in the original). Although Gould directed his criticism at IQ tests, his remarks apply equally to any trait inferred from statistical data.

Although the psychologist Gordon Allport (1966) also expressed reservations about factor analysis, he had little doubt about the existence of traits. Without a stable source of influence within the person, how can behavior remain stable over 20- and 30-year periods? If there is not some organizing source within the person, how can different observers come to see an individual in the same way (Kenrick & Funder, 1988)? Allport acknowledged that when people sweat outdoors, they do so because the temperature is hot. Nonetheless, the mechanism of behavioral adaptation lies within the individual: Evolution has given humans nerve sensors to detect temperature change and sweat glands to release cooling fluids. Dogs, with an absence of sweat glands in the skin, fail to adapt to temperature changes by sweating. The basic trait of sweating does reflect something real and physical in the design of human glands and the nervous system.

Allport failed to offer perhaps the strongest justification for identifying traits with brain structure and function: the behavioral resemblance of reared-apart MZ twins. When two separated MZ twins enter a laboratory and begin checking similar self-descriptions on a 400-item questionnaire, one has to wonder what source of resemblance could be responsible other than neurological similarity. The laws of physics do not permit extrasensory perception or brain-to-brain telecommunication; the source of reared-apart MZ twins' behavioral resemblance must lie within their nervous systems. (I have noted in Chapter 2 that the hypothesis of similarity in physical appearance is a red herring.) In one of the Minnesota twin study's well-publicized cases, one twin was reared in Czechoslovakia as a Nazi and the other in Trinidad as a Jew (Begley & Kasinborf, 1979)! Despite these nearly opposite life histories, their answers on the Minnesota Multiphasic Personality Inventory (MMPI) were extremely similar. Although some of their attitudes were different—the Jewish-raised twin was more liberal than the other—different life histories may still lead to behavioral expressions of similar trait dispositions that have one neurological foundation. Thus, although "reification" is a somewhat unpleasant-sounding word, it describes a proper activity—looking for the neurological roots of behavioral dispositions. And given the heritability of personality traits, biological foundations will be found eventually for many of them.

In Figure 3.1, the left-hand boxes show the causes of sociability. In statistical terms, they are "causal indicators" because their arrows point toward the latent trait, whereas the boxed behaviors are "effects indicators" because the latent trait's arrows point at them (Bollen & Lennox, 1991). The direction of causality is clearly the most important and defining difference between the two sets of indicators: We say that attending a party reveals the trait of sociability, not that it causes it. Another subtle difference has to do with the intercorrelations among the indicators. Positive correlations will be found among the effects indicators, and often these will be large. In this diagram, effects correlations can be calculated as the product of the numerical weights on their respective arrows. For instance, the correlation of "attend parties" and "break into discussions" is .49 (i.e., .7 × .7), and the average correlation among all pairs of effects indicators is .41. On the other hand, the weights on the causal indicators cannot be used to calculate the correlations among the causal indicators. Rather, their degree of intercorrelation is shown by the double-headed arrows, and causal indicators unconnected by double-headed arrows do not correlate. Two kinds of causal influences are shown: genes at various loci and specific experiences. The genes, being unlinked, do not all correlate with one another; this reflects the random assortment of genes, as described in Chapter 2. Some experiences may correlate, and others may be totally uncorrelated. Figure 3.1 thus visualizes the idea that uncorrelated and numerous influences may combine to produce a trait that is then inferred from its various manifestations (effects indicators). This book's thesis is that the experiential arrows in Figure 3.1 are neither child-rearing factors nor other environmental factors tied particularly to the family unit.

One difficulty is that we seek a general answer about family influence. The number of traits generated in the history of psychological research has been huge, and many traits going under different names may be similar. For instance, "self-esteem" may be defined as how much a person respects and likes himself or herself, whereas "general anxiety" may be defined as a person's feeling tension and a knot in his or her stomach. Although on the surface the two concepts appear different, questionnaire measures of anxiety and self-esteem usually correlate negatively, making it unlikely that heritable influence on anxiety would be totally absent in a measure of self-esteem. Thus, part of the task is knowing the domain of traits. As each trait is investigated, we can determine whether it is heritable and whether it shows family environmental influence. As the number of traits showing the same pattern of genetic and environmental influence grows, the greater the strength of any generalization. If three, four, or five uncorrelated traits are investigated, and if they support a conclusion of genetic influence without composite shared environmental influence, the likelihood diminishes that any new trait that is named and discovered will be totally unrelated to the known traits. Thus, it becomes implausible that a new trait awaits discovery that will somehow reveal an entirely different pattern of genetic and environmental determination.

Behavior Genetic Studies of Personality Traits

The literature on the behavior genetics of personality is voluminous. But a new review of hundreds of twin and adoption studies is unnecessary to enable us to reach conclusions about personality variability. Instead, I rely on previous reviews and selective studies that have addressed issues commonly raised in this area relating to the strengths of the methods and their assumptions. One word of warning is in order: With the selection of a single study, just about any point can be made. Sampling variation is an inherent feature of the landscape of behavioral research—and it is often a serious problem, because investigators usually do not have the finances to study giant samples and employ representative sampling procedures that would minimize sampling variations. The practical science of opinion polling, however, has not foundered on the occasional miscalled election where the poll said that a losing candidate would win by a margin of a few percentage points. In the long run, opinion polling calls most elections correctly; in the long run, behavior genetic studies point in the direction of the underlying truths. When single studies are offered here, their results are representative of others in the field, and exceptions and qualifications are mentioned later.

In the personality field, a consensus has been reached that a "Big Five" set of trait dimensions spans the major naturalistic personality traits. These dimensions are found repeatedly in self-report questionnaires and in rating data (Digman, 1990). Many of the premier personality inventories—including Cattell's Sixteen Personality Factor Questionnaire (16PF), the Eysenck Personality Inventory, and the renowned MMPI—can be reduced to all, or a subset, of these five personality dimensions. The dimensions have been replicated in five language groups, from English to Japanese. They appear in studies from 1949 to the present. If these dimensions do not encompass the entire range of adult traits, they appear at least to capture a large portion of traits mentioned in everyday language as people describe one another. Each of the "Big Five" personality trait dimensions is named here according to one end of the continuum it represents:

1. Extraversion: traits such as "gregarious," "sociable," "dominant," and "adventurous."
2. Agreeableness: traits such as "kind," "affectionate," and "friendly."
3. Conscientiousness: traits such as "reliable," "organized," and "planful."
4. Emotional stability: traits such as "calm," "not worrying," and "stable."
5. Intellectual openness: traits such as "original," "insightful," "wide interests," and "inventive."

Reviewing the world's scientific literature on the "Big Five," we can reach general conclusions about the types of genetic and environmental influences operating to produce trait variation (Loehlin & Rowe, 1992; Loehlin, 1992). A colleague and I (Loehlin & Rowe, 1992) examined two kinds of family environmental influences. One was the environment shared by siblings (c^2), and the other was the environment shared by parent and a child, symbolized by the product pc. The first component of this product (p) represents the influence of parental phenotype on family environment; the second (c) is the effect of family environment on the child (the same environment that also contributes to siblings' resemblance).

Loehlin and I reviewed a heterogeneous set of studies that used neither exactly the same questionnaires, age groups, nor geographic locations (indeed, some studies took place oceans apart). These included a diverse range of behavior genetic research designs: (1) the comparison of resemblances in MZ twins and DZ twins; (2) the comparison of adoptive and biological parent–child resemblances; (3) the comparison of adoptive and biological sibling resemblances; (4) the comparison of resemblances in the families of MZ twin pairs; and (5) the comparison of resemblances in MZ twins reared apart and together.

A sense of the richness of these data can be obtained by considering some observations for extraversion. In the extraversion data set, the sample-size-weighted correlation for MZ twins raised apart was .38; for MZ twins raised together, .55; for biological siblings, .20; and for all biologically unrelated siblings reared together in adoptive families, –.06. This pattern can be simply interpreted: *Individuals who share genes are alike in personality regardless of how they are reared, whereas rearing environment induces little or no personality resemblance.*

Data from twin-family studies elaborate these conclusions. In a twin-family study, adult MZ twins are recruited, and they are tested with their children. The unique genetic relatedness of MZ twins teases apart genetic and family environmental influences. For example, being a genetic duplicate, an MZ twin father should correlate as highly with his nephews and nieces as with his own children, because he correlates .50 genetically with both. The nephews and nieces, possessing the same genetic fathers, should correlate as highly as half-siblings, although they are raised as cousins (often in different towns or cities, with social contact mainly limited to holidays and special occasions). As shown in Table 3.1, the extraversion correlations we found (Loehlin & Rowe, 1992) followed lines of genetic relatedness. What family environmental mechanism could have generated correlations that were the same for parents and their own children as for uncles/aunts and the children of their brothers and sisters? What family environmental mechanism could have made cousins as alike as half-siblings? Only the adult MZ twins themselves showed a higher correlation (.43) than the first-degree biological relatives. Excluding the MZ twins, the overall heritability estimate (weighted by sample size) for Table 3.1 was .47, about the same as that estimated by the MZ twin correlation.

Table 3.2 summarizes our results for fitting the "Big Five" personality traits to various models (with the most information available on extraversion and emotionality). In the best-fitting models, the largest component of trait variation was unshared environment, followed closely by broad-sense heritability, while the component of siblings' shared

TABLE 3.1. Averaged Extraversion Correlations in Two Twin-Family Studies

	Mean r	No. of pairs	$r_g{}^a$	Social relation
MZ twins	.43	116	1.00	Twins
Siblings in twin families	.23	177	.50	Full siblings
Twin parent to own child	.22	413	.50	Parent–child
Twin parent to brother's or sister's child	.21	192	.50	Uncle/aunt–nephew/niece
Cousins via MZ twins	.16	138	.25	Cousins

Note. Correlations reflect weighted average of two twin-family studies. Original sources: Price, Vandenberg, Iyer, & Williams (1982) and Loehlin (1986). Adapted from Loehlin & Rowe (1992). Copyright 1992 by Harvester Wheatsheaf. Adapted by permission.
$^a r_g$ is the relatives' genetic correlation.

environment was much smaller. The contribution of the rearing environment was statistically significant for all traits except extraversion, but accounted for only 2% to 9% of the total variation. The least important component was parent–child environmental influence: *The parameter p could be set to zero in all trait models.*

These results do not mean that the structure of personality trait variation is completely resolved. The statistical model just presented emphasizes nonadditive genetic influences as an additional source of MZ twins' behavioral resemblance. An alternative model is that MZ twins share a special environmental similarity that no other pairs of relatives experience. These two models, although differing in assumptions, gave nearly identical statistical fits to the observed correlations.

TABLE 3.2. Parameter Estimates for "Big Five" Personality Dimensions

Dimension	Unshared environment	Broad-sense h^2	Narrow-sense h^2	Siblings' shared environment
I. Extraversion	.49	.49	.32	.02
II. Agreeableness	.52	.39	.29	.09
III. Conscientiousness	.55	.40	.22	.05
IV. Emotional stability	.52	.41	.27	.07
V. Intellectual openness	.49	.45	.43	.06
Mean	.51	.43	.31	.06

Note. Adapted from Loehlin & Rowe (1992). Copyright 1992 by Harvester Wheatsheaf. Adapted by permission.

Although these statistical data were indecisive, I find the biological interpretation of genetic nonadditivity more intellectually compelling than one based on special MZ twin environments. A nonadditive trait's hallmark is an MZ twin correlation more than double that of first-degree relatives (e.g., siblings). Physical traits, such as brain midfrequency alpha level, show this property, correlating about .80 in MZ twins but only .13 in DZ twins (Lykken, McGue, Tellegen, & Bouchard, 1992). In addition, nonlinear combinations of ordinary traits may also correlate more than twice as strongly in MZ as in DZ twins. For instance, Lykken et al. (1992) found that the squared difference of height minus weight correlated .62 in MZ twins but only .15 in DZ twins. Thus, MZ twins were much more alike than DZ pairs in whether their weight was proportionate to their height. A further argument against the hypothesis of a special MZ twin environment is that MZ twins raised apart typically possess the same extraordinary resemblance for different traits as those raised together.

Lykken et al. (1992) have given this genetic nonadditivity a special name, "emergenesis"—that is, the "emergent properties of configurations of monomorphic genes." As mentioned in Chapter 2, unlike first-degree relatives, MZ twins share the entire *configuration* of their genes. For instance, a rare trait—say, charismatic leadership—conferred by a five-locus, recessive-gene system would appear only once in about 20 million random matings, but it would be shared by a pair of MZ twins. And whereas both MZ twins would possess world-class leadership skills, one would not be likely to find these in either their nontwin siblings or their parents. Thus, a trait can have a high degree of genetic determination without "breeding true" in families. As Lykken et al. (1992) remark, the random halves of genes from each parent may work additively, or may result in some unique new combination:

> Your tall mother held four queens, and she passed three of them along to you. Combining them (additively) with a queen from the paternal line, you can stand as tall as Mom. . . . The exciting thing about emergenesis is that you *might* receive the 10 and king of spades from Dad, and the jack, queen, and ace of spades from Mom, cards that never counted for much in either family tree but whose combination in you might produce a Ramanujan [a mathematical genius], a new Olympic record—or a True Crime miniseries for television. (p. 1575)

Or they might produce, as recounted by Lykken et al., a pair of reared-apart MZ twins who discovered, upon reunion, that they both used

Vademecum toothpaste, Canoe shaving lotion, Vitalis hair tonic, and Lucky Strike cigarettes.

Our model-fitting exercises (Loehlin & Rowe, 1992) were consistent in weakening the claims of the two major avenues of family environmental transmission of traits. First, there was a total absence of evidence that children resemble their parents in behavioral traits because some environmental process in the family transmits them from parent to child, whether that process be imitation, emotional identification, or anything else. The expectable parent–child resemblance would be merely one-half the *additive* (i.e., narrow-sense) heritability shown in Table 3.2. With mean additive heritability of .31, we would expect a rather modest parent–child correlation of about .16 for most personality traits. Note that the trait with the greatest additive heritability in Table 3.2, intellectual openness, is linked with the domain of intellectual ability (where, as we shall see later, additive genetic influences are more pronounced than they are for personality traits). Second, there was little evidence for environmental influences shared by siblings. This parameter estimate was weak, both in absolute terms and by comparison to unshared environmental influences. Children may grow up in one family, with many of the same objective experiences, yet they are nearly as unlike one another in personality as children reared in different families.

Family adoptions played a prominent role in our reaching these remarkable conclusions. The utter lack of familial resemblance in adoptive families—despite the early occurrence of adoption in infancy—directly implies that a family's emotional climate or parental example fails to set the direction of personality development. The socialization science view of strong family effects might be salvaged if parental treatments in adoptive homes were so different from those in biological families as to vitiate family influences. Hoffman (1985, 1991) suggests that merely knowing a child is adopted may place personality development on a different course:

> Simply knowing [that a child is] adopted may lessen the parents' efforts to mold the child to their own image either because the parents' identification with the child is less or because the parents feel more of an obligation to let the adoptive child develop independently. (1985, p. 132)

On the other hand, this response to adoption is speculative and *post hoc*. No one has demonstrated that adoptive families have parenting styles so original and different as to separate them from the normal channels of socialization. In the Colorado Adoption Project, adoptive families were not exactly the same in rearing styles as the biological families with which they had been matched (Plomin, DeFries, & Fulker, 1988, pp. 73–74). For example, the adoptive families were more religious (the adoptees had been placed through a church-affiliated adoption agency) and exercised greater control over their children's behavior. Less family conflict also existed in the adoptive homes. The adoptive parents did not treat their children with greater warmth than the non-adoptive ones, however, and these *mean* group differences accounted for only a small part of the total variation in rearing styles. Even if adoptive parents could invent new rearing approaches, it is unclear that such innovations would necessarily lead to less parent–child resemblance. For instance, adoptive parents who express a lack of concern with whether their children strive academically (because they supposedly value the adoptive children's independent development) may nonetheless model a high regard for academic achievement in their own behavior (e.g., attending parent–child conferences, participating in school fund–raising activities) that belies their overt beliefs. One can more easily imagine the intentional socialization of behavior in some different direction than a complete absence of such mechanisms as modeling and imitation in adoptive families as opposed to biological families.

The Texas Adoption Study provides some unique data with which to evaluate these two different views (Loehlin, Willerman, & Horn, 1987). We have here the strong behavior genetic design of comparing biological and adoptive children raised in the same households; this should eliminate quarrels about whether two different sets of families are well matched. We also have rare personality data on the birth mothers of the adoptees. As noted in Chapter 2, the families recruited into this study all adopted children through a private agency in Texas; fortunately for research, the agency routinely administered personality and IQ tests to the unwed mothers before their children's birth. With these records available, the adoption design was completed by locating the adoptive families and administering tests to both the parents and children. About 40% of the adoptive families had biological children of their own, born either before or after the adoptive placement (contrary to popular mythology, adoption does not cure infertility, but some subfertile parents are able eventually to have a biological child). All the children were first tested at an average age of 7 years. In the initial round of the study, few personality resemblances were found in either biological or nonbiological comparisons; of course, however, these young children could not complete the same personality inventories as were administered to adults. In a follow-up, children from 181 of the 300 families in the original study were recontacted; at this point, the adoptive children averaged about 17 years old. Their birth mothers had been on average just 2 years older (19 years old) at the time of the births. Thus, we can ask this question: Did do the adoptees become like their birth mothers while living apart from them? These older adoptees were also able to complete the adult personality inventories.

I illustrate the Texas Adoption Study's general conclusions with the specific results for the MMPI. Developed at the University of Minnesota during the 1950s, the MMPI is widely known to clinicians, and it now enjoys wide use throughout the United States. Its nine scales—tagged with titles such as Hypochondriasis, Hysteria, and Schizophrenia—were originally intended for the diagnosis of psychopathology. Nonetheless, the inventory can also be used with normal populations, and response variability is great.

The Texas Adoption Study presents nearly an ideal design for evaluating familial effects on the MMPI. The adoptees were placed within a few days of birth and were permanently adopted; the adoptions were closed, so that adoptive parents did not have contact with the adoptees' biological relatives; nor could the adoptive parents be aware of the birth mothers' MMPI outcomes. Selective placement was minimal: The median correlation of the MMPI clinical scale scores from the birth mothers to the adoptive mothers and fathers were only .03 and .00, respectively.

Table 3.3 summarizes median correlations taken over eight MMPI scales. When relatives lacking biological relatedness were compared,

TABLE 3.3. Median MMPI Scale Correlations for Biologically Unrelated and Related Children

	Adoptive child	Biological child
Adoptive father	.02 (180)	.12° (81)
Adoptive mother	.00 (177)	.12° (81)
Adoptive midparent–midchild	.03 (135)	.24°° (61)
Birth mother	.18°° (133)	—

Note. n's are in parentheses. Each correlation is a median of correlations taken over eight MMPI Scales. Data are taken from Loehlin, Willerman, & Horn (1987).
°$p < .10$.
°°$p < .05$

MMPI scale scores did not correlate. The median midparent (i.e., average of mother's and father's score)–midchild correlation was just .03 (n = 135). Thus, rearing influences were negligible. In contrast, when relatives possessed biological relatedness—that is, a birth mother and her adopted-away child, or an adoptive mother and her own biological child —correlations were positive. Although the small sample size does not make the adoptive parent–biological child correlation of .12 statistically reliable, it is well within sampling variation of our expected value of a familial correlation for nonintellectual personality traits (.15). Heritability can be calculated as either the midparent–midchild correlation (h^2 = .24) or as twice the correlation between the birth mother and adoptee (h^2 = .36).

These data constitute a direct response to Hoffman's (1985, 1991) suggestion that adoptive parents treat adoptive and nonadoptive children differentially. It is true that an adoptive parent resembles only one kind of child in his or her own family, the biological child. And the Texas adoptees' MMPI traits could not be predicted from the adoptive parents'. Yet the adoptees' MMPI traits could be predicted from their *birth mothers'* MMPI traits (r = .18, n = 135). Thus we fully recover the fully expected degree of familial resemblance once we have information on a biological parent—even a biological parent whose contact with her child was limited to a few hours or days after birth. These observations lead strongly to the inference that what creates parent–child resemblance in natural families is biology, and that no process of imitation, modeling, or emotional identification is required to induce it. Table 3.4 drives this point home by showing birth mother–adoptee MMPI scale correlations. What we see here is the same amount of personality similarity as exists with shared rearing experiences (Hill & Hill, 1973).

The comparison of twins raised apart and together is another natural laboratory for weighing rearing influence. As noted earlier, the samples of twins raised apart tend to be more haphazard and idiosyncratic than those of twins raised ordinarily. The Minnesota study of twins reared apart also provides data on the resemblance of twins reared together, who completed the same physiological tests and personality inventories as the separated twins (Bouchard, Lykken, McGue, Segal, & Tellegen, 1990). The amount of variance on each measure that could be attributed to siblings' rearing was obtained by subtracting the raised-apart twins' correlation from the raised-together twins' correlation. As illustrated in Table 3.5, estimates of rearing influences were very low across a broad range of physical and personality measures. Indeed, in no case

TABLE 3.4. MMPI Correlations between Mothers and Children When Children Raised Apart

MMPI scale	r
Hypochondriasis	.06
Depression	.26
Hysteria	.13
Psychopathic Deviate	.27
Paranoia	.07
Psychasthenia	.18
Schizophrenia	.28
Hypomania	.17
Median	.18
Pairs	133

Note. From Loehlin, Willerman, & Horn (1987). Copyright 1987 by the American Psychological Association. Reprinted by permission.

did the difference between the separated and unseparated twins attain statistical significance—the correlations differed to within what sampling variation would allow.

No one can deny that occasional evidence for shared environmental influences crops up in twin and adoption studies. The evidence regarding parent-to-child influence, however, must be viewed in light of the many disconfirmations of such influences over a broad range of traits. The occasional statistically significant correlation between an adoptive parent and child may be merely a case of sampling chance. Indeed, the weight of evidence suggests that a higher standard of proof is needed for putative shared environmental influences than for putative genetic ones: The shared environmental result should be replicated across several studies before one begins to think about a family environmental mechanism to account for it.

What about that small rearing influence that is occasionally significant for some traits? Does this mean that something is going on environmentally in the family? Perhaps not, because the evidence for c^2 is strongest when data from MZ twins are included in the models discussed earlier. Environments may be able to induce resemblance when genetically identical people are exposed to similar circumstances or when twins and siblings are able to influence one another directly. In one of my studies of teenagers, I found that nontwin siblings who spent time with

TABLE 3.5. Resemblance in MZ Twins Reared Together (MZT) and Apart (MZA): The Minnesota Study of Twins Reared Apart

Measure	MZA	MZT	Variance attributable to shared environment
Fingerprint ridge count	.97	.96	−.01
Height	.86	.93	.07
Weight	.73	.83	.10
Brain alpha activity (two measures)	.80	.81	.01
	.80	.82	.02
Systolic blood pressure	.64	.70	.06
Heart rate	.49	.54	.05
Mean of 11 Multidimensional Personality Questionnaire scales	.50	.49	−.01
Mean of 18 California Personality Inventory Scales	.48	.49	.01
Mean of 23 Strong–Campbell Vocational Interest Inventory scales	.39	.48	.09
Mean of 17 Minnesota Occupational Interest Inventory scales	.40	.49	.09

Note. Adapted from Bouchard, Lykken, McGue, Segal, & Tellegen (1990). Copyright 1990 by the American Association for the Advancement of Science. Adapted by permission.

the same friends were more similar in smoking and drinking behavior than were siblings who did not spend time with the same friends (Rowe & Gulley, 1992). It is not particularly surprising that an older sibling or the friend of such a sibling can give a cigarette or beer to a younger brother or sister. Adult twins who stay in contact with each other may frequent the same "watering holes" or teetotaling social groups, and so may influence each other's drinking. Twins and nontwin siblings may sometimes also be "partners in crime," committing delinquent acts together; sibling correlations for delinquency are greater than for other traits (Rowe & Gulley, 1992). In a sample of reared-apart MZ twins, time spent in direct social contact was also associated with personality similarity, independently of the twins' age or age at separation (Rose, Kaprio, Williams, Viken, & Obremski, 1990). These contemporaneous sibling influences, however, may not be mechanisms of long-term socialization, because their effects depend on siblings' immediate social contacts— influences that may dissipate once contact is lost. An observation of contemporaneous environmental influences would not be proof that *rearing* environmental variation matters.

This review has slighted some areas of research that should be mentioned before I move on to studies of psychopathology. In an extensive series of behavior genetic studies, Robert Plomin and Arnold Buss (Buss & Plomin, 1984) have investigated childhood temperament, with particular emphasis on the traits of sociability, activity, and emotionality. In twin and adoption studies, these traits, as aspects of childhood personality, show a broad-sense heritability of .40 to .50. DZ twin correlations are often very low in childhood, sometimes even negative. Although additive genetic variation may be less important in childhood than in adulthood, a more plausible interpretation is that parents, who make these personality ratings, may contrast their children while rating them—scoring them as a bit more different than they are in actuality. The small sample size of many childhood twin studies also contribute to estimates' instability. On environmental effects, the twin and adoption studies of young children are in close agreement with the adult studies: There is little evidence of family environmental influences on temperamental traits assessed during childhood.

Another research focus is the issue of longitudinal stability versus change in personality. As Francis Galton (the English polymath who was the founder of modern behavior genetics) observed, twins who were alike at birth fail to develop great dissimilarities later in life, despite the accumulation of different experiences (Galton, 1876). I have concluded that directional change in personality traits is usually attributable to unshared environment, because MZ twins do not show a more similar profile of personality *change* than DZ twins (Rowe, 1987). That is, one MZ twin may become more sociable between the first time he or she takes a personality test and the second time, a year or a few years later. But the direction or amount of change in this MZ twin should *not* predict the direction or amount of personality change in his or her cotwin.

Conversely, "stability" refers to the tendency of individuals to maintain their same rank order on a trait dimension over time. It is apparently the result of genetics, as genetic factors continue to influence a trait throughout life. In my earlier article, I acknowledged that definitive proof could only come from lifelong studies of twins. Nonetheless, I asserted:

> The similarity of adult twins reared together, who have lived the greater part of their lives apart, is just a bit less surprising than the resemblance

of reared apart twins. Certainly, these results hint at a genetically driven stability to adult personality. (1987, p. 222)

Behavior Genetic Studies of Psychopathology

Problems of nomenclature and breadth of behavioral traits apply to psychopathology as well as to normal traits. One way to divide this domain is as follows: schizophrenia, mood disorders (bipolar disorder and unipolar depression), externalizing disorders (e.g., aggression and conduct problems), and internalizing disorders (e.g., high levels of anxiety). In this section, I briefly review relevant evidence on the influence of family environments in each of these types of disorders.

Schizophrenia

In both the popular mind and scientific circles, schizophrenia is the most devastating type of mental illness, with its great severity and sometimes bizarre symptomatology. Affecting about 1% of the population, schizophrenia includes such symptoms as an inability to form lasting emotional ties with friends and spouses; an absence of normal emotional responses to events; and delusions and hallucinations (usually auditory). I heard a women display symptoms of schizophrenia on one radio talk show when she complained that the government was listening to her while she shopped at the local supermarket. She thought that a large radar antenna at a local military base had been focused on her as she moved about the store. Although her beliefs were wildly delusional, her conversation with the talk show's host was otherwise quite reasonable. This example holds a bit of humor, but the life course of seriously ill schizophrenics can be tragic; their inability to hold jobs or to form lasting emotional bonds leaves them outside the friendships and pleasures of everyday life. Indeed, schizophrenics appear in disproportionate numbers in the population of the homeless and destitute in the United States.

During the dominance of Freudian influence from the 1920s to the 1950s (Torrey, 1992), the blame for schizophrenia was often placed on the "schizophrenogenic mother"—a women lacking in any emotional resonance toward her child. Postulating the existence of such a parent was reasonable, because about 10% of the offspring of one schizophrenic parent are affected with schizophrenia. And when observed in clinic or interviewed, a mother with schizophrenia does not exhibit ideal parenting styles: She often lacks normal affect toward her children because she lacks emotional response in general, and the household is disorganized because she herself is disorganized in her behavior. Few would deny that a schizophrenic mother violates the tenets of good parenting; if there is a family environmental influence able to "mess up" children, it should be this one.

Yet the "schizophrenogenic mother" explanation of psychopathology is dead. The chinks in the explanation were always there: The majority of the children of such mothers failed to display psychopathology, and the ability of many children to develop normally in a hostile environment was impressive. Consider this story of a schizophrenic mother with three children (Segal & Yahraes, 1979). The mother said she was poisoning the food. The oldest child, a girl, tended to believe her, and so she refused meals. A second daughter would eat when the (normal) father was present in the home. But the youngest child, a 7-year-old boy, noted that "I'm not dead yet," and continued to accept the meals produced by a delusional mother. The so-called "shared" family environment was experienced very differently by the children in this family.

But what of the evidence for the familial effect—the 10% incidence in the children of one schizophrenic parent? I believe that this similarity of parent and child is genetically induced. Pooling data across adoptive studies yields a rate of schizophrenia in the children of a schizophrenic biological parent who are then relinquished and raised by normal adoptive parents of about 1 in 10 (DeFries & Plomin, 1978). Yet this rate is about the *same* as that of children who are raised with a schizophrenic parent (9.4%, $n = 1,678$; McGue & Gottesman, 1989). Thus, adding the environmental disadvantage to the genetic one does not increase risk over what is already seen with genetic disadvantage alone. In contrast, genetic disadvantage alone does elevate risk (10%, vs. 1% in the general population). More complex model-fitting analyses also confirm the absence of rearing influence attributable to schizophrenic disease in a parent (McGue, Gottesman, & Rao, 1985).

Although its generalizability is limited by a small sample size, a study of the families of Danish MZ and DZ twins who were discordant for schizophrenia (i.e., one twin in each pair had a diagnosis of schizophrenia, while the other had no mental illness) illustrates the subtlety of the environmental influences (Gottesman & Bertelsen, 1989). More of the normal twins (64%) had children than the abnormal twins (29%), consistent with schizophrenics' having fewer children than other people.

Rates of diagnosed schizophrenia in the 150 offspring followed lines of genetic relatedness. As many offspring of MZ twins who displayed schizophrenia (16.8%) were diagnosed as offspring of MZ cotwins who did *not* display the illness (17.4%). A lack of illness in a parent failed to reduce the risk to children who were at risk genetically, as described in this brief case history: One twin developed schizophrenia after the birth of her second child, at age 25 years. Her cotwin also had two children, but was described as completely normal throughout her life. The cotwin's daughter developed paranoid schizophrenia, the same diagnosis as her affected aunt. No other child was affected. In the DZ pairs, more schizophrenia was evident in the children of the twins displaying schizophrenia (17.4%) than in the children of the cotwins who were free of the illness (2.1%), because the latter presumably had fewer genes tending toward schizophrenia.

These data, like the main findings of combined twin and adoption studies, show that the putative environmental effect is not a shared one (i.e., child-rearing practices), in which one would see an increase in schizophrenia risk to the children of an affected MZ twin. Rather, the environmental influences were *unshared* ones uncorrelated with rearing environment (they were just as prevalent in the "bad" homes as in the "good" homes). Whatever these influences were, they caused a schizophrenia genotype to go unexpressed in some individuals—so-called "false negatives," who appeared outwardly normal, but still carried some genes that put their own offspring at risk for the disease. These unshared environmental influences may have had nothing whatsoever to do with stresses in individuals' social environments. The source of discordance in psychopathology could have been accidents of embryological development, exposure to viruses, or some other biological process differentiating the MZ cotwins during their development. In a study using brain imaging methods, affected MZ twins had smaller ventricular areas (which contain spinal fluid but not nerve cells) and smaller anterior hippocampi (a brain area associated with the ability to form immediate memories) than their unaffected cotwins (Suddath, Christison, Torrey, Casanova, & Weinberger, 1990). Thus, a defect in the brain has been associated with schizophrenia in an affected twin of a discordant pair, suggesting that the psychopathology originates in some biological process or processes that have damaged one twin more than the other.

Given these data and other adoption data on schizophrenia, it is clear that exposure to a schizophrenic parent is not critical for the development of the illness. As Gottesman (1991) observed, "Both the necessity and the sufficiency of the specific kinds of schizophrenogenic environments provided by schizophrenic parents have been weakened by the adoption results. Recall that almost 90 percent of schizophrenics do not have schizophrenic parents" (p. 149). He cautions, however, that the adoption results permit gene × environment interactions, whereby children with schizophrenia-disposing genotypes would be more susceptible than nondisposed children to particular family influences (but not ones unique to schizophrenic parentage).

A Finnish adoption study (Tienari et al., 1990, 1991) searched for interactions between schizophrenia-disposing genotypes and family environments. Their research design compared children of schizophrenic biological mothers adopted by nonrelatives with a case-by-case matched group of adoptive children of normal biological mothers. As in other adoption studies, rates of psychotic disorders were elevated only among adopted-away children of schizophrenic biological mothers (9.3% in index adoptees vs. 1.1% in controls; Tienari et al., 1990). This result again shows how the transmission of disposing genes may increase schizophrenia risk.

In all adoptive families, environmental quality was assessed through lengthy home interviews leading to clinical evaluations of family mental health. Healthy adoptive families were those in which conflicts were rare, anxiety and depression were mild, and role functioning was appropriate to a family's stage in the life cycle. The most disturbed adoptive families either had major unresolved conflicts or were openly chaotic. Poor mental health functioning in the adoptive families was associated with the degree of psychiatric disturbance in the adoptive offspring. An interaction between genetic background and family environment held, because this relationship was stronger for the genetically disposed index adoptees (who had schizophrenic biological mothers) than for the control adoptees. Of the index adoptees with mentally healthy adoptive families, 3.5% had psychotic spectrum mental disorders, as compared to 62.2% of those with severely disturbed adoptive parents.

In summary, these adoptive findings indicate a possible interaction between genotype and family environment for the development of psychosis. Two cautions must be mentioned, however. The majority of adoptive offspring in the Finnish study were adults when their adoptive families were interviewed. Hence, the study did not start prior in time to the offspring's development of psychiatric illness. This research design means that the direction of causality is a concern; it is possible that a severely disturbed child may harm an adoptive family's mental health status, rather than vice versa. Second, the interviewing clinicians were aware of the offspring's mental health status, which may have confounded their reports of family mental health status. If the Finnish study leads to replications of the same type, then an exciting possibility of gene × environment interactions for psychosis would be assured. At least in this behavioral domain, familial influences may interact with children's genetic dispositions.

Although the genetics of schizophrenia fall outside this chapter's main focus, I present a brief summary of these results in Table 3.6. As would be expected for a familial genetic disorder, the risk to the relatives of affected individuals closely reflects their genetic relatedness. Still at issue is the exact mode of inheritance of schizophrenia (e.g., do genes with major effects exist?). Reviewing this evidence, McGue and Gottesman (1989) concluded that the evidence is most consistent with a polygenic model, because the nonlinear decline in concordance with degree of genetic relatedness is best satisfied by a multigene model. Nonetheless, the last word has not been heard on the issue, and a search is underway to find large-effect schizophrenia genes by means of linkage analysis with molecular genetic markers.

Mood Disorders

Two mood disorders constitute another major branch of mental illness. The two disorders are unipolar depression, which manifests itself as cyclic periods of severe depression; and bipolar disorder, in which depression cycles with mania (a state of high energy, euphoria, and sometimes delusional beliefs). Lifetime prevalences are greater for unipolar (about 6%) than for bipolar (about 0.5%) illness, with prevalences greater in women than in men (Tsuang & Faraone, 1990). Mood disorders have an unusual family correlate—greater creativity among the normal or mildly disturbed relatives of psychiatrically ill individuals. Greater creativity may be a biologically adaptive advantage conferred by the genes for mood disorders, when their number is below the threshold for severe illness (Andreasen, 1978; Richards, Kinney, Lunde, Benet, & Merzel, 1988).

Family, twin, and adoption data on mood disorders are less extensive than those on schizophrenia. Reviews in the area, however, suggest conclusions in accord with the schizophrenia findings (Moldin, Reich, & Rice, 1991; Tsuang & Faraone, 1990). Adoption studies demonstrate

TABLE 3.6. Schizophrenia Rates among the Relatives of Schizophrenics

Familial relationship	Sample size	% affected
Monozygotic twins	106	44.3
Offspring of two schizophrenic parents	134	36.6
Dizygotic twins	149	12.1
Siblings	7,523	7.3
Offspring of one schizophrenic parent	1,678	9.4
Half-siblings	442	2.9
Nieces or nephews	3,965	2.7
Grandchildren	739	2.8
First cousins	1,600	1.6
Spouses	399	1.0

Note. Sample size adjusted for age–risk curve (see Gottesman, Shields, & Hanson, 1982). Adapted from McGue & Gottesman (1989).

some familial genetic influence on both disorders. To date, the attempts to identify specific genes associated with the disorders through linkage analysis have been unsuccessful. Common family environmental influences are not suggested in the adoptive outcomes.

The twin data on mood disorders, however, are inconsistent with this book's thesis. The DZ twin correlations are more than one-half the MZ ones, suggesting considerable rearing influence. Tsuang and Faraone (1990) estimate that about 40% of variation in mood disorders is attributable to rearing.

At first glance, we would seem to have a puzzling exception to the general rule of a lack of influence from family differences. The growing skepticism about this influence, based on the general studies of personality that have been reviewed already, suggests looking for other possible explanations before too readily accepting some form of rearing experience here. One possibility immediately presents itself: nonrandom mating. Unhappy people preferentially marry each other. This does not mean that the unhappy necessarily prefer one another; the unhappy may have fewer choices in the marriage "marketplace" if happy people reject them. Nonrandom mating effects can mimic rearing influence in twin studies, because matched matings tend to increase the DZ twin correlations but cannot affect the MZ ones (because MZ twins cannot be made more alike genetically than they already are, whereas nonrandom mating tends to bring similar genes together in siblings). Given that the twin estimate of common sibling environment (c^2) is $2r_{DZ} - r_{MZ}$ (see chapter 2), a greater DZ correlation tends to be "read" as shared environment even when it is induced by assortative mating. Thus Tsuang and Faraone (1990) conclude:

> The effects of common [shared] environment will be overestimated and those of heritability underestimated in the presence of assortative mating. Thus, the true magnitude of the genetic effect is likely to be larger than variance components suggest, because assortative mating is common among patients with mood disorders. (p. 91)

Externalizing Disorders

In childhood and adolescence, poor attention span, high activity levels, and conduct problems (i.e., disobedience, aggression) are more prevalent in boys than in girls. As with the major mental illnesses, a single diagnostic category may conceal considerable heterogeneity in pathways of genetic and environmental causation. Moreover, although these disorders often co-occur, they are imperfectly correlated. Some cases exist in which problems with attention span or activity level only are displayed, without co-occurring conduct problems; other cases exist in which conduct problems co-occur with normal attention span. The strong relationship of these "externalizing" behaviors—so called because these behavioral problems are easily seen by teachers and parents—to later crime and delinquency makes them of major concern in crime-ridden U.S. society.

Although behavior genetic studies of this disorder are not numerous, high-quality twin and adoption studies can serve to illustrate the absence of rearing influences. The twin study was completed in England by Goodman and Stevenson (1989), using 102 MZ and 111 DZ twin pairs. Parents, teachers, and observers provided ratings of the twins' hyperactivity. Table 3.7 presents the correlations for DZ twins and two kinds of MZ twins. One group consisted of MZ twins diagnosed as MZ on the basis of a standard questionnaire[1] (including questions such as "Are your twins as alike as two peas in a pod?"), but believed to be DZ by their parents. The other MZ twins were twins diagnosed as MZ and identified by their parents as MZ. (It may seem surprising that parents may not know what kinds of twins they have; one reason is that parents may be provided incorrect information at the time of their twins' birth, because delivery room doctors and nurses room must base their opinions about twin type on placental tissue, which can be unreliable for this

TABLE 3.7. Mean MZ and DZ Twin Correlations for Inattentiveness and Hyperactivity

Group	Twin r	No. of pairs
Recognized MZ	.62	64
Unrecognized MZ	.53	22
All MZ	.58	93
All DZ	.23	98

Note. Correlations reflect unweighted averages over different data sources in all categories of twins. Seven MZ pairs whose parents were uncertain or in conflict over twin classification were grouped with all MZ twins. Adapted from Goodman & Stevenson (1989). Copyright 1989 by Pergamon Press. Adapted by perrmission.

purpose.) The importance of this comparison is that it tested whether a *parental belief* that twins were MZ can make them more alike in behavior—a labeling bias influence, so to speak. As shown in Table 3.7, both kinds of MZ twins are about twice as similar as the DZ twins. The estimate of rearing influence was also effectively zero ($c^2 = -.12$).

Because twins experience high rates of premature birth, they constitute an ideal population for studying whether birth traumas have developmental consequences. Goodman and Stevenson (1989) examined this question as well. An MZ twin with a low birth weight (below 2,000 grams), however, was not more likely to be hyperactive than the genetically identical cotwin with a high birth weight. Regarding this discovery, Goodman and Stevenson commented: "In the absence of 'hard signs' of structural brain damage, childhood hyperactivity is unlikely to be the result of perinatal adversity, *even* if the child was at high perinatal risk, *e.g.* as a low birth weight twin" (1989, p. 707).

As in other samples, poor parenting practices were associated with hyperactivity in this study. Yet, given the lack of evidence for rearing influences from the twin analyses, the causality of this association must be viewed skeptically, as Goodman and Stevenson observed: ". . . hyperactivity is more likely to be a cause than a consequence of distorted family relationships" (1989, p. 706). Or both could be attributable to genes shared by parent and child—a possibility to which I will return in Chapter 5.

Parental treatments fared no better when evaluated in a study of adoptions. Jary and Stewart (1985) used a full adoption design (although information could not be obtained on *all* biological parents of the adoptees) and a comparison group of nonadopted children. All the children were diagnosed as conduct-disordered. More antisocial traits appeared in the biological parents than in the adoptive parents, in whom these traits were nearly absent. For example, 0% of the adoptive fathers were diagnosed as antisocial, as opposed to 11% of the adoptees' biological fathers and 14% of the nonadoptees' biological fathers. The rates of diagnoses in the adoptees' biological parents were conservative because information was available for only 34% of their fathers, but the full sample size was used to compute the 11% rate. The unmistakable implication is that children can develop serious problem behaviors without being raised by problem parents:

> If it is true that these disorders in fathers are largely responsible for the factors known to be associated with aggressive conduct disorder, such as broken homes, wife and child abuse, and inconsistent discipline, then our findings suggest that these social factors are not necessary to the origin of the disorder. (Jary & Stewart, p. 10).

Again, the link between rearing experiences and child outcome is weakened.

Internalizing Disorders

People with a variety of psychological problems report the negative emotions of depression, fear, and anxiety (commonly referred to as "internalizing" disorders, because they are not usually outwardly evident). Given the lack of rearing influences on personality traits of normal intensity, it is unsurprising that when these same emotions are experienced more intensely, they show the same mix of determinants. This point can be made by considering adult twins (n = 3,798 pairs) who completed a short questionnaire for symptoms of anxiety and depression (Kendler, Heath, Martin, & Eaves, 1986). About 30% of the twins admitted symptoms of anxiety, such as feelings of panic and worry. About 4% reported that they had suicidal thoughts. A finding relevant to one assumption of the twin method was that the frequency of the twins' current social contact was unassociated with the similarity of the reported symptoms. Various statistical models were fitted to the individual items; the main finding was genetic influence on all symptoms, and a singular lack of rearing influence on them. In the cautious phrasing of scholarly writing, Kendler et al. ventured:

... an etiologic role for familial factors could not be unambiguously demonstrated for any of the items studied. . . . Though these results do not eliminate a possible role for common [shared] environmental variables, they do suggest that factors such as rearing environment and culture play a smaller role than has previously been thought in the etiology of common symptoms of anxiety and depression. (1986, pp. 220–221)

Summary

In summary, the picture for psychopathology is not different from that for normal traits: There is little influence of common rearing experience on child or adult psychopathology. Exceptions may be found to this general rule, but they are not many. Delinquency in the teenage years is one trait that does not seem to fit the pattern; as noted by Cloninger and Gottesman (1987), twin resemblance for delinquency is not much greater in MZ than in DZ pairs. But this exception may be merely the result of the tendency of both types of twins to be "partners in crime" and to run around with the same adolescent crowd, as noted earlier (Rowe & Gulley, 1992). The general pattern for personality and psychopathology is now so reliable that it must be explained.

Behavior Genetic Studies of Social Attitudes

People hold beliefs about a wide variety of political, social, and religious topics. Socialization science assumes that many of these beliefs are acquired via social learning in the family. One can easily imagine exposure to an "Archie Bunker" father, who spouts racial slurs and advocates conservative social policies to anyone who will listen. All children old enough to understand Archie's political views will be exposed to them, and may therefore acquire them. At the other extreme, politically liberal parents may encourage humanitarian impulses toward the less fortunate, and may use the abundance of the American dinner table as an object lesson in the need for social generosity. Our intuition is that rearing effects are strong, because we know that social attitudes must be learned somewhere. Unlike physical activity or emotional outbursts, attitudes do not seem to spring immediately from physiology. Yet the fact that these attitudes must be learned does not mean that family experiences are crucial exposures for acquiring them. It is easy to forget that even a young child's life is wider, more varied, and more rich in experiential opportunities than most parents will readily acknowledge.

In their review of earlier studies and report of original findings, Eaves, Eysenck, and Martin (1989) applied the full armamentarium of behavior genetic model-fitting research to explore underlying influences on social attitudes. They examined both individual attitudinal items from major attitude self-report inventories and composite, multifactor scales. Their data consisted of twin samples in England and Australia, with sample sizes in the hundreds of pairs; hence, they reported empirical replications across continents.

It was quickly apparent that social attitudes do not present the same kinds of data patterns as personality traits do. DZ twin correlations were higher for social attitudes than for personality traits. Thus, from basic model fitting, it looks as though *both* heredity and rearing experience influence social attitudes. For example, male twins' authoritarianism correlated .74 in MZ pairs and .44 in DZ pairs. According to our algebraic rules, the estimates of heritability (h^2) and rearing influence (c^2) would be 60% and 14%, respectively. For males twins' religion (a scale of belief in particular religious precepts, not membership in a particular religious faith), the respective correlations were .66 and .51, with $h^2 = .30$ and $c^2 = .36$. For female twins' prejudice, they were .61 and .48, with $h^2 = .26$ and $c^2 = .35$. Other examples could be given, but the pattern is clear: The twin data include a component of genetic influence *and* a component of rearing influence. Table 3.8 presents short one- and two-word items from the Australian questionnaire, separated according to whether the items had large or small rearing effects. For each item, respondents indicated whether they approved, disapproved, or were indifferent. No difference in content or emphasis is immediately apparent in the items where variation was statistically more versus less "family environmental." Possibly the difference between the items was merely one of sampling variation.[2]

The conclusion that family environments influence social attitudes has one important caveat, however, that could entirely undermine our inference of nongenetic family influence. That is, nonrandom marriage effects are also greater for social attitudes than for personality traits, or even for intellectual ability. For instance, in one British study, the spouse correlation for religion was .52; for authoritarianism, .56; for socialism, .54; and for prejudice, .35 (Eaves et al., 1989, p. 378). As we have seen for mood disorders, if spouses match on a behavioral trait, greater genetic similarity may be induced in offspring, which in turn can inflate the value

TABLE 3.8. Social Attitudes with High and Low
Family Environmental Influence (Marriage
Assortment Not Considered)

Low family environmental influence, high genetic influence

1. Death penalty
2. Self-denial
3. Working mothers
4. Military drill
5. White superiority
6. Cousin marriage
7. Chaperones
8. Empire building
9. Computer music
10. Fluoridation
11. Women judges
12. Conventional clothes
13. Teenage drivers
14. Apartheid
15. Censorship
16. White lies
17. Strict rules
18. Jazz
19. Learning Latin
20. Divorce
21. Inborn conscience

High family environmental influence, low genetic influence

1. School uniforms
2. Birth control
3. Divine law
4. Nudist camps
5. Bible truth
6. Co-education

Note. Adapted from Eaves, Eysenck, & Martin (1989). Copyright 1989
by the Academic Press Ltd. Adapted by permission.

of a DZ twin correlation in a way that mimics the effects of family environment. These high spousal correlation coefficients did not appear to be the result of social influence in the marriage; people who had been married a long time were not more alike in their attitudes than were newlyweds. Initial assortment, rather than influence, thus seems to be the cause of spousal behavioral resemblance.

Readers may notice an ironic parallel here with this book's theme. I have argued that rearing experiences do not influence the traits of children—whose youth, potential for developmental growth, and inexperience make them seem like potential candidates for an influence process. Yet we accept quite readily the idea that our spouses are hard to influence; it is easier to avoid an area of divergent opinion than to try to get our wives or husbands to agree. How intuitive it is that spouses are hard to change! Yet the great change that occurs in children does not mean that their *direction* of change is any more malleable to our wishes than that of our spouses, to whom we also apply pressure by social example and by levers of reward and punishment, but to little advantage.

In statistical models including nonrandom mating, Eaves et al. (1989) were able to show that a statistical parameter representing parental influence on children's social attitudes could be omitted without degrading statistical model fits:

> The degree of assortative [nonrandom] mating for attitudes is so high that its genetic consequences could account for all the additional resemblance between twins that our earlier analyses had ascribed to the "family environment." . . . This result does not agree with our initial intuition that cultural factors derived from parents are major determinants of family resemblance in attitudes. (p. 387)

Given these countervailing models, Eaves et al. (1989) concluded that one must turn to other behavior genetic designs to rule out rearing influences decisively. The nonrandom mating model suggests that an adoptive parent and child will lack resemblance for social attitudes, whereas a rearing environment model expects familial resemblance among biologically unrelated individuals raised in one household.

Not many adoptive data exist for social attitudes, but the few existing examples are consistent with a lack of rearing influence. In the Minnesota study of twins raised apart, separated twins correlated as highly as unseparated twins for religious traditionalism (Bouchard et al., 1990). Another important test comes from Sandra Scarr's (1981) adoption study of authoritarianism (as assessed via the F or Fascism scale). This area of research has been described in Chapter 1; although Adorno, Frenkel-Brunswik, Levinson, and Sanford (1950) viewed the F scale as tapping into an underlying dimension of personality, the items themselves refer to generalized social attitudes. Table 3.9 presents a few items from the F scale. Reading through items 3, 4, and 8, where agreement represents authoritarianism, one can sense an extremity of emphasis. Phrases such as "complete faith," "somehow get rid of," and "publicly whipped or worse" suggest a conservative extreme on some dimension of opinion— Archie Bunker rather than Thomas Jefferson. And such broadly stated

TABLE 3.9. Illustrative Authoritarianism Items

1. One of the most important things children should learn is when to disobey authorities. (R)
2. People ought to pay more attention to new ideas, even if they seen to go against the American way of life. (R)
3. Most of our social problems could be solved if we could somehow get rid of the immoral, crooked, and feebleminded people.
4. Every person should have complete faith in a supernatural power whose decisions he obeys without question.
5. The artist and professor are probably more important to society than the business man and the manufacturer. (R)
6. The findings of science may some day show that many of our most cherished beliefs are wrong. (R)
7. In spite of what you read about the wild sex life of people in important places, the real story is about the same in any group of people. (R)
8. Sex crimes, such as rape and attacks on children, deserve more than mere imprisonment; such criminals ought to be publicly whipped or worse.

Note. R = agreement means lack of authoritarianism. From Adorno, Frenkel-Brunswik, Levinson, & Sanford (1950). Copyright 1950 by the American Jewish Committee. Reprinted by permission of HarperCollins Publishers Inc.

opinions invite disagreement from people who hold a more differentiated view of the social world.

Scarr (1981) compared parent–child and sibling attitudinal resemblance in 112 adoptive families and 120 matched biological families in Minnesota. All children were placed with adoptive families before their first birthdays. The adoptive parents held more authoritarian attitudes than the biological ones; Scarr speculated that this difference was partly attributable to the location of relatively more adoptive families in small towns and rural areas. The mean differences, however, were not great compared to the variability of attitudes held within the two groups of families: Some parents were highly authoritarian, others just the opposite, and children in both sets of families were exposed to a wide range of beliefs. As we have seen for social attitudes generally, nonrandom mating effects existed for authoritarian attitudes (the spouse correlation for biological families was .43, and that for adoptive families was .34).

Scarr's data can be used to test the expectation that variation in rearing should influence authoritarianism, if adoptive family members' authoritarian beliefs correlate. But Scarr did not find this. Adoptive relatives' attitudinal resemblance was weak (and, statistically, could have been attributable to chance). In contrast, biological family members resembled one another strongly. The mother–child authoritarianism correlations showed the greatest contrast: In the adoptive families this correlation was .00, whereas in the biological families it was .41. The sibling correlations were .14 and .36, respectively, and the father–child correlations were .06 and .44, respectively. Thus similar beliefs occurred whenever families shared genes, but not when they shared rearing experiences alone. It takes a small act of imagination to think of the possible mismatches represented by a correlation of zero: a mother who believes that criminals should get the gallows, while her adolescent adoptive son would vote against the death penalty; or a mother who belongs to the Sierra Club and votes Democratic, while her adolescent adoptive daughter would think that social problems can be solved, in Adorno et al.'s (1950) phrase, by ridding the world of the "immoral, crooked, and feebleminded."

What happened? Why didn't the adolescent adoptive children share their parents' beliefs? Scarr's data contain several clues suggesting a possible explanation, the first being the strong association of verbal IQ and authoritarian attitudes: The Adorno et al. items were endorsed in the authoritarian direction by *less* verbally bright individuals. Of course, this does not mean that high-IQ individuals never hold authoritarian beliefs; however, such individuals may better sense the social opprobrium attached to endorsing authoritarian items, and thus may not choose not to make a public expression of these beliefs. Authoritarian beliefs also may be truly rarer among highly intelligent individuals, who may be loath to respond to social complexities with the blunt instrument of authoritarian solutions. Whatever the exact process, the general lesson is that individuals reason according to their own beliefs, independently of parental example. The genes for IQ congregate in biological families, and therefore so do the reasoning abilities that lead to similar attitudes.

In Scarr's data, authoritarian attitudes were also positively associated with personality traits reflecting fear in social situations. More fearful individuals may grope for direct solutions to social conflicts. Genes for personality traits, like those favoring intellectual traits, congregate in biological families, and therefore so does the tendency to develop similar social attitudes when personality favors one belief over another. In Scarr's (1981) words, "authoritarian attitudes are not learned in rote fashion from one's associates (parents, teachers, colleagues) but rather represent conclusions one has reached by applying one's cognitive skills to social and political experiences" (p. 423). Thus we reach the final conclusion that, most likely, both genes (for IQ and personality traits) and nonrandom mating give the appearance of rearing influences in twin studies of social attitudes. The people one is raised with have little lasting importance for what one finally believes.

Behavior Genetic Research
on Religious Affiliation

Variation in rearing does matter, however, for religious affiliation. It is true that religious denomination is neither a personality trait nor a social attitude, and as such does not qualify as a trait. Nonetheless, exceptions are interesting because behavior genetic methods seem so regularly to fail to show rearing influence that, if nothing else, we need to see an example where they can come to the opposite conclusion. In Eaves, Martin, and Heath's (1990) twin-family study in Australia, religious denominations (mainly Anglican, other Protestant, and Catholic) revealed what was missing from other traits: Children were like the parents who reared them in religion, and the twin siblings were also like each other. Resemblances were not perfect, because some individuals changed religious denominations; furthermore, when children grew up and left home, they became less like their parents. I do not intend to describe Eaves et al.'s statistical analysis in detail. Their model-fitting procedures led to the main conclusion that these patterns of imitation were environmental—that they were rearing effects.

At first glance, the environmental inheritance of religious denomination may seem to conflict with the genetic transmission of social attitudes; however, once one realizes the wide range of belief and opinion held within a large denomination, the conflict vanishes. Some Catholics use birth control and have had abortions, whereas others are ardently pro-life. Some Anglicans are politically conservative, whereas others are liberal. What Eaves et al. (1990) tested was merely the transmission of a religious label—not whether the professed faith was accepted, not whether religious ceremonies were observed, and not whether faith was shallow or deep. Indeed, the implication of a religious life is unverified in naming a denomination. Genetic influence appears strongly in the transmission of religious *beliefs* (Waller, Kojetin, Bouchard, Lykken, & Tellegen, 1990).

Nonetheless, certainly pollsters and church leaders care to count their numbers, and we must ask why religious denomination shows rearing influence. One answer may be that it takes time and effort before the doctrine and ceremonies of a faith are learned. Parents provide the opportunity for this learning, so a choice based on a child's own genetic disposition is impossible. Once the child becomes an adult, the discomforts of switching faiths are many: Neither the liturgy, the music, the doctrines, nor the traditions of a new faith are known, nor are they conveniently acquired. It is easy to find friendship and emotional support from members of one's own faith, and easy to step into its comfortable routines. If another faith would be inherently more attractive (e.g., Unitarianism in place of Catholicism for the religiously dubious), there is still the cost of time and effort in making the transition from one faith to another. So it may be simply that the costs of exploring new alternatives outweigh the immediate benefits of staying in the original faith. People may remain ensconced in their own faith, unless pulled away from it by an interfaith marriage or by movement into a different social class, where opportunities to practice the faith learned in childhood become greatly reduced. Ironically, the Eaves et al. (1990) data gave a hint of genetic influence on female twins' choice of religious denomination, once the twin sisters had left home. In an environment of greater choice and opportunity, genetic dispositions may begin to influence choice, when they may not have before.

Niche Picking

In his book *The Extended Phenotype*, Richard Dawkins (1982) cleverly imagines how genotypes may extend beyond the confines of nucleic acid to encompass a constructed environment that nurtures, protects, and supports the organism. The extended environment is as much a creation of the genes as is the body that houses them. To pick two of many illustrations, the paper wasp creates a paper-like nest to house its young and protect them from rain and wind. The beaver plays construction worker, deftly cutting down trees with its razor-sharp teeth and building dams that rechannel streams, flooding a basin for its mud and wood home. How can these acts be regarded as acts of DNA, when genes code only for proteins and do not contain within them a blueprint of a paper nest or dam? The answer is that the genes may construct a nervous system— and that hormones and neurotransmitters may then motivate behaviors resulting in the dramatic redesign of an environment. The way a beaver will restructure its environment is as genetically shaped as its flat tail and keen hearing.

The extended phenotypes of paper wasps and beavers emerge from a hard-wired, instinctive sense of what things ought to be. Little tutoring is needed for the expression of either behavior, although I suspect that the dam building of a beaver must improve with experience, as even bees show a capacity for learning.

Dawkins's examples are undeniably examples of instincts—of stereotyped inherent patterns of behavior (Wessells & Hopson, 1988). Such instincts are shared by most individuals in a species, but the present topic is individual differences in traits. Yet the conceptual distance between the human expression of individual differences and the extended phenotype of a species may not be so great. Genes can produce dispositions, tendencies, and inclinations, because people with subtly different nervous systems are differently motivated. Admittedly, the process of causality is a probabilistic one—but it is reliable, on the average, when one looks at enough people, or examines a long enough period in a single person's life. The genes themselves do not pick the environment; only the whole person, not DNA sheltered within the nuclei of trillions of cells, can act. Yet, given enough environmental opportunities, the ones chosen are those most reinforcing for a particular nervous system created by a particular genotype.

The role of "genotypes" in modifying and selecting environments has been labeled in behavior genetics with the terms "reactive" and "active" gene–environment correlations (Plomin, DeFries, & Loehlin, 1977; Scarr & McCartney, 1983). The reactive correlation refers to other people's responses to one's genetic disposition. For instance, a highly active child triggers more parental surveillance than an inactive one. A beautiful woman attracts the attention of more men than an unattractive one. The other type is the active correlation, whereby individuals with different genetic dispositions eventually discover and frequent the environmental contexts that reinforce them. The chess-playing prodigy, who spends hours practicing, reading about chess, and competing in tournaments, fertilizes an innate talent with the kinds of challenges that will nurture it.

In a behavior genetic study, the gene–environment correlation, like the extended phenotypes of wasps and beavers, counts as part of *genetic variation* because the direction of the growth curve of development, and the limit ultimately attained, is set in the genes and in their effects on the environment. Perhaps this is unfair, because the environment plays a direct causal role in developing and maintaining a genetic disposition; certainly, without the environmental opportunities, neither the talent of a chess prodigy nor the creativity of a recording artist could flourish.

But the character of these environmental influences is qualitatively different from that of rearing ones. Rearing environments are imposed on children, whereas the reactive and active environments are created in response to the particular genotype. To some extent they are chosen, as Scarr and McCartney (1983) observe: ". . . most differences among people arise from genetically determined differences in the experiences to which they are attracted and which they evoke from their environments" (p. 433). Socialization science looks to rearing to change developmental growth curves, but it is exactly the *imposed* rearing environment that loses its sway over development until, as we have seen, adoptive children no longer resemble their (biologically unrelated) siblings or parents, and until the similarity seen in biological families is merely the happenstance of overlapping heredity. In biological families too, the genetic differences among siblings often generate very different life courses as, through the reactive and active processes, children discover the environmental opportunities for the genes' extended phenotype. In a newspaper column, Curtis Austin (1991) warned against attributing too much influence to rearing:

> Yet I can't help but feel another side of the story receives far less attention. It's not always the parents' fault. Sometimes, truly loving and caring parents have troubled kids. . . . In the middle-class neighborhood where I was raised, the Wheeler boys were a study in contrast. Gary, the older by about two years, was well-mannered, hard-working and a straight-A student. Carlton, was loud, abrasive and a constant trouble-maker. Gary went on to college, got married and raised a family. His brother became a professional criminal, spending his life in and out of prison. (p. D1)

In the diversity of American society, the environmental opportunities exist to manifest almost any behavioral disposition. Children may discover friends among peers whose values are as foreign to their own parents as another culture's. In Austin's example, Carlton Wheeler, despite being reared under the same roof with the same caring parents as Gary, displayed a very different developmental trajectory. The implication is that parents are often given too much credit for children who turn out well, and too much blame for children who turn out poorly. The source of causal influence is not in rearing variation, but in the genes and in unshared environmental variation.

This chapter has covered the nonintellectual personality traits. Historically, intellectual abilities have held a more central position in the nature–nurture debate because their social importance merges a scholarly concern with the concerns of social policy makers and parents. So the next chapter returns to this old battlefield, and examines the hypothesis of rearing influences on IQ.

Notes

[1]The questionnaire could not assign 8% of the cases, which were omitted from the analysis. Questionnaire identification of twin type is usually quite accurate (about a 95% hit rate) when compared to biological means of determining twin type, such as human blood groups.

[2]Differences in the heritability of beliefs may be important. Tesser (1993) found that more heritable beliefs are more resistant to change in response to social pressure.

References

Andreasen, N. C. (1978). Creativity and psychiatric illness. *Psychiatric Annals*, 8, 113–119.

Adorno, T. W., Frenkel-Brunswik, E., Levinson, D. J., & Sanford, R. N. (1950). *The authoritarian personality*. New York: Harper.

Allport, G. W. (1966). Traits revisited. *American Psychologist, 21,* 1–10.

Austin, C. (1991, November 16). Kids' wrong turns don't always lead back to parents. *Dallas Times Herald*, Section D, 1.

Begley, S., & Kasindorf, M. (1979, December 3). Twins: Nazi and Jew. *Newsweek*, 139.

Bollen, K., & Lennox, R. (1991). Conventional wisdom on measurement: A structural equation model perspective. *Psychological Bulletin, 110,* 305–314.

Bouchard, T. J., Lykken, D. T., McGue, M., Segal, N. L., & Tellegen, A. (1990). Sources of human psychological differences: The Minnesota study of twins reared apart. *Science, 250,* 223–228.

Buss, A. H., & Plomin, R. (1984). *Temperament: Early developing personality traits*. Hillsdale, NJ: Erlbaum.

Cloninger, C. R., & Gottesman, I. I. (1987). Genetic and environmental factors in antisocial behavior disorders. In S. Mednick, T. Moffit, & S. Stack (Eds.), *The causes of crime* (pp. 92–109). New York: Cambridge University Press.

Dawkins, R. (1982). *The extended phenotype: The gene as the unit of selection*. Oxford: Oxford University Press.

DeFries, J. C., & Plomin, R. (1978). Behavioral genetics. *Annual Review of Psychology, 29,* 473–515.

Digman, J. M. (1990). Personality structure: Emergence of the five-factor model. *Annual Review of Psychology, 41,* 417–440.

Eaves, L. J., Eysenck, H. J., & Martin, N. G. (1989). *Genes, culture and personality: An empirical approach.* London: Academic Press.

Eaves, L. J., Martin, N. G., & Heath, A. C. (1990). Religious affiliation in twins and their parents: Testing a model of cultural inheritance. *Behavior Genetics, 20,* 1–22.

Funder, D. C. (1991). Global traits: A neo-Allportian approach to personality. *Psychological Science, 2,* 31–39.

Galton, F. (1876). The history of twins as a criterion of the relative powers of nature and nurture. *Royal Anthropological Institute of Great Britain and Ireland Journal, 6,* 391–406.

Goodman, R., & Stevenson, J. (1989). A twin study of hyperactivity: II. The aetiological role of genes, family relationships and perinatal adversity. *Journal of Child Psychology and Psychiatry, 30,* 691–709.

Gould, S. J. (1981). *The mismeasure of man.* New York: Norton.

Gottesman, I. I. (1991). *Schizophrenia genesis: The origins of madness.* New York: W. H. Freeman.

Gottesman, I. I., & Bertelsen, A. (1989). Confirming unexpressed genotypes for schizophrenia: Risks in the offspring of Fischer's Danish identical and fraternal discordant twins. *Archives of General Psychiatry, 46,* 867–872.

Gottesman, I. I., Shields, J., & Hanson, D. R. (1982). *Schizophrenia: The epigenetic puzzle.* Cambridge, England: Cambridge University Press.

Hill, M. S., & Hill, R. N. (1973). Hereditary influence on the normal personality using the MMPI: I. Age-corrected parent–offspring resemblances. *Behavior Genetics, 3,* 133–144.

Hoffman, L. W. (1985). The changing genetics/socialization balance. *Journal of Social Issues, 41,* 127–148.

Hoffman, L. W. (1991). The influence of family environment on personality: Accounting for sibling differences. *Psychological Bulletin, 110,* 187–203.

Jary, M. L., & Stewart, M. A. (1985). Psychiatric disorder in the parents of adopted children with aggressive conduct disorder. *Neuropsychobiology, 13,* 7–11.

Kendler, K. S., Heath, A., Martin, N. G., & Eaves, L. J. (1986). Symptoms of anxiety and depression in a volunteer twin population. *Archives of General Psychiatry, 43,* 213–221.

Kenrick, D. T., & Funder, D. C. (1988). Profiting from controversy: Lessons from the person–situation debate. *American Psychologist, 43,* 23–34.

Loehlin, J. C. (1986). Heredity, environment, and the Thurstone Temperament Schedule. *Behavior Genetics, 16,* 61–73.

Loehlin, J. C. (1992). *Genes and environment in personality development.* Newbury Park, CA: Sage.

Loehlin, J. C., & Rowe, D. C. (1992). Genes, environment, and personality. In G. Caprara & G. L. Van Heck (Eds.), *Modern personality psychology: Critical reviews and new directions* (pp. 352–370). New York: Harvester Wheatsheaf.

Loehlin, J. C., Willerman, L., & Horn, J. M. (1987). Personality resemblance in adoptive families: A 10-year follow-up. *Journal of Personality and Social Psychology, 53,* 961–969.

Lykken, D. T., McGue, M., Tellegen, A., & Bouchard, T. J., Jr. (1992). Emergenesis: Genetic traits that may not run in families. *American Psychologist, 47,* 1565–1577.

McCrae, R. R., & Costa, P. T., Jr. (1990). *Personality in adulthood.* New York: Guilford Press.

McGue, M., & Gottesman, I. I. (1989). Genetic linkage in schizophrenia: Perspectives from genetic epidemiology. *Schizophrenia Bulletin, 15,* 453–464.

McGue, M., Gottesman, I. I., & Rao, D. C. (1985). Resolving genetic models for the transmission of schizophrenia. *Genetic Epidemiology, 2,* 99–110.

Moldin, S. O., Reich, T., & Rice, J. P. (1991). Current perspectives on the genetics of unipolar depression. *Behavior Genetics, 21,* 211–242.

Plomin, R., DeFries, J. C., & Fulker, D. W. (1988). *Nature and nurture during infancy and early childhood.* Cambridge, England: Cambridge University Press.

Plomin, R., DeFries, J. C., & Loehlin, J. (1977). Genotype–environment interaction and correlation in the analysis of human behavior. *Psychological Bulletin, 84,* 309–322.

Price, R. A., Vandenberg, S. G., Iyer, H., & Williams, J. S. (1982). Components of variation in normal personality. *Journal of Personality and Social Psychology, 43,* 328–340.

Richards, R., Kinney, D. K., Lunde, I., Benet, M., & Merzel, A. P. C. (1988). Creativity in manic–depressives, cyclothymes, their normal relatives, and control subjects. *Journal of Abnormal Psychology, 97,* 281–288.

Rose, R. J., Kaprio, J., Williams, C. J., Viken, R., & Obremski, K. (1990). Social contact and sibling similarity: Facts, issues, and red herrings. *Behavior Genetics, 20,* 763–778.

Rowe, D. C. (1987). Resolving the person–situation debate: Invitation to an interdisciplinary dialogue. *American Psychologist, 42,* 218–227.

Rowe, D. C., & Gulley, B. (1992). Sibling effects on substance use and delinquency. *Criminology, 30,* 217–233..

Scarr, S. (1981). *Race, social class, and individual differences in I.Q.* Hillsdale, NJ: Erlbaum.

Scarr, S., & McCartney, K. (1983). How people make their own environments: A theory of genotype → environment effects. *Child Development, 54,* 424–435.

Segal, J., & Yahraes, H. (1979). *A child's journey: Forces that shape the lives of our young.* New York: McGraw-Hill.

Suddath, R. L., Christison, G. W., Torrey, E. F., Casanova, M. F., & Weinberger, D. R. (1990). Anatomical abnormalities in the brains of monozygotic twins discordant for schizophrenia. *New England Journal of Medicine, 322,* 789–794.

Tesser, A. (1993). The importance of heritability in psychological research: The case of attitudes. *Psychological Review, 100,* 129–142.

Tienari, P., Kaleva, M., Lahti, I., Laksy, K., Moring, J., Naarala, M., Sorri, A., Wahlberg, K. E., & Wynne, L. (1991). Adoption studies of schizophrenia. In C. Eggers (Ed.), *Schizophrenia and youth: Etiology and therapeutic consequences* (pp. 40–51). Berlin: Springer-Verlag.

Tienari, P., Lahti, I., Sorri, A., Naarala, M., Moring, J., Kaleva, M., Wahlberg, K., & Wynne, L. C. (1990). Adopted-away offspring of schizophrenics and controls: The Finnish adoptive family study of schizophrenia. In L. N. Robins & M.Rutter (Eds.), *Straight and devious pathways from childhood to adulthood* (pp. 365–379). Cambridge, England: Cambridge University Press.

Torrey, E. F. (1992). *Freudian fraud: The malignant effect of Freud's theory on American thought and culture.* New York: HarperCollins.

Tsuang, M. T., & Faraone, S. V. (1990). *The genetics of mood disorders.* Baltimore: John Hopkins University Press.

Waller, N. G., Kojetin, B. A., Bouchard, T. J., Lykken, D. T., & Tellegen, A. (1990). Genetic and environmental influences on religious interests, attitudes, and values: A study of twins reared apart and together. *Psychological Science, 1*, 138–142.

Wessells, N. K., & Hopson, J. L. (1988). *Biology.* New York: Random House.

CHAPTER 4

LIMITED REARING EFFECTS ON INTELLIGENCE (IQ)

n *Nature's Gambit* (Feldman, 1986), we can read case histories of extraordinary intellectual achievement. Adam Konantovich could speak in grammatical sentences at 3 months of age and read simple books at 1 year. At the age of 5 years, when attending a puppet show for preschoolers at the Boston Museum of Science, Adam answered a rhetorical question about what whales eat as follows: "Krill, they're small shrimp, but they're not microscopic." Billy Delvin was reading about particle physics at age 7 and scored better on the mathematics Scholastic Aptitude Test (SAT) than many junior high school students. Yet another story of precocity was told to me by a friend who is a professor at Harvard. His young daughter, then only about 18 months old, was greeted in the supermarket by a women who smiled and said, "Coochie, coochie, coo." His daughter then turned to her mother and asked, "Is she trying to talk to me?" These stories tell us that some children are born with unusually great aptitude for intellectual achievement. We recognize intuitively that no amount of "intellectual stimulation" (even the 3,000 books in the home of Adam Konantovich) could produce such talent in a child lacking special "gifts," but these unusual cases cannot tell us how important rearing environment is for intellectual development more generally—the issue broached in this chapter.

General Intelligence: Definitions and Controversies

Most social scientists recognize that "academic intelligence" refers to the ability to acquire the kinds of information taught in schools. Indeed, the first IQ tests were developed in France by Alfred Binet for the express purpose of early identification of children having difficulty with academic subjects. Beyond this common-sense statement, there is less agreement about a definition of "intelligence" because the kernel of skills needed for schooling is difficult to summarize in a short statement. Consensus definitions of intelligence among psychologists and educational specialists with expertise on intelligence included "abstract reasoning and thinking," "the capacity to acquire knowledge," and "problem solving ability" (Snyderman & Rothman, 1987). *Webster's Third International Dictionary* (1968) gives as one definition of intelligence "the faculty of understanding: capacity to know or apprehend." Another definition, clearly influenced by the development of psychometrics (i.e., the scientific study of individual differences in intelligence), is as follows: "the available ability as measured by intelligence tests or by other social criteria to use one's existing knowledge to meet problems, to use symbols or relationships, to create new relationships, to think abstractly" (p. 1174).

Although intelligence is a fuzzy concept, it provides enough narrowing criteria to exclude many rankable areas of human performance. In an unfortunate choice of terminology, Gardner (1983) discusses multiple human "intelligences," including such diverse types as musical ability, personal intelligence, and bodily/kinesthetic ability. As in math and English, individual differences in each of these other domains would cover a huge range, be relatively stable, and be rankable. However, these are not areas of "intelligence" according to our definition, because individual differences in abstract reasoning and problem solving are not strongly associated with individual differences in these other performance domains. For instance, professional tennis players, although sharing an inordinate degree of athletic talent, have IQ scores ranging from borderline retarded to brilliant, and so on for the other areas of performance. There would be less to quibble about had Gardner chosen the phrase "multiple talents" rather than "multiple intelligences," which confuses these other areas of ability with IQ.

Even if we restrict our consideration to the verbal and mathematical problem-solving skills of academic intelligence, questions about generality versus specificity remain. It is clear that in rare cases, specificity is so extreme that masterful performance in one domain of human accomplishment accompanies great retardation in nearly all others. Consider the case of Leslie Lemke, who was born profoundly retarded and suffering from cerebral palsy (Feldman, 1986). He was blind, his eyes having been surgically removed after birth for unexplained medical reasons. When he was about 18 years old, Leslie's mother added music to his daily routine, but she was unprepared for what came next: Leslie sat down at the piano and played (despite a total absence of musical training) Tchaikovsky's Piano Concerto No. 1 with a certain touch. His musical gifts were those of an "idiot savant"—a specialized brilliance in someone who is otherwise far below average (indeed, at the time, Leslie could not speak).

More typically, however, abilities in the academic domain show much closer integration. Subtest scores on an IQ test intercorrelate positively with one another in the .40 to .60 range—a positive relationship meaning that someone who scores below average on one IQ subtest is also likely to score below average on the others. This positive relationship occurs despite disparate test content. IQ subtests on the Wechsler Adult Intelligence Scale (WAIS) and the Wechsler Intelligence Scale for Children (WISC) include a General Information test, in which general "cultural literacy" is tested (e.g., number of weeks in a year, distances between major cities); a Comprehension subtest; a Vocabulary subtest; a Block Design subtest, in which a presented design must be reproduced quickly with red and white blocks; a Digit Span subtest, in which numbers heard must be repeated back; and several other subtests. The subtests either require previously acquired knowledge, or require quick reasoning but place fewer demands on accumulated past knowledge. When subtest scores are combined to form a total score, this score is said to represent "g," or general intelligence—the commonality of performance across different intellectual domains.

In his book *The Mismeasure of Man*, Stephen Jay Gould (1981) has stridently attacked the concept of a g underlying the domain of academic intelligence. His historical review covers debates among factor analysts over the number of dimensions underlying performance on IQ tests containing substantively diverse subtests. Spearman defended the concept of g, focusing on the commonality among subtests; at the other extreme, Guilford identified 120 separable ability dimensions within IQ tests. More commonly, the tests are seen as factoring into just a few dimensions, such as Thurstone's primary mental abilities of verbal comprehension and spatial visualization.

The two views of IQ tests, however, are really compatible. When the general population is broadly sampled to include people of diverse ability levels, g stands out in the positive intercorrelation of subtests, and one dimension may be used profitably to rank people. At the same time, further factor analysis of the subtests should identify specific factors that are themselves intercorrelated. Thus, separating factors provides a more exact ranking of individuals in particular subdomains of intellectual ability—allowing one, for instance, to identify more exactly the most and least mathematically skilled individuals, rather than using the more general ranking provided by a total test score that includes verbal as well as mathematical components. On the other hand, because of the correlation of the factors, the total score is just a more general ranking, not a dishonest or useless one, and for many purposes may serve as well as or better than a subtest score. After all, the civil service does not want to identify future mathematicians, but merely wants to find the people who are brighter (in a broad sense) than others.

Gould admits many of these facts, but puts a different emphasis on them. Although he acknowledges that Spearman's g factor extracted from a group of tests can encompass over half the variation in them (p. 314), he treats the factor-analytic solutions as purely arbitrary. He argues that g is a chimerical statistical artifact, just one mathematical solution among many equivalents. He calls it the "rotten core" (p. 320) of the hereditarian view of intelligence.

As a consumer of SAT scores, however, Gould must be aware that even in the restricted population of students ambitious enough to seek a college education, mathematical and verbal subtests correlate about .70, sharing about half their variance. The rank order of test takers on the total SAT score does not deviate greatly from their rank order on the basis of either the verbal or mathematical portion alone. This practical phenomenon, observed across many intellectual tests when administered to diverse populations, is enough alone to justify the use of the total score g rather than a component score in many applied and theoretical contexts. In sum, g is neither chimerical nor rotten, because the general population includes few people with skills as disjunctive as Leslie Lemke's. The "idiot savant" view of intelligence promoted by Gould is neither endorsed by modern factor analysts nor influential in the practical uses of IQ tests (Snyderman & Rothman, 1987).

The crux of IQ testing—or any measurement of intellectual achievement in academic work—is its relationship to socially valued outcomes (Barrett & Depinet, 1991). Parents care about IQ ability because of its power to forecast academic success. But the IQ test is embedded in a richer set of correlates than merely years of schooling, and these additional correlates, if anything, intensify the emotions surrounding the interpretation of IQ scores. IQ is particularly important for entry into and success in high-prestige occupations, such as medicine, law, and university teaching. It is unlikely that one would find a natural scientist, lawyer, or doctor with an IQ below 110, but this cutoff would exclude 75% of the white population or 95% of the black population in the United States from eligibility, according to current score distributions.

Decades of research in organizational psychology reveal that IQ determines job performance in a variety of occupations, and although validity coefficients are slightly higher for intellectually demanding occupations than for intellectually undemanding ones, they are important in occupations from the executive suite to the janitorial staff. Because of this connection with job performance levels, the use of ability test scores to match people to occupational niches can contribute to national productivity by making the best use of the national talent pool:

> . . . the use of the Programmer Aptitude Test in place of an invalid selection method to hire 618 entry-level computer programmers leads to an estimated productivity improvement of $54.7 million ($68 million in 1981 dollars) over a 10–year period if the top 30% of applicants are hired. . . . the gross national product would be increased by $80 to $100 billion per year if improved selection methods were introduced throughout the economy. (Schmidt & Hunter, 1981, p. 1129)

The basis for these striking conclusions is simple: observing people of low versus high IQ perform in a variety of occupations. Higher IQ test scores predict the acquisition of more job-relevant knowledge, both during training and later on the job (Hunter, 1986). Greater knowledge and better problem-solving skills together explain the association of IQ scores with superior job performance, whether rated by supervisory personnel or assessed by direct observation. As Hunter notes, "learning on the job goes on at a high rate for at least five years and continues at a slower rate out to 20 years, which is as far as the data goes [*sic*] . . . even simple jobs require far more learning than is evident to outsiders" (1986, p. 360).

Explanations for Intellectual Growth

The intuitive explanation of intellectual development is that it depends on various kinds of exposures to intellectually stimulating environments. How can this intuition be contradicted? The knowledge that Darwin wrote *The Origin of Species* or that $2x + 5 = 11$ solves for $x = 3$ cannot be encoded directly in the human genome; although the latter relationship might be discovered by a very gifted child without much formal training in algebra, the former must be directly taught or learned incidentally on exposure to this piece of information. The self-evident importance of exposure leads naturally to an emphasis in socialization science on rearing, because families own different numbers of books, use different vocabulary levels, and discuss topics of different intellectual complexity around the dinner table (or more commonly today, around the TV set).

But, of course, the home is not the only source of exposure to intellectual subjects. The "lighthouses of knowledge" envisioned in the 19th century—the U.S. system of universal education—may not live up to the ideal of providing the highest-quality education to every American child, but America's schools, good and poor, reach most children and offer a source of "intellectual stimulation" separate from the family of origin. Indeed, the importance of schooling has led the Cornell psychologist Steven Ceci (1990a) to the conclusion that schooling *is* the cause of IQ test performance:

> The processes associated with schooling influence performance on IQ tests through a combination of *direct* instruction (e.g., it is in school that most children learn the answers to many IQ questions such as "In what continent is Egypt?" "Who wrote Hamlet?" and "What is the boiling point of water?") and *indirect* modes or styles of thinking and reasoning (e.g., schools encourage taxonomic/paradigmatic sorting and responding, rather than thematic/functioning responding, and this happens to be the valued form of responding on IQ tests). (pp. 71–72, emphasis in the original)

Following Ceci's line of argument, we could replace variation in family environments with variation in school environments as the source of individual differences in intelligence. And Ceci marshals several arguments to illustrate the importance of schooling. For example, intellectual growth is slower in the summer, when children are out of school, than during the school year; unschooled children are not as bright as children who attend school; and the children who are in school the longest have the highest IQ scores. The last point was illustrated by substantial correlations between years of completed schooling and IQ. Ceci (1990a) remarks, ". . . it has been known for many decades that a child's experience of schooling exerts a strong influence on intelligence test performance. Overall, there is an adjusted correlation of .68 between the number of years of school completed and IQ" (p. 73).

Ceci is definitely onto something, but I cannot accept his conclusion that schooling alone is responsible for the individual differences in IQ that we see. Ceci ignores temporal order when, for whatever reason, he fails to mention while making this argument that IQ scores obtained much *earlier* in the academic career—even at the point of school entry in preschool and first grade—also predict the number of years of completed schooling. Unless we are willing to accept time travel as a premise, the accumulated exposure to indirect and direct benefits of instruction cannot cause these early differences in IQ scores. Rather, given this temporal order in the absence of time travel, we are forced to conclude that IQ, or some third factor associated with IQ and years of schooling, directly causes the number of years of schooling completed.

Consider the acquisition of vocabulary. Most vocabulary is learned incidentally from exposures to spoken and written language. During childhood, vocabularies grow from just a few words to thousands of words—a pace of acquisition so rapid that few parents have any idea about the origin of each new word. Schooling contributes importantly to this growth of vocabulary when words are acquired incidentally as children read texts—that is, when they infer the words' meaning from their natural context in a written passage (Nagy, Herman, & Anderson, 1985). During the middle school years, children acquire about 3,300 words each year. According to Nagy et al.'s (1985) estimates, they read about a million words per year and encounter from 15 to 55 unknown words in each 1,000 words of text. On the basis of their experimental results, a child has a 5% to 11% chance of correctly inferring a word's meaning from context on a single exposure; thus, children in the middle grades learn approximately 3,125 words from reading in a year, or nearly enough words to account for their annual vocabulary growth.

What accounts for individual differences in vocabulary acquisition? Clearly, individual differences in the amount read are part of the story, because the more reading is done, the more unknown words will be encountered and possibly acquired once their meaning is inferred from context. Another important process is the ability to extract a word's meaning from context when it is encountered in a passage. Using constructed passages, research studies have demonstrated that the ability to extract word meaning from context varies greatly by IQ level. In these studies, passages of simple vocabulary are constructed that contain one unknown word—a nonsense word, but one having a meaning in its new context. High-IQ individuals more successfully extract the meaning of the unknown word from its context in the otherwise simple passage (Sternberg, 1985, pp. 233–234). Readers may want to try the following passage:

> Two ill-dressed people—the one a tired women of middle years and the other a tense young man—sat around a fire where the common meal was almost ready. The mother, Tanith, peered at her son through the *oam* of the bubbling stew. (Sternberg, 1985, p. 233)

If this process holds, we can infer that brighter individuals will more easily acquire the meaning of unknown real words encountered in natural texts, and thus develop larger vocabularies, than less capable individuals.

Although we have a sense of why some individuals' vocabularies are larger than others, we still do not know what the crucial environments are. One view is that the rearing environment makes a large difference, because parental vocabularies differ markedly. But this view may miss the richness of the total environment to which any child who is not severely deprived is exposed. Even in the Arizona desert children can discover the meaning of the word "umbrella," because exposures are available, although perhaps not so commonplace as in London. The word "penguin" may be learned from a *National Geographic* special, from a cartoon, from reading a story about Antarctica, and from many other sources. The total number of exposures (a million words in text, millions more in spoken language) may reduce the variability in the size of vocabulary that is attributable to rearing environments, because the family environment is only a small part of the total social environment, and all aspects of this environment are rich in incidental learning opportunities.

This view that applies to vocabulary may hold for intellectual development generally. The total stimulation needed for intellectual development may be available to any child in families from the working class to the professional class; the environmental differences noticed among families may be relatively unimportant for the eventual intellectual growth attained. The critical environments may not be those *imposed* on children by virtue of accidents of birth, but those actively sought by children, and shaped by how children parse the stream of experience to which they are exposed. Even minority children do not exist in poor social environments, although their environments may be culturally *different* from the majority's. The process described in Chapter 3—the active gene–environment correlation—would then explain intellectual development, much as it does the development of character.

Behavior Genetic Studies of Rearing Environments and IQ

The behavior genetic literature on IQ is vast and is not comprehensively reviewed here. This literature unambiguously establishes the inheritance of intellectual abilities in families: Shared genes lead to resemblance in intellectual abilities, regardless of whether the pairs of relatives live together and experience similar environmental influences or live apart and experience different ones. Heritability estimates range from 40% to 70%, indicating that substantial variation in intellectual ability has substantial genetic basis.

Table 4.1 presents a list of IQ correlations, admittedly from heterogeneous studies, showing the typical decline of resemblance with decreasing genetic relatedness (Loehlin, 1989). For instance, MZ twins raised apart correlated .72, whereas cousins (who possess some environmental similarity, as do imperfectly separated MZ twins) correlated only .15. There are many ways to estimate heritability. Directly, from the correlation of MZ twins raised apart, it would be 72%; indirectly, from the correlation of parent and offspring reared apart, it would be 48%; from siblings reared apart, it would also be 48%. Model-fitting the correlations shown in Table 4.1, Chipuer, Rovine, and Plomin (1990) settled

TABLE 4.1. IQ Correlations for Different Pairs of Relatives

Group	Mean correlation	No. of pairs
MZ twins reared apart	.72	65
MZ twins reared together	.86	4,672
DZ twins reared together	.60	5,533
Siblings reared together	.47	26,473
Parent and child reared together	.42	8,433
Cousins	.15	1,176
Biological siblings reared apart	.24	203
Parent and child reared apart	.24	720
Unrelated siblings reared together[a]	.29	345
Unrelated siblings reared together[b]	.34	369
Parent and adopted child	.19	1,491

Note. Correlations for unrelated family members reared together come from older studies. The children were young, and selective placement effects were present. Original source: Bouchard & McGue (1981). Adapted from Loehlin (1989). Copyright 1989 by the American Psychological Association. Adapted by permission.
[a]Biological child of adoptive parent with adopted sibling.
[b]Adopted siblings from successive adoptions.

on a broad-sense (additive plus dominance) heritability of 51%. Loehlin (1989) fitted several different statistical models to the same correlations and arrived at broad-sense heritabilities ranging from 47% to 58%.

The surprise in the table is not the evidence for IQ heritability, but rather the evidence for an influence of different rearing environments. The adopted siblings correlated .34, suggesting that rearing environment accounts for 34% of variation in IQ (the correlation is not doubled because these siblings shared the full common environmental effect, despite sharing none of their genes). The estimate from adoptive parent and offspring was weaker (19%), but perhaps a parent and child share fewer experiences relevant to intellectual development than siblings do. These data raise a possibility of an ecumenical resolution of the nature–nurture debate in regard to IQ, as they imply that rearing experiences combine additively with inherited advantage or disadvantage in intellectual development.

Yet we have already seen that caution is needed in considering the sparse evidence for rearing influence. The adoptive data summarized in Table 4.1 contain two pitfalls. The first is selective placement (i.e., an adoptee's being placed in a family of social background similar to that of the biological parent)—a problem common in adoption studies of IQ, but virtually nonexistent in adoption studies of personality traits. As noted in Chapter 2, selective placement can lead to a genetic influence's being read as an environmental one. A second problem is that many adoption studies have used as subjects young children of preschool or early grade-school ages; the correlations in Table 4.1 represent a mix of ages, mostly young children. If the model of active gene–environment correlation is correct (Scarr & McCartney, 1983), then as environmental opportunities outside the family accumulate, children's IQ should be more greatly affected by their genetic potential and less influenced by their rearing experiences. In other words, early exposure to a large vocabulary and parental encouragement of achievement in the home should boost IQ test performance—not because the advantaged children are made any brighter, but merely because they are exposed to material that is relatively lacking in the home environments of less advantaged children. This real advantage cannot be maintained into adolescence and adulthood, however, because eventually most children (except those living in the most depriving environments) should encounter sufficient intellectual stimulation to reach their potential for intellectual growth.

One way to test this notion is to put age directly into the models of intellectual development. In a meta-analysis of 103 reports of twin studies, McCartney, Harris, and Bernieri (1990) explored the relation of twins' ages to the size of the rearing (shared) environment component inferred from the twin study design. For intelligence, the correlation of the estimate of rearing influence with twins' ages was –.37, indicating less influence of rearing environment as the twins became older. In contrast, the heritability of intelligence increased with age as rearing influences lessened (r = .36). In late adulthood (average age = 66 years), the heritability of IQ may be higher than that found earlier in life (about 80%; Pedersen, Plomin, Nesselroade, & McClearn, 1992).

New adoption studies completed with older children also give less credence to a lasting influence of rearing. Sandra Scarr and Richard Weinberg (1978) completed a study of children between 16 and 22 years of age in adoptive and biological families. Although none of the families in either the adoptive or the matched biological family groups were extremely deprived, they did represent a broad range of socioeconomic statuses, from the working to the professional social classes; incomes ranged from under $10,000 to more than $40,000 (1978 dollars). Scarr and Weinberg reported:

> Occupations of the fathers in the two samples varied from janitor, auto mechanic, small farmer (income < $10,000), telephone installer, and sheet metal worker at the low end to physician, engineer, college professor, and radio station owner at the high end of the scale. Most occupations were in the middle range of carpenter and printer to insurance agent and building contractor. (p. 678).

All the children had been adopted prior to 12 months of age.

Thus these were early-adopted children, now entering early adulthood (mean age = 18½ years), who had had years of exposure to varied rearing environments—years that should have acted to make the unrelated children reared together alike in IQ, and also to make them resemble their adoptive parents in intellectual abilities. The statistical results were unkind to this expectation. In the biological families, the IQ correlations were as follows: father–child, .40; mother–child, .41; and sibling, .35. In the adoptive families, they were .16, .09, and –.03, respectively. Consider now the interpretation of the unrelated siblings' correlation, –.03. Siblings who had been raised together for an average of 18½ years, but who lacked biological relatedness, were no more alike than randomly paired children raised in different families of similar social class backgrounds. Scarr and Weinberg (1978) drew the substantive conclusion revealed in these bare statistics:

If we observe that professional families take their children to the theater more often than working-class families, or hang mobiles above their cribs more frequently, some social scientists feel justified in recommending to everyone that they take in plays frequently, rather than play baseball in the backyard, or hang mobiles over the crib, rather than carry the baby about wherever they go. Since these are the child-rearing practices of the professional class, whose children excel at IQ tests and in school, all parents are advised to alter their child-rearing practices to follow suit. *It has not been demonstrated that these variations in child rearing are functionally different in their effects on the children*. . . . (p. 690; italics in original)

Another new adoption study was started in Denver, Colorado, in the early 1970s. The Colorado Adoption Project (Cyphers, Fulker, Plomin, & DeFries, 1989) employed a full adoption design, with the biological parents of the adopted-away children tested through a private adoption agency prior to the birth of their children. The children's average age at placement was just 27 days. Added to the adoptive families and the biological parents of the adoptees was another set of families— biological families matched for social class, child's gender, and family size with the adoptive families. The most unusual aspect of this study is a near-absence of selective placement: The IQs of the adoptive parents were unassociated with those of the biological parents who had relinquished their children for adoption. The social class range of the families was more restrictive than in Scarr and Weinberg's (1978) study, with adoptive fathers having a mean of 15.7 years of schooling (Plomin, DeFries, & Fulker, 1988, p. 46); nonetheless, educational levels did vary in the range from the working to professional social classes.

Although the children were young when tested, rearing influence in the family did not appear to affect their IQ scores. As Cypher et al. dryly wrote, "Environmental resemblance between parents and offspring is nonsignificant for all four specific cognitive abilities as well as the general [IQ] composite" (1989, p. 380). Consistent with McCartney et al.'s (1990) meta-analysis, heritabilities increased with the children's age: at 3 years, .13; at 4 years, .18; and at 7 years, 28%. Thus as the children became older, their IQ scores expressed their genotypic potentials more strongly and their influences in the rearing families not at all.

Ideally, we should find a diminishment of rearing influences in one group of children as they grow up. The Texas Adoption Study, described in Chapter 2 and 3, provides this rare opportunity because the same adopted children were tested once when they were 3 to 14 years old and a second time when they were 13 to 24 years old (Loehlin, Horn, & Willerman, 1989). As in the other adoption studies, the Texas adop-

tive families represented a social class range without extreme depriva-
tion; nearly all the adoptive fathers had at least a high school education
(Horn, Loehlin, & Willerman, 1982). Table 4.2 shows the mean correlations for adoptive parent and adopted child and for unrelated siblings
(either more than one adoptee in a family or an adoptee and a biological child of the adoptive parents). When the children mostly attended
elementary school, rearing influence accounted for 16% of IQ variation
($r = .16$ in both cases); at the follow-up, however, when the children were
in high school or had graduated, rearing accounted for none of the variance ($r = -.01$ or .08). More complex model-fitting analyses of the total
adoptive data set, including data on the biological mothers of the
adoptees, arrived at this same conclusion—no influence of variation in
rearing on the IQs of the older children.

As implied in Scarr and Weinberg's (1978) remarks quoted above,
our estimates of rearing variation (c^2) are far more important for a sense
of the malleability of IQ than are estimates of heritability. If different
rearing makes a difference, IQ may be very malleable despite considerable heritability, because the final level of intellectual attainment will be
dependent on the additive effects of rearing environment and heredity.
If the rearing environments imposed on children in the family make little
difference, then IQ cannot be significantly altered by the kinds of social
interventions we can foresee—because adoption is probably the most
comprehensive, practical intervention for changing a child's level of intellectual stimulation that can be imagined. A compensatory preschool
educational intervention lasts 1 or 2 years (at most, a few years); adoption covers the entire childhood. Moreover, a compensatory educational
intervention chiefly changes curriculum, although some such interventions also work with families; adoption can put a child from a working-
class background into a family with high-IQ parents who have large

TABLE 4.2. Rearing Influence on IQ in the Texas Adoption Study

	Round 1		Round 2	
	Mean r	Mean no. of pairs	Mean r	Mean no. of pairs
Adoptive parent and adoptee	.16	250	.08	250
Unrelated siblings reared together	.16	91	–.01	91

Note. The data are from Loehlin, Horn, & Willerman (1989).

vocabularies, intellectual tastes and preferences, and access to good schools of the professional class. The aggregate data presented first in Table 4.1, with the rearing environment effects of .19–.34, raise bright hopes for rearing influence. However, the results from the Minnesota, Colorado, and Texas adoption studies, and from other adoption work not detailed here, inevitably reduce the estimate of rearing influence to some small value when rearing environments fall in the range from the working to professional social classes. Indeed, the consensus estimate is *zero* influence of rearing variation for adolescents and young adults (McGue, Bouchard, Iacono, & Lykken, 1993).

Although these are not directly comparable to correlational data, the mean IQ scores of adoptive children are not any more encouraging for a belief in IQ malleability (Locurto, 1990). The mean IQ of adoptees across eight adoption studies was 106, only six points greater than the population mean of 100. It was considerably less than the mean of the biological children of adoptive parents (114 in three studies) with whom the adoptees were raised, suggesting that they failed to reach the intellectual potential afforded by their rearing environments. If we ignore the possible methodological flaws detailed in Locurto's article, the adoption studies indicate gains or losses in only the 10- to 12-point range— a rearing influence "far less than the predictions made during the early 1960s by Hunt . . . and Bloom . . . who spoke of changes on the order of 50 to 70 points," and "more cautious still than recent estimates which have been described as occupying a more middle ground but which nonetheless average 20 to 25 points" (Locurto, 1990, p. 290).

This lack of rearing influence may come as a shock to readers used to hearing the successes of compensatory educational programs for young children touted in the popular press. The sad reality is that findings from compensatory educational programs do not contradict the present conclusions, because the universal pattern is only a short-term gain in IQ (on the order of 10–20 points immediately after a compensatory educational program), followed by the loss of these IQ gains in first, second, or third grade. In the winter 1969 issue of the *Harvard Educational Review*, Arthur Jensen became an apostate to the educational establishment by challenging the value of these intervention programs:

> The chief goal of compensatory education—to remedy the educational lag of disadvantaged children and thereby narrow the achievement gap between "minority" and "majority" pupils—has been utterly unrealized in any of the large compensatory education programs that have been evaluated so far. (cited in Jensen, 1972, p. 69)

At the time, Jensen was pilloried for disputing the conventional wisdom with such frank and uncompromising language, but his iconoclastic views no longer lie outside the mainstream (Spitz, 1986; Haskins, 1989).

Consider first Haskins's (1989) sympathetic review of compensatory education outcomes. He concluded that both for Head Start and for "model" compensatory education programs, "gains on standardized IQ and achievement tests as well as on tests of socioemotional development decline within a few years (or even less in the case of Head Start studies)" (p. 278). And he went on to caution that it has not been proven on the basis of available evidence that Head Start-type programs improve either the school performance or life chances of poor children, noting that "policy recommendations call for humility" (p. 280).

In a review of broader scope and more critical intent, Spitz (1986) considered efforts to raise the IQs of mildly retarded individuals (IQs = 50–75) from the 1800s to the present, noting throughout a cycle of bright hopes followed by profound disappointments as program after program was found to be either fraudulent or empirically unfounded. Under his cold gaze, even the claims of "model" compensatory educational programs seem hollow. For example, in the widely publicized Perry Preschool Program, 58 disadvantaged black children aged 2–4 years in the experimental group received 2 years of a special preschool program, whereas 65 children in the control group received none. The experimental group showed a rise in the typical IQ after the program, but a fall by 9 to 10 years of age, so positive reports of the study have since focused on late-adolescent (19-year) outcomes that appear on the surface to be more favorable. Haskins (1989) picked several such outcomes from the Perry study to report:

> By the time they reached age 19, 31% of Weikart's [Perry] program children as compared with 51% ($p < .02$) of control children had been arrested or detained. Moreover, 12% of program children but 25% of control children had been arrested three or more times, and program children had 42 arrests for nonminor crimes whereas controls had 80 such arrests. (p. 276)

But Spitz (1986) added to these observations other findings from the original research reports:

- The average grade of the experimental group was C; that for the control group was C–.
- Both groups earned poverty-level wages.

- The groups did not differ in the number of criminal *convictions*.
- The experimental and control groups had equal IQs.
- Although 35% of the control group versus 15% of the experimental group were classified as mentally retarded, the experimental children spent more time receiving "remedial education."

Certainly neither the Perry project nor others like it have broken the cycle of poverty. Spitz (1986) concluded that people have taken the self-evident fact that extreme social isolation or physical barriers (e.g., deafness) can lead to reversible mental retardation, and have come to the logical but not empirical conclusion that most intellectual retardation in children living in economically poor but socially rich social environments is therefore reversible. This last belief has been unsupported by 180 years of efforts in compensatory interventions.

The temporary rise in IQ produced by early intervention programs still requires explanation. It may be partly an exposure effect, as is the early environmental advantage of adopted children placed in adoptive homes of higher socioeconomic status. In this case, the advantage should diminish as other children receive equivalent exposures at later ages in normal school and home settings. Other processes, though, may contribute to perceived program influence. One is a statistical artifact called "regression to the mean," whereby a group of children selected for very low test scores tends to score higher on retaking the test without any intervention. I call statistical regression the "George Steinbrenner effect," after the owner of the New York Yankees who liked to buy the league's best batters from other teams, only to find the next year that their batting averages failed to meet the banner performance of the previous one; they were still good players, but Lady Luck chose someone else. In the case of low-scoring test takers, performance improves because any bad luck resulting in an extremely low score does not select the same children again; of course, the children are still intellectually retarded, but they score 5–10 points higher on the IQ test on the second test occasion than on the first. Finally, some programs teach the test or frankly give answers to test questions—a method that can raise test scores at any level (Spitz, 1986).[1]

In an adoption study with aims like those of early intervention studies, two French scientists looked at the intellectual outcomes for a small group of children (average age = 14 years) born to biological parents of either extremely high or low social class, and then adopted by adoptive parents of extremely high or low social class (Capron & Duyme, 1989). The four combinations of biological parentage and rearing backgrounds produced a "cross-fostering" design with which to examine the relative impacts of biological and adoptive parentage. For both types of parentage, high social class was advantageous for the IQs of the adoptees, with the environmental difference between the poor and well-to-do families increasing IQ by about 12 points (high social class, IQ = 111.6; low social class, IQ = 99.95). These adoptive placements represented environmental extremes, and we see that they had an effect (although the nature of the environmental influence remains unknown and could be anything from diet to schooling; McGue, 1989). However, the effect size (12 points) is more modest than many policy makers would have imagined.

In summary, the accumulated data fail to demonstrate that variation in rearing influences IQ, once children are older. Nor do compensatory educational intervention programs offer any "quick fixes" for the low IQs of children reared in poverty. No large-scale adoption study has observed children from the poorest areas raised later in the richest ones, but the few data that do exist suggest only modest IQ gains. If there are limits to malleability, why should social scientists attempt to deny them, any more than a physical scientist would want to wish away the principles of theromodynamics that outlaw the existence of perpetual motion machines? We live in a world of very real biological and physical limits, even if the fecundity of human imagination is boundless. It should be remembered, though, that "retardation" on IQ tests is not equivalent to failure in life. As Spitz (1986) has observed:

> It has been shown that even when IQ remains the same over a 40–year period, most persons in the mildly retarded and borderline range of intelligence are no longer labelled retarded when they leave school and enter the work force. . . . They are better able to adjust to the lesser intellectual demands of unskilled and semi-skilled jobs than to the academic demands of the classroom. (p. 219)

The other lesson of this review is that exposure to intellectual stimulation is crucial for intellectual development. As Ceci (1990a) maintains, increases in vocabulary, problem-solving skills, and general knowledge all depend on environmental exposures—but on ones *outside* the family (particularly schooling, but also television, peers, and personal efforts to improve oneself intellectually). The rate of intellectual growth does not appear to be primarily limited by the number or quality of exposures available to the intellectually curious child. Moreover, as part of rearing environment, schools of widely different per-student dollar expenditure are functionally equivalent in their influence on the rate of intellectual development. Thus as children grow older, phenotypic IQ becomes much more diagnostic of genotypic potential and much less diagnostic of family rearing environments. These facts imply that children who differ in IQ make more or less *effective* use of their intellectual environments—a supposition supported by information-processing approaches to the analysis of IQ.

Studies of IQ, Speed, and Capacity

In successive generations of computer equipment, users have noticed two areas of dramatic improvement: speed and capacity. The clock cycle of a computer is a timed electrical circuit that coordinates all activities of its memory and its central computational processor. Improvements in computer chip design have decreased the clock cycle, so that many more activities can be run in the same period of time on a newer computer than on an obsolescent model. Computer programs are brought into the active memory of the computer from some type of long-term storage device (e.g., magnetic disk, optical disk), and the size of a program that a computer can run cannot exceed the capacity of its active memory store. With the huge increase in active memory capacity in the last several generations of computers, larger programs with greater capabilities and more features can now be run—programs that would disable a computer with less of this capacity.

Although the computer is mechanically very different from the mind—a collection of transistors and wires as opposed to nerve cells and axons—some differences in brain "wetware" may account for differences in IQ. Indirect evidence for this thesis can be found in cognitive science, which probes the operation of the brain through elemental tasks that measure the processes of cognition, including the speed and capacity of mental operations. We now have evidence that people who score higher on traditional tests of IQ tend to share two advantages over people who score less well: Their minds (or brains) are faster and have greater working memory capacity. A full review of the human information-processing literature is beyond the scope of this book, but some highlights can serve to illustrate the growing connections between older, psychometric notions of intelligence and information-processing theories concerning the disassembly of complex thoughts into simpler, component processes.

Thoughts, though quick, are not instantaneous. In less than a second, the brain can send commands to the feet that propel a world-class basketball player 3 feet into the air. For a full mental operation, 0.001 second is not enough time, but 0.2 second is. As children get older, their brains operate more rapidly; their speed on a variety of timed tasks has been found to improve developmentally. Kail (1991) discovered a natural developmental law: a single curve describing the speeding up of mental operations across diverse cognitive and noncognitive tasks, such as tapping a finger, mental addition, quickly releasing a button, and picture matching. On all tasks, improvement was "exponential," meaning that most of the increase in response speed occurred early (between the ages of 7 and 13 years), followed by a slowing of the rate of improvement until the rate leveled out during the later teens.[2]

Figure 4.1 shows the developmental change in reaction times on Kail's tapping task—tapping a key as rapidly as possible with one finger. Seven-year-olds emitted a tap about every 0.4 second; 21-year-olds, about every 0.2 second. Kail's interpretation of these results uses a computer metaphor like the one I have offered above:

> If two computers have identical software but one machine has a slower cycle time (i.e., the time for the central processor to execute a single instruction), that machine will execute all processes more slowly. . . . The human analog to cycle time might be the time to scan the productions . . . in working memory. . . . (1991, p. 266)

If development produces greater intelligence and also produces greater speed of response, then perhaps at any one age response speed will correlate with IQ—an inference now confirmed in studies using many different reaction time paradigms. Not that reaction time explains all the variation in IQ; the information-processing basis of IQ is likely to be composed of multiple processes, each one making its own independent contribution to intelligence.

To illustrate the IQ–reaction time association, I use the Hick task, a simple test of reaction time that requires the subject to lift his or her finger from a "home" button when one of a set of lights comes on and then to push another button to terminate the light (see Figure 4.2). "Reaction time" is how long it takes to lift the finger. "Movement time" is how long it takes to turn the light out (i.e., to move from the "home" button to the one next to the light). Although this is not self-evident,

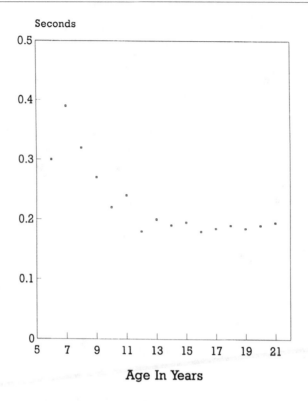

FIGURE 4.1. The relation of speed of finger tapping and age. Adapted from Kail (1991). Copyright 1991 by the American Psychological Association. Adapted by permission.

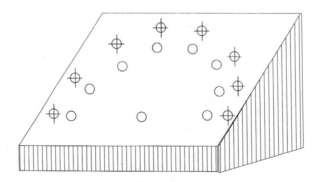

FIGURE 4.2. An apparatus for testing reaction time. Adapted from Jensen (1987). Copyright 1987 by Ablex Publishing Corporation. Adapted by permission.

reaction times are slowed by the mere presence of several lights: Reaction times are slower when six or eight lights are showing on the apparatus, as opposed to just two or four lights.

Faster movement and reaction times on the Hick task were associated with higher IQ scores (Jensen & Vernon, 1986). These associations became stronger when the apparatus was made more complex (six or eight lights) than when it was simpler (two or four lights). Averaged over three studies, the Hick reaction times correlated –.15, –.23, –.27, and –.40 with IQ for two, four, six, and eight presented lights, respectively. The Hick task is just one of many simple tasks (in the sense that most respondents have little trouble making correct responses) on which faster responding has been associated with higher IQ scores (Vernon, 1987).

In research on infants, the use of tasks closer to the physiological bases of intelligence has resulted in a breakthrough—the prediction of childhood IQ from tests given to infants under 1 year of age. Whereas traditional infant tests assessed motor development and (crudely) attention, and failed to reliably predict later IQ in early childhood, the new tests focus on infants' cognitive responses to simple stimuli, which predict later intelligence. One robust measure of abilities in the first year is "duration of fixation" (Colombo, Mitchell, Coldren, & Freeseman, 1991). Older infants look more briefly at a novel stimulus than younger infants do. Corresponding with this developmental trend, smarter babies also have shorter fixation times than duller ones in a simple habituation task, such as viewing a projected color slide of a woman's face. Surreptitiously, the duration of a baby's gaze at the woman's face is recorded; this is averaged over all looks until interest in the face stimulus has been lost (i.e., until the baby has habituated to the stimulus). At 4 months of age, the duration of gaze ranges from about 5 seconds to 2 minutes per fixation. Babies with quick fixation times ("short-look" babies) outperform babies with long fixation times ("long-look" babies) on other cognitive tasks and on later IQ tests. Although the exact process underlying these performance differences is still being investigated, one interpretation is that it represents a global superiority in information processing time: ". . . the findings lend support to the interpretation that fixation duration reflect[s] differences in the speed with which visual stimuli are processed, such that short lookers simply process stimuli more rapidly than long lookers" (Colombo et al., 1991, p. 1255).

Although speed is good, it is not the sole component in an explanation of intellectual abilities. Cognitive capacity—the ability to juggle several pieces of information simultaneously in working memory—is also important. One simple task of memory capacity is Digit Span, one of the subtests of the WAIS and WISC described earlier. Like processing speed, Digit Span performance increases developmentally: At the start of elementary school, children can repeat back only four to five digits immediately after hearing them, but high school students can repeat back six to eight digits. Better reliability can be obtained by combining several measures of working memory capacity. For example, another simple measure is alphabet recoding. Several letters are computer-presented, and the one that follows next in the alphabet must be supplied. The computer might show the following: S L R + 1 = ? For a correct response, these letters must first be reordered in memory (L R S + 1 = ?), leading to the answer, T. Holding and reordering the letters in memory tax working memory capacity, and thus test for the relevant ability.[3]

In contrast to the mentally taxing but intellectually barren tests of working memory, tests of reasoning ability seem to capture the essence of human intelligence. What is poetry without deftly drawn analogies and metaphors? Among the most widely used tests of reasoning abilities are verbal analogies. For young children, these may be mundane ("Brother is to boy as sister is to _____"). At the college level, they may be more subtle and sophisticated ("Bench is to judge as pulpit is to _____") or more poetic ("Sand is to beach as star is to _____"). Other higher-order reasoning tasks would include the use of mathematics, grammatical understanding, and reasoning about numbers. The ability to reason well, in general, correlates with measures of "crystallized" intelligence such as general word and science knowledge—again, the generality of human intelligence (g).

In an article provocatively entitled "Reasoning Ability Is (Little More Than) Working-Memory Capacity?!," the intercorrelations of sets of working memory tests and sets of reasoning tests in four separate studies were explored (Kyllonen & Christal, 1990). The amazing result was that the simple tasks of working memory correlated, as a set, about .80 with a set of reasoning tests. Working memory and the capacity to reason abstractly are therefore virtually identical.

In developing a general theory of working memory capacity, Just and Carpenter (1992) were able to simulate differences between good and poor comprehenders of verbal material with a computer program. Good comprehenders were assumed to possess greater working memory capacity. Just and Carpenter's theory predicted the specific kinds of verbal material that overtax the abilities of those individuals with less memory capacity than others. For instance, sentences with embedded clauses (e.g., "The reporter *whom the senator attacked* admitted the error") pose greater information-processing demands than simple ones, and individuals with less memory capacity have more difficulty with these sentences than those with greater memory capacity. Just and Carpenter's computer program was able to simulate the exact point in a sentence at which comprehension is most influenced by differences in memory capacity. On some sentences, greater memory capacity leads to *longer* processing time, because it allows the individual to explore possible interpretations that are simply missed by individuals with less capacity. Finally, because performance degradation and enhancement, under different conditions of verbal complexity, are exact processes, this theory tends to rule out motivational explanations sometimes offered for a lack of comprehension of verbal material.

In summary, both speed and capacity are essential components of intelligence as measured in traditional tests of intellectual abilities. Behavior geneticists have recently turned their attention to the genetics of information-processing speed (Baker, Vernon, & Ho, 1991). Their main discovery has been that variation in the more componential information-processing abilities, like IQ score variation, is heritable (but with little evidence of rearing influence). The statistical association of the componential abilities with IQ scores appears to be attributable to the same set of genes underlying both phenotypic measures of performance; in other words, the same physiology that affects reaction time and memory capacity also affects IQ. But what is this physiology? I next turn briefly to this question.

Preliminary Research on Physiology and IQ

The ultimate biological understanding of individual differences in IQ will come only when both the underlying genes and the physiological basis of human intelligence have been discovered. Although the 1990s have been called the "decade of the brain" in neuroscience research, progress toward understanding the biology of human intelligence is just now beginning (Matarazzo, 1992).

One correlation is striking: that between brain size and intelligence. This correlation is remarkable because, *a priori*, it would seem unlikely that the gross anatomy of the brain would predict individual differences in IQ in the normal range, where no brain damage is evident.

The mere mention of this association, however, conjures up the most reprehensible forms of biological determinism and the (in retrospect) ludicrous claims of 19th-century scientists that every aspect of human character could be inferred from the shape of the cranium. Gould (1981) has taken some delight in dismantling the 19th- and early 20th-century evidence on this association. On postmortem examination, the brain sizes of men of eminence violated the hypothesis that bigger is always better. Gould cites the example of Anatole France, who in 1924 "opted for the other end of Turgenev's [brain size > 2,000 grams] fame and clocked in at a mere 1,017 grams" (p. 92). If nothing else, Gould's summation of the 19th-century data shows that the correlation of brain size and IQ is far from perfect; however, one would not expect a single parameter of brain anatomy or function to predict more than a small fraction of total IQ variability. To address the issue, one needs to collect better data than postmortem results on elderly novelists—results confounded by different procedures for preparing the brain, the decrease in brain size associated with aging, and the haphazard sampling of brains. With the new technologies of brain imaging, better methods now exist for examining the brain size–IQ association, and such an empirical question should be addressed by more refined technologies and data collection. Gould's approach—embarrassing the 19th-century advocates of the IQ–brain size association—is a kind of science that would make Francis Bacon roll over in his grave.

The brain size–IQ association has been recently replicated by means of magnetic resonance imaging (MRI)—a medical technique for visualizing the anatomy of the brain within a living person, which can be applied to taking measurements of brain areas in healthy people (Andreasen et al., 1993; Willerman, Schultz, Rutledge, & Bigler, 1991). In the study by Willerman and his colleagues (1991) forty students at the University of Texas–Austin were put on an MRI machine at a local medical facility. Each MRI brain image caught a slice of the brain about 0.2 inch thick. The students selected were either very bright (IQs ≥ 130) or close to average (IQs about 90). The sample selection ruled out possible confounding explanations of brain size, such as variation in body size: The average-IQ students were actually taller than the high-IQ students, and associations of brain size with height or weight were statistically controlled even though they were quite weak ($r = .09$ to $.10$). Both groups came from middle-class backgrounds (the parents had an average education level of 2 years of college), rendering undernutrition explanations of brain size variation implausible.

Within each "slice" of brain, a computer counted the total amount of dark area containing brain cells, and this served as an index of brain area. As shown in Figure 4.3, high-IQ students had larger brains (adjusted for body size) than average-IQ students; moreover, males had larger brains than females.[4] The magnitude of the brain area difference varied with brain region, with the largest brain area differences in the brain regions that include the neural substrates of language. The overall correlation between brain area and IQ was .51, accounting for 26% of IQ variance. Using a statistical adjustment yielded a correlation of .35

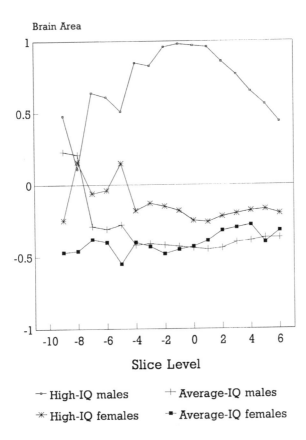

FIGURE 4.3. The relationship between IQ level and brain area. Adapted from Holden (1991). Copyright 1991 by the American Association for the Advancement of Science. Adapted by permission.

between brain area and IQ in more representative samples. The exact explanation for the area difference is, at this time, unknown; it could reflect greater myelination of brain axons, a greater number of nerve or glial cells, less neuronal death in the brains of brighter individuals, or a combination of processes.

Another new imaging technique—positron emission tomography (PET)—also yields physiological correlates of intelligence (Haier et al., 1988). PET scanning produces images of areas of the brain that are more or less metabolically active, according to how much they draw radioactive sugar from the blood for cell metabolism. Higher-IQ subjects (again, all subjects put through the PET scanning machine had normal-range IQs) used less sugar in those brain regions involving higher cognitive functions while they solved IQ test items. Thus, their brains appeared to be more efficient in the processing of information than those of lower-IQ individuals.

Given the kinds of results just outlined, neuroscience is clearly on a frontier of discovery of the biological basis of intelligence. As Haier (1990) has said in an article addressed to psychologists, "Sooner or later, however, all psychology research leads into the human brain. The search for brain mechanisms that are relevant to intelligence is no more reductionistic than a search for cultural or social mechanisms" (p. 373).

Genes and IQ: Possibilities for Future Research

The genes determining IQ lie buried among the 100,000 genes estimated to exist in our 46 chromosomes. Even if three-quarters of human genes were monomorphic (and hence unable to contribute to variation in IQ), the remainder of 33,000 genes would be a vast domain to search. To use a simile employed in Chapter 2, the IQ-determining genes are like needles in a haystack.

As of this writing, the IQ genes remain undiscovered, but strategies exist for eventually locating them. Already, more than 200 genes expressed solely in the human brain have been placed into bacterial colonies from which they can be extracted and used to identify the genotype of an individual. If genotypes are known for brain-expressed genes, their association with IQ scores can be examined directly by correlating individuals' genotypic scores (e.g., AA = 1, Aa = 0, and aa = −1) against their IQs. Genotypes that predict IQs can be flagged for further investigation. Known genotypes can also be used in linkage analysis, in which the association of particular alleles with IQ is followed through family pedigrees.

At the present time, it is difficult to know whether we should be optimistic or pessimistic about these efforts to find specific genes. True, a small number of gene pairs can generate tremendous genetic variability. As few as five gene pairs, with some measurement error added, could conceivably produce a normal-looking trait distribution, with each pair contributing about 20% of the total genetic variability. Yet it is hard to imagine that as few as five loci contribute all genetic variability in a trait as complex as IQ; more likely, many more gene pairs are responsible for IQ variation. If specific loci contributing to IQ are to be detected successfully, they must contribute at least 1–3% to the genetic variation in IQ, and preferably more. Given that it is unlikely that all genetic loci have *equally* small effects, there is hope that some loci will contribute more than others and thus will be over a threshold of detectability. We can be cautiously optimistic that some loci contributing to IQ variability will be discovered with molecular genetic techniques, but no single, spectacular discovery is to be expected.

A Model of Intelligence

Figure 4.4 summarizes many of the ideas presented in this chapter. The left side of the figure depicts the "ultimate" causal influences on IQ variation: unshared experiences and genes. Genes influence the development of the nervous system, as well as its ability to interact with the broad social environment, by creating nervous system differences in speed, capacity, and perhaps as-yet-undiscovered mental operations. Once exposed to a social environment, these physiological differences influence variation in the latent trait of "intelligence" that is assessed through verbal and mathematical test scores (boxes on the right).

Another influence on the test scores themselves is measurement error, which includes everything from mistakenly darkening the wrong box on an answer sheet to unexpected social influences such as a moment's distraction. Thus test scores do not absolutely indicate the genetic characteristics of any individual, although they are strongly associated with them. Measurement error is represented by the arrows entering the "Verbal Test Score" and "Math Test Score" boxes from above and below.

Rearing influences have been omitted from Figure 4.4 because, in

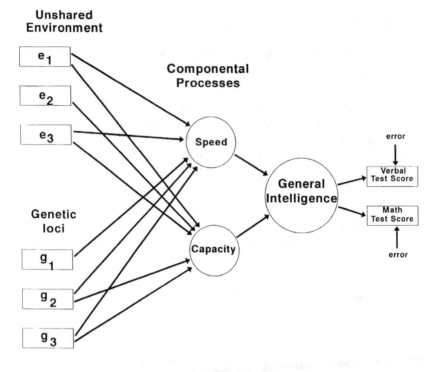

FIGURE 4.4. A model of general intelligence.

the range from the working to professional classes, they wash out as children enter their teenage years. Contrary to what is widely believed by the U.S. public, the literature review in this chapter shows that home environments from that of a factory or clerical worker to that of a doctor or lawyer offer *equivalent* environmental stimulation for intellectual growth. In concrete terms, a near-zero IQ correlation for older "unrelated siblings reared together" means that two (adoptive) children in a doctor's family do differ on the average by as much as 17 IQ points (the average difference of randomly paired children). And a lack of association between adoptive parents' and adolescent adoptees' IQs means that the adoptee raised by a carpenter has a 50–50 chance of obtaining a higher IQ score than a lawyer's adoptee. Some three-quarters of American families fall into this range of social class categories, where rearing effects have been proven weak, despite massive differences in levels of funding for their public schools and massive differences in home intellectual environments. Of course, I do not intend to imply that intelligence develops without exposure to schools, books, television shows, magazines, and good conversations. I mean simply that these exposures can be found in three-quarters of American society in significant abundance to support full intellectual growth.[5]

I know that my conclusion is counterintuitive, because we can listen to the differences in speech patterns in working- and professional-class parents; because we are aware of their different habits and life interests; and because we can see a resemblance of a bright child to professional-class parents. How easy it is, then, to fall into the trap of inferring causality from behavioral resemblance—to assume that because a child is like a parent in intellectual abilities, some parental action has produced this outcome. I am reminded of a news report about an Asian boy who won a prestigious Westinghouse award for achievement in science. The reporter constantly referred to the work ethic of Asian families and the strong encouragement of achievement in Asian culture. But this adolescent boy politely reminded the reporter that his own efforts deserved credit—that excellence in science was a personal goal he had long sought. When social sciences offers counterintuitive discoveries, the lay public, not to mention some social scientists, have difficulty grasping them because reasoning and gut reaction may differ. These discoveries also oppose widespread cultural beliefs that parental treatments environmentally mold children's traits. Cultural beliefs, however ancient and pervasive, can be misleading. We must instead dependably infer causation from experimental and quasi-experimental studies, as we have been painstakingly trained to do in the conduct of science.

Figure 4.4 omits the process of gene–environment correlation, such as that of the Asian boy determined to excel in science who read advanced science texts, or the chess prodigy studying position after position and badgering adults for games. Gene–environment correlation has not been shown diagrammatically because it can be read in the figure as genetic variation: The genotype and environment become so correlated as to become inseparable by ordinary experimental methods.

The only environmental influence shown explicitly in the diagram is unshared environment. Unshared experiences certainly influence IQ: MZ twins differ (nongenetically) by 6–8 IQ points, and not all of that difference is attributable to measurement error. My lack of attention to unshared environment reflects the difficulty of identifying just what these environmental influences are. These influences are not the active efforts by which children increase their knowledge; as mentioned earlier, active gene–environment correlations are associated with genotypes and are counted in genetic variation in most behavior genetic models. Rather, they influence each child uniquely, are uncorrelated (by mathematical definition) with family background, and are also uncorrelated with genotype (a good genotype does not accrue more good unshared effects than a poor one). And they may consist of both social and biological processes. During embryogenesis, randomly occurring environmental events trigger different developmental pathways, so that even the nervous systems of identical twins fail to match exactly at birth. Random somatic mutations in DNA can further slightly reduce the identity of MZ twins' genotypes in all body cells. Such environmentally induced differences in brain function may contribute to IQ variation. Moreover, numerous social influences may contribute to the unshared effect: an inspiring teacher who, at the right time and with the right child, fires enthusiasm for an intellectual subject; a child's stumbling on a personal area of interest (e.g., a future paleontologist's initial fascination with dinosaurs); an unexpected failure on an important test that leads a child to abandon one academic route for another; a car accident, resulting in debilitating brain damage; and many other, more minor environmental influences that lead children apart, step by step, year after year. Unlike family backgrounds (for which variation in environments are easily discernible, although they lack effects on IQ variation), the unshared experiences have effects on IQ but are difficult to observe and measure.

I have focused mainly on IQ because IQ tests have been the center of controversy for so long. The same conclusions stated for IQ, however, apply with equal force to academic achievement in general. Indeed, IQ and achievement tests fall on a continuum of item specificity. General information items on IQ tests are ones that come up more frequently than items that must be learned in a specialized class (e.g., "Who is Charles Darwin?" vs. "Who ruled England in 1350?"); the problem-solving items require less specialized knowledge about a particular field than would an achievement test in physics or chemistry. No IQ test is independent of cultural experience, but some tests make more specialized demands than others. Because academic achievement is so dependent on underlying intelligence, however, conclusions about components of variance are not different for the two types of outcomes. Scarr and Weinberg (1983) found that unrelated siblings correlated –.11 and .11 for math and reading achievement, respectively, as compared with .35 and .27 in a matched sample of biological siblings.

This chapter has not discussed the policy implications of these findings. Understanding that for most individuals IQ score differences represent mainly genetic differences, with a pound of unshared environment and several ounces of measurement error, does not mean that IQ tests should necessarily be used either in the selection of individuals for jobs or in the placement of children into special classes for the educationally retarded. Such decisions must reflect our values and goals as a society. Nonetheless, any reasonable choice of policy alternatives must acknowledge that ignoring IQ differences has potential costs for economic productivity, as mentioned earlier, and that variation in rearing has limited effects. Let us not, as social scientists, sell the "snake oil" of unrealistic expectations for changing educational performance merely by placing children in schools with Olympic-sized swimming pools and with a cadre of well-educated teachers. Nature develops via nurture, but we must be modest about our control over children's fates while making our best efforts to secure their futures.

Notes

[1]Occasional newspaper stories suggest that some reports of rapidly rising test scores may be fraudulant. For instance, rising test scores in an upper-middle-class school on Chicago's North Side led to the following allegations against the principal, Linda Chase:

> Two third grade teachers . . . testified that last spring Chase gave them an essay question used on a standardized written examination and told them to familiarize students with the question before the exam . . . a third grade teacher said that four years ago Chase told her to change answers on completed tests . . . (*Arizona Daily Star*, 1992, p. 9)

[2]My example deals with improvement during childhood in mental speed and capacity. But a less sanguine analysis can be made of the latter part of the lifespan: During adulthood, decreases in speed and working memory capacity may be primarily responsible for declining reasoning and problem-solving powers (Salthouse, 1991).

[3]In his book *On Intelligence . . . More or Less,* Ceci (1990a) attacks the line of reasoning put forward in this chapter. One of the flaws of his argument—his neglect of temporal order—has been noted earlier in this chapter. Another flaw—his lack of appreciation of environmental variance estimates in behavior genetic studies—is, of course, a broad theme of this book. But Ceci is also critical of information-processing research because massive training can improve performance on some information-processing tasks. For example, after hundreds of training trials, a college student managed to increase his digit span memory from

the usual 6–8 digits to 80 digits! Eleven-year-old children, given 3,000 training trials, managed to rotate images of letters and numbers mentally back to their original orientations as quickly as adults did. But the way in which tasks are done mentally also changes with extreme training, as Kail (1991) has commented: "Greater task experience means that performance is more likely to reflect retrieval of a stored response, which means that speed is no longer constrained by available resources" (p. 266).

A point-by-point rebuttal to Ceci's book would take this work too far afield. I do not deny that much remains to be learned about human information processing—and the tasks used, although simple on the surface, are not simple at the level of mental actions. But I think Ceci himself senses that his position is a defensive one, because the argument for a biological basis to intelligence has been strengthened by the new evidence. In an editorial in *Intelligence*, he complained:

> It is not a simplification to assert that the once disreputable slogan "biology is destiny" has returned with a vengeance. As we enter the 1990s the evidence for this position is more abundant and more interconnected than was true when Herrnstein proffered a version of it 20 years ago. (1990b, p. 143)

The interested reader may peruse references cited in this chapter and in Ceci's (1990a) book to form an independent judgment of what the evidence means.

[4]A sex difference in brain size, after height and weight were controlled for, was an unexpected result. Willerman et al. (1991) cite some evidence that men and women have the same number of cortical neurons, despite differences in overall brain size. There is increasing evidence for sex differences in brain organization and function; a popular account of this research is given by Moir and Jessel (1991).

[5]Flynn (1987) documented IQ gains ranging from 5 to 25 points in the post-World War II period in 14 industrialized countries. If real, these historical gains may have many causes, including biological ones (e.g., better nutrition and the conquest of childhood infectious diseases). Further exploration of historical IQ change is a worthy research endeavor.

References

Andreasen, N. C., Flaum, M., Swayze II, V., O'Leary, D. S., Alliger, R., Cohen, G., Ehrhardt, J., & Yuh, W. T. C. (1993). Intelligence and brain structure in normal individuals. *American Journal of Psychiatry, 150*, 130–134.

Arizona Daily Star. (1992, January 3). Illinois school scandal highlights "obsession" to boost test scores. Section A, 9.

Baker, L. A., Vernon, P. A., & Ho, H. (1991). The genetic correlation between intelligence and speed of information processing. *Behavior Genetics, 14,* 351–367.

Barrett, G. V., & Depinet, R. L. (1991). A reconsideration of testing for competence rather than for intelligence. *American Psychologist, 46,* 1012–1024.

Bouchard, T. J., Jr., & McGue, M. (1981). Familial studies of intelligence. *Science, 212,* 1055–1059.

Capron, C., & Duyme, M. (1989). Assessment of the effects of socio-economic status on IQ in a full cross-fostering study. *Nature, 340,* 552–554.

Ceci, S. J. (1990a). *On intelligence . . . more or less.* Englewood Cliffs, NJ: Prentice Hall Press.

Ceci, S. J. (1990b). On the relation between microlevel processing efficiency and macrolevel measures of intelligence: Some arguments against current reductionism. *Intelligence, 14,* 141–150.

Chipuer, H. M., Rovine, M. J., & Plomin, R. (1990). LISREL modeling: Genetic and environmental influences on IQ revisited. *Intelligence, 14,* 11–29.

Colombo, J., Mitchell, D. W., Coldren, J. T., & Freeseman, L. J. (1991). Individual differences in infant visual attention: Are short lookers faster processors or feature processors? *Child Development, 62,* 1247–1257.

Cyphers, L. H., Fulker, D. W., Plomin, R., & DeFries, J. C. (1989). Cognitive abilities in the early school years: No effects of shared environment between parents and offspring. *Intelligence, 13,* 369–386.

Feldman, D. H. (1986). *Nature's gambit: Child prodigies and development of human potential.* New York: Basic Books.

Flynn, J. R. (1987). Massive IQ gains in 14 nations: What IQ tests really measure. *Psychological Bulletin, 101,* 171–191.

Gardner, H. (1983). *Frames of mind: The theory of multiple intelligences.* New York: Basic Books.

Gould, S. J. (1981). *The mismeasure of man.* New York: Norton.

Haskins, R. (1989). Beyond metaphor: The efficacy of early childhood education. *American Psychologist, 44,* 274–282.

Haier, R. J. (1990). The end of intelligence research. *Intelligence, 14,* 371–374.

Haier, R. J., Siegel, B., Jr., Nuechterlein, K. H., Hazlett, E., Wu, J., Paek, J., Browning, H. L., & Buchsbaum, M. S. (1988). Cortical glucose metabolic rate correlates of abstract reasoning and attention studied with positron emission tomography. *Intelligence, 12,* 199–217.

Holden, C. (1991). Brains: Is bigger better? *Science, 257,* 1584.

Horn, J. M., Loehlin, J. C., & Willerman, L. (1982). Aspects of the inheritance of intellectual abilities. *Behavior Genetics, 12,* 479–516.

Hunter, J. E. (1986). Cognitive ability, cognitive aptitutes, job knowledge, and job performance. *Journal of Vocational Behavior, 29,* 340–362.

Jensen, A. R. (1972). *Genetics and education.* New York: Harper & Row.

Jensen, A. R. (1987). Individual differences in the Hick paradigm. In P. A. Vernon (Ed.), *Speed of information-processing and intelligence* (pp. 101–175). Norwood, NJ: Ablex.

Jensen, A. R., & Vernon, P. A. (1986). Jensen's reaction-time studies: A reply to Longstreth. *Intelligence, 10,* 153–179.

Just, M. A., & Carpenter, P. A. (1992). A capacity theory of comprehension: Individual differences in working memory. *Psychological Review, 99,* 122–149.

Kail, R. (1991). Processing time declines exponentially during childhood and adolescence. *Developmental Psychology, 27,* 259–266.

Kyllonen, P. C., & Christal, R. E. (1990). Reasoning ability is (little more than) working-memory capacity?! *Intelligence, 14,* 389–433.

Locurto, C. (1990). The malleability of IQ as judged from adoption studies. *Intelligence, 14,* 275–292.

Loehlin, J. C. (1989). Partitioning environmental and genetic contributions to behavioral development. *American Psychologist, 44,* 1285–1292.

Loehlin, J. C., Horn, J. M., & Willerman, L. (1989). Modeling IQ change: Evidence from the Texas Adoption Project. *Child Development, 60,* 993–1004.

Matarazzo, J. D. (1992). Psychological testing and assessment in the 21st century. *American Psychologist, 47,* 1007–1018.

McGue, M. (1989). Nature–nurture and intelligence. *Nature, 340,* 507–508.

McGue, M., Bouchard, T. J., Jr., Iacono, W. G., & Lykken, D. T. (1993). Behavioral genetics of cognitive ability: A life span perspective. In R. Plomin & G. McClearn (Eds.), *Nature, nurture, and psychology* (pp. 59–76). Washington, DC: American Psychological Association.

Moir, A., & Jessel, D. (1991). *Brain sex: The real difference between men and women.* New York: Lyle Stuart.

McCartney, K., Harris, M. J., & Bernieri, F. (1990). Growing up and growing apart: A developmental meta-analysis of twin studies. *Psychological Bulletin, 107,* 226–237.

Nagy, W. E., Herman, P. A., & Anderson, R. C. (1985). Learning words from context. *Reading Research Quarterly, 20,* 233–253.

Pedersen, N. L., Plomin, R., Nesselroade, J. R., & McClearn, G. E. (1992). A quantitative genetic analysis of cognitive abilities during the second half of the life span. *Psychological Science, 3,* 340–345.

Plomin, R., DeFries, J. C., & Fulker, D. W. (1988). *Nature and nurture during infancy and early childhood.* Cambridge, England: Cambridge University Press.

Salthouse, T. A. (1991). Mediation of adult age differences in cognition by reductions in working memory and speed of processing. *Psychological Science, 2,* 179–183.

Scarr, S., & McCartney, K. (1983). How people make their own environments: A theory of genotype → environment effects. *Child Development, 54,* 424–435.

Scarr, S., & Weinberg, R. A. (1978). The influence of "family background" on intellectual attainment. *American Sociological Review, 43,* 674–692.

Scarr, S., & Weinberg, R. A. (1983). The Minnesota adoption studies: Genetic differences and malleability. *Child Development, 54,* 260–267.

Schmidt, F. L., & Hunter, J. E. (1981). Employment testing: Old theories and new research findings. *American Psychologist, 36,* 1128–1137.

Snyderman, M., & Rothman, S. (1987). Survey of expert opinion on intelligence and aptitude testing. *American Psychologist, 42,* 137–144.

Spitz, H. H. (1986). *The raising of intelligence: A selected history of attempts to raise retarded intelligence.* Hillsdale, NJ: Erlbaum.

Sternberg, R. J. (1985). *Beyond IQ: A triarchic theory of human intelligence.* New York: Cambridge University Press.

Vernon, P. A. (Ed.). (1987). *Speed of information-processing and intelligence.* Norwood, NJ: Ablex.

Webster's third international dictionary. (1968). Springfield, MA: Merriam.

Willerman, L., Schultz, R., Rutledge, J. N., & Bigler, E. D. (1991). *In vivo* brain size and intelligence. *Intelligence, 15,* 223–228.

CHAPTER 5

UNITING NATURE AND NURTURE: THE GENETICS OF ENVIRONMENTAL MEASURES

n *Nature's Thumbprint*, a New York City psychiatrist and his son present a case history of early-separated identical twins who were raised apart:

> Identical twin men, now age thirty, were separated at birth and raised in different countries by their respective adoptive parents. Both kept their lives neat—neat to the point of pathology. Their clothes were preened, appointments met precisely on time, hands scrubbed regularly to a raw, red color. When the first was asked why he felt the need to be so clean, his answer was plain.
>
> "My mother. When I was growing up she always kept the house perfectly ordered. She insisted on every little thing returned to its proper place, the clocks—we had dozens of clocks—each set to the same noonday chime. She insisted on this, you see. I learned from her. What else could I do?"
>
> The man's identical twin, just as much a perfectionist with soap and water, explained his own behavior this way: "The reason is quite simple. I'm reacting to my mother, who was an absolute slob." (Neubauer & Neubauer, 1990, pp. 20-21)

In hindsight, how easily we can explain any behavior by drawing upon our experiences in for childhood! To one twin, blissfully unaware of the other, his mother's obsessiveness had produced his own. To the other twin, blissfully unaware of the first, his mother's slovenly habits produced an opposing impulse in himself—a compulsion toward neatness and cleanliness. Neither twin thought to look inside himself for the causal influence—to the genes that instruct biological development, to their similar minds), but we, as neutral observers, can forgive their common error of believing that what their parents did made them who they are. Rearing explanations may be seductive and flexible, but false.

This chapter discusses genetic variation in "environmental measures." We already understand that variation in rearing experiences, beyond rare extremes, has little influence on personality development. Nonetheless, rearing measures do possess statistical associations with personality and intellectual traits, as verified in hundreds of studies of biological families in the working-class to professional-class range. These associations are usually interpreted as "influence," although as social scientists we understand that correlation does not mean causation—a piece of advice often ignored in studies of childhood socialization. A lack of inferred rearing influence implies that these statistical associations cannot be causal ones; instead, they must be *spurious*, depending on genes shared by parents and children (in biological families) to create an appearance of causality. The insights needed to understand this phenomenon are simple. First, we need to recognize that variation in "environmental measures" may contain genetic variation; second, we need to see that this genetic variation may produce an appearance of rearing influences on children.

The Genetics of Social Class

Changes in Explanations for Class and Racial Differences

The most widespread explanations of behavioral differences among both children and adults are social class and culture. Socialization science relies on social class and culture for environmental explanations of behavioral pathologies (such as criminality and insanity), as well as of variation in IQ and scholastic achievement. During the period from 1900 to the beginning of World War II, class and cultural explanations replaced the formerly pervasive biological theories of racial and class differences in behavior.

Environmentalism prevailed for diverse reasons (Degler, 1991). One was that conceptions of inheritance changed. A Lamarckian could both believe in the genetic superiority of Caucasians and be a social reformer, because Lamarck's theory held that new traits acquired during one's lifetime could be passed on genetically to the next generation. In genetics, when scientific advances showed that the Lamarckian doctrine was false, social reformers had to abandon it for some form of cultural influence if the "lower" races were to be raised, or the socially disadvantaged improved. The excesses of the eugenics movement also drove scholars away from biological explanations. In the United States, liberals vehemently opposed the political successes of the eugenics movement, which encouraged laws in many states permitting compulsory sterilization of the intellectually retarded. Geneticists, who formerly supported the movement, also abandoned it. One reason was scientific: For some traits, eugenics would be a slow and halting process, because deleterious, recessive genes respond to selective pressures only slowly.

In the period from 1900 to the 1930s, the anthropologists, psychologists, and sociologists who joined a movement toward cultural and class explanations expressed views that are now widely accepted (Degler, 1991). The psychologist Klineberg used a cultural explanation for the poor performance of Native Americans on speeded tests of intellectual ability (i.e., that their cultural values placed less emphasis on speed than did economically competitive American mainstream society), and he used both cultural and social class explanations for African-Americans' poorer test performance (i.e., their lack of educational and economic opportunity, surely evident in the United States in 1935). The anthropologist Kroeber assumed equal moralities and potentialities in all races; in his view, any observed difference could be attributed to a lack of exposure to rearing environments able to activate them. The sociologist Kelsey, once he had abandoned Lamarckianism, found that cultural inheritance made him more optimistic that racial and class differences in behavior could be eliminated, as soon as better environmental provisions were given to all. When Nazi racial theories furnished a final proof that biology could be used to justify the most horrendous acts of inhumanity, environmental explanations came to dominate the social sciences completely.

Today, socialization science depends, without much reflection or analysis, on variations in social class and culture as environmental explanations of the seemingly intractable class and racial differences seen in the United States—intractable because many additional years have not ended disparities in IQ and scholastic achievement favoring whites over blacks, and favoring professional occupations over working-class ones. Modern college textbooks commonly repeat the cultural and class explanations that first drove biology from social science in the 1920s and 1930s:

Poor diets, poor health, poor schooling, and a way of life that does not require or reward abstract thinking, all can reduce intellectual capacities regardless of genetic potential. In this way, Sowell's careful study demolished notions of inborn [white over black] racial superiority. (Stark, 1985, p. 110)

Racial and social-class differences in IQ test results are adequately explained by cultural factors. The problem is, however, that IQ tests are widely used as a basis for labeling and tracking students, providing yet another opportunity for the self-fulfilling prophecy of academic success or failure to occur. (Robertson, 1981, p. 393)

The raw emotion with which any challenges to class and cultural explanations are greeted reflects this historical fact: Such explanations freed socialization science, at least temporarily, from hereditarian arguments about class- and race-related developmental outcomes, and thus provided social scientists with a platform for social reform. But a disquieting threat to environmentalism lies in the idea that racial or class variation may itself be genetically based. This line of reasoning so threatens concerns for social welfare that its avoidance has undermined thorough research on sensitive topics such as race and class. It is one reason why some theories of socialization prefer to avoid genetics altogether.

Of course, "race" and "class" are not equivalent constructs. Social class levels are permeable to people of diverse ethnic backgrounds and individual characteristics; physical, racial characteristics are evolutionary legacies, and they are unchanging attributes ascribed to people. Specialized research designs can be applied to studying possible genetic bases of racial differences in behavior, including transracial adoption and genetic admixture research designs.[1] Although this research can be done, such studies are difficult to conduct, and data from them are sparse. Furthermore, standard behavior genetic research designs work well with social class variation, but poorly with racial variation: Among identical twins separated and raised apart, cases may be found where one twin is middle-class and another is lower-class, but one cannot find a case in which one twin is Caucasian and another is African-American. Because there is better evidence on class than on racial variation, the remainder of this section focuses on the former.

My thesis here is that social class may capture not variation in rearing and environmental social background, but instead variation in genes. This idea returns genes to socialization science by a back door—*by the very variable (social class) thought to have liberated social science from hereditarian thinking!* The present argument requires a somewhat different perspective: My question is not "What does social class predict?," but rather "What makes for social class differences in the first place?"

Social class can be measured by means of several popular indices: (1) years of education completed; (2) occupational prestige; and (3) family income. Unlike the violent storms that regularly hit Florida's coasts to wreck homes and property, class attainments do not represent environments imposed on adults by natural events beyond their control; rather, they represent what individuals *earn or find* through years of effort, mixed with good and bad luck. As was not the case in the rigid monarchies of pre–World War I Europe, social mobility between generations is a fact of life in the industrialized West today, nearly as persistent as death and taxes. Some children rise to a social class status above that of their fathers (and in this more liberated era, mothers); other children fall to a status below that of their parents; and still others remain in about the same place. If individuals' social class partly results from their behavior, then it can reflect genetic variation in the traits and abilities that may determine whether people rise, fall, or remain static. What we call "environment" can be, in part, genetic (Herrnstein, 1973).

Although these observations seem simple, social scientists have studiously avoided them. Apparently, we do not want to wrestle with the implications of admitting that 5%, 10%, or 25% of social class variation may be genetic. A common statement such as "the IQs of middle- and working-class children are more alike when equated for years of parental education" loses its cogency if variation in a social class measure is itself partly genetic. If so, equating groups on class matches them genetically as well as environmentally. And if genes can cause behavioral variation, then it may come as no surprise to us that genetically matched groups are no longer as different from one another as unmatched ones. This reasoning does not prove that class differences are genetic in origin, of course, but it does shake the habitual confidence that they are not.

Genetic Influence on Social Class Variation: Jencks's Model and an Alternative

Not all postwar scholars ignored their intellectual obligation to deal with how genetic variation may influence social class variation. In his seminal book *Inequality*, Christopher Jencks (1972) attempted to evaluate genes' contributions to social status. He used data on the genetic inheritance of IQ in his statistical models of income, concluding that the genes' contribution to men's income variation was a rather small one: "First, genes account for no more than 10 percent of the [income] difference. As usual, biological explanations for the inheritance of privilege do not take us very far" (p. 215).

More specifically, Jencks attributed 7–9% of income variation between men in the upper and lower social classes to IQ genes; 16–20% to IQ advantage attributable to the superior environment of the upper class; 24–29% to the extra schooling for those with equal IQs; 18% to higher-status occupations for those with equal IQs and equal schooling; and the 30% remaining to an additional income advantage of higher-status men after the men were equated on all other factors. Now even a 7–9% contribution of genes to income should deserve some consideration in socialization science, but Jencks's conclusion, and even his concern, are somehow absent from the pages of many social science textbooks. The feeling may be that although a genetic contribution exists, it is small enough to be neglected (although a correlation of .30 is a typical magnitude in socialization science and explains 9% of variation).

Matters become more serious, however, if flaws in Jencks's methods resulted in his underestimating genes' influence on social class differences. I can identify one such subtle flaw in Jencks's logic, and this must be understood before other data on the transmission of social advantage are considered. Table 5.1 presents correlations among genes, IQ at age 11 years, years of education, and adult income, provided by Jencks or derived from his data. Jencks inferred the genes' correlations with other variables from a particular statistical model—one based upon "causal chains". In such a model, one variable causes the next in a chain, along with new influences unrelated to the prior variables, which enter at each new place. With causal chain models, a well-established prin-

TABLE 5.1. Illustrative Correlations under Christopher Jencks's Model

	Genes	IQ, age 11 years	Years of education	Income (adult)
Genes	1.00			
IQ, age 11 years	.71[a]	1.00		
Years of education	.16[a]	.58[b]	1.00	
Income (adult)	.14[a]	.24[a]	.35[b]	1.00

[a]The correlations are derived from Jencks's (1972) data by means of various path-analytic models.
[b]The correlations are from Jencks (1972).

ciple is that the correlation of a variable at the chain's tail with any variable downstream is simply the product of the statistical associations linking them.

Figure 5.1 (top) illustrates the causal assumptions embodied in the more complex chain models that Jencks actually used. The "head" variable is IQ genes, which affect IQ at age 11, which in turn affects education, which then leads to the chain's "tail" (income). The path coefficient is the correlation of each variable with the next one in the chain. Each variable downstream from IQ genes is also affected by other influences, as represented by the vertical arrows. Since they are unmeasured influences, we do not need to concern ourselves with them.

Suppose we want to know the correlation between IQ genes and income. It is simply the product of the numbers along the chain: .71 ×

JENCKS' VIEW

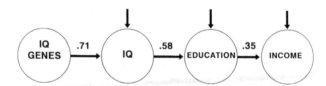

GENES EXPLAIN 2% OF INCOME

COMMON FACTOR VIEW

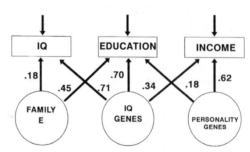

GENES EXPLAIN 50% OF INCOME

FIGURE 5.1. Genetic variation and income levels: two views.

.58 × .35 = .14. Thus, according to a chain model, genes explain just 2% of the variation in income (.14² = .02), an estimate actually below Jencks's 7–9%. His higher estimates came from a model containing more variables and pathways, but this model does reproduce the *logic* of Jencks's more complicated ones.

What is seriously wrong with Jencks's chain model? Its problem is that genes do not produce a test score at age 11, which next directly causes years of years of education, which next directly causes incomes. Rather, genes produce a phenotype—a person with particular intellectual abilities and weaknesses. Persons' strengths and weaknesses affect their encounters with the IQ test at age 11, the demands of schooling, the opportunities of the job market, and the rigors of succeeding in a job. Thus the influence of the genes is not mediated through the test score itself, and Jencks's model as a literal representation of genetic influence becomes misleading.

Figure 5.1 (bottom) shows an alternative representation of influences on social status. IQ genes, personality genes, and family environment influence IQ at age 11, education, and income simultaneously. Personality genes have been added because, as Jencks acknowledged, "Genes may . . . influence certain personality traits, and these may influence a man's earning power" (1972, p. 262). The figure neglects the temporal lags between events by assuming that the same IQ genes that affect adult income also affect IQ at 11 years. This assumption is warranted because considerable overlap exists between genes influencing intelligence in childhood and adulthood.[2] The figure also omits any correlation of family environment and genes, but we know that more intellectually capable parents will provide their children with more intellectually stimulating home environments. More complex behavior genetic models can estimate the effects on IQ of this genotype × environment correlation (Loehlin & DeFries, 1987), but for the present illustrative purposes this complication is omitted.

As before, the correlations among variables can be calculated by multiplying the statistical associations on the pathways that connect them. Figure 5.1 has been drawn to replicate the correlations among observable variables in Table 5.1. So income and IQ correlate .24 (.71 × .34), education and IQ correlate .58 (.71 × .70 + .45 × .18), and education and income correlate .35 (.70 × .34 + .18 × .62). Figure 5.1 shows the same correlation between IQ and IQ genes as Table 5.1 (r = .71). However, IQ genes correlate .70 with years of education and .34 with income, as opposed to .16 and .14 in Table 5.1. The model in Figure 5.1 has been chosen as a conceptual illustration, not as a true partition of the variation in IQ, education, and income.

The common-factor world view depicted in Figure 5.1 departs from Jencks's original in one major respect. The influence of genes becomes much greater than before—the squares of the statistical associations on the arrows pointed at the measured variables. Thus IQ genes now explain 12% (.34 × .34) of variance in adults' incomes, as opposed to a mere 2% in the pure chain model (Figure 5.1, top). The addition of personality genes increases the genetic contribution to income variation by 38% (.62 × .62), so that gene substitutions, in total, explain about 50% of income variation! The model allows rearing to influence education: One-fifth of education variation (.20 = .45 × .45) is attributable to rearing, whereas 49% is attributable to IQ genes (.49 = .70 × .70).

But which view of the world is more correct—Jencks's view that "biological explanations . . . do not take us very far" in the explanation of income, or the view that a major part of income variation is attributable to genes and that little is attributable to variation in family environments? The answer must come from behavior genetic studies that use social status itself as the outcome. Neither education nor income is a trait in the same sense as eye color or brain dopamine concentrations; however, heritable traits can create genetic variation in education and income through an influence on levels of accomplishment, in classroom learning and later in the workforce. Thus a behavior genetic analysis can be done on years of education or on income as though they were individual traits, and it can seek the degree of total genetic variation in them.

Behavior Genetic Studies of Social Status

An economist, Paul Taubman (1976), tried this approach with one of the largest and most representative American twin samples: the World War II Veterans Twin Panel. These adult male twins all served in the military during World War II and were identified through their military records. Except for the physically handicapped, felons, and people with serious mental or psychological handicaps, the population of World War II veterans spanned a wide cross-section of American society—with a wide range of years of completed schooling, and incomes from poverty to wealth. The twin registry included about 1,000 MZ twins and

1,000 DZ twins. Years of education yielded twin correlations of .76 for identical pairs and .54 for fraternal pairs (or, in terms of variance components, 44% for heritability, 32% for rearing environment, and 24% for unshared environment). For income, the results were even less encouraging to rearing influences. The MZ twin brothers correlated .52, whereas the DZ brothers correlated only .30 (or, in terms of variance components, 44% for heritability, 8% for rearing, and 48% for unshared environment). Ironically, Jencks's low estimate of family influence on attained income would be correct—but for *rearing* environments rather than for genes, as only 8% of variation in income in Taubman's study owed to the environmental advantages some families were able to confer on their children.

Some children, of course, do inherit fortunes from their parents. However, this is true in only a very small percentage of cases, so that monetary inheritances fail to alter the picture of little overall family environmental advantage for children's incomes in adulthood in the population at large. Indeed, years of education is a better "environmental" variable than is income, because at least some variation in years of education can be attributed to environmental advantages conferred by rearing. In Norway, however, even variation in educational attainment is primarily genetic rather than attributable to rearing environment (allowing for assortative mating, h^2 = .60; Tambs, Sundet, Magnus, & Berg, 1989). And as the last two chapters have shown, these rearing differences, though effectively influencing years of schooling completed in the United States, lack influence on most personality or intellectual capacity traits, because rearing influences on these traits are for the most part nil. Behavior genetic studies conducted in other countries also demonstrate genetic variation in standard social class measures (Tambs et al., 1989; Teasdale, 1979; Teasdale & Owen, 1981).

As I have noted already, social class measures thus contain genetic variation because heritable traits are associated with life accomplishments. Richard Herrnstein proposed the following syllogism relating abilities to social standing (1973, pp. 197–198):

1. If differences in mental abilities are inherited, and
2. If success requires those abilities, and
3. If earnings and prestige depend on success,
4. Then social standing (which reflects earning and prestige) will be based to some extent on inherited differences among people.

Mobility effects—"success," in Herrnstein's syllogism—can be seen in the fate of children who move up and down the occupational ladder, relative to the status of their families of origin. In each generation in industrialized societies, about 30% of children move upward in social class (relative to their class of origin), about 30% move downward, and the remainder stay in place. In light of the data summarized here and in previous chapters, each statement in the syllogism is noncontroversial. In presenting them, however, Herrnstein offered no evidence for the influence of heritable traits on social mobility, other than the general correlation of IQ and social status.

A more direct demonstration of the influence of heritable IQ variation on social mobility comes from *within*-family comparisons. In the quiet suburbs of an English city, the IQs of upwardly mobile sons averaged 7 points higher than those of their fathers, whereas those of downwardly mobile sons averaged 8 points lower (Mascie-Taylor & Gibson, 1978). In Minnesota, the IQs of downwardly mobile sons were consistently lower than those of their fathers, and those of the upwardly mobile sons, were consistently higher. Moreover, as shown in Figure 5.2, the proportion of sons rising or falling in social class increased systematically with the departure of their IQs from their fathers' (Waller, 1971). About 40% of those sons with IQs 15 points below their fathers' fell in social standing, whereas an equal number of those with IQs 15 points above their fathers' rose in social standing. The more discrepant a son's IQ from his father's, the more likely the son was to fall or rise in social standing. Herrnstein's (1973) syllogism has thus received empirical support in studies conducted in England and the United States. Although one might prefer larger and more representative studies than these two, I think it unlikely that a massive National Institute of Health study would discover that children duller than their parents tend to rise in social class, or that the brighter ones tend to fall.

In summary, social mobility explains why genes in a professional-class person differ, on average, from those in a working-class person. If people were randomly allocated to social class levels, then no systematic genetic differences would exist among them. However, this is not the case: It is by dint of individual effort, and by the presence or absence of favorable traits, that people with different genotypes become reassorted into different social classes. The situation is like that of a species of mollusks that find different depths in a tidal plain. Genotypic variants able to survive better in deeper, cooler waters become more common there, whereas in the shallower, warmer waters, other genotypes

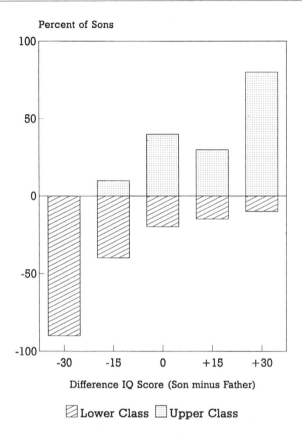

Percent of Sons

Difference IQ Score (Son minus Father)

Lower Class Upper Class

FIGURE 5.2. Social class mobility based on sons' IQs. Adapted from Waller (1971). Copyright 1971 by the Society for the Study of Social Biology. Adapted by permission.

are favored. Through this selective action, genetic variation may arise between mollusks in deep and shallow waters. That is, the existence of environmental "niches," each more compatible with one particular genotype than with another, supports gene variation at particular loci because one genotype (AA) thrives in one niche, whereas another (aa) thrives in a different niche (Kari & Avise, 1992).

In each generation, countervailing forces try to eliminate the genetic basis of social class. One force is the reassortment of genes occurring within marriages. Although a college student is more likely to marry another college student than to marry a laborer, mate choice is far from perfect for traits such as IQ (with a strong influence on social success), and imperfect for other traits as well. The husband–wife correlation on IQ is only about .35 (Johnson, Ahern, & Cole, 1980). Children, receiving genes from the parent with the genotype more favorable to mobility as well as from the other parent, usually enter social competition with a more average genotype than that of the better parent's. For a typical family at the upward social class extreme, downward social mobility (toward the population mean) is to be expected, because less favorable genes tend to be received from the more average parent. For a typical family at the social bottom, upward social mobility (toward the population mean) is to be expected, because more favorable genes tend to be received from the more average parent.

This reassortment, however, fails to imply a continuing progression toward the average. The loss of very favorable and very unfavorable genotypes from extreme families is compensated for in their recreation in the children of average parents. The real world is unlike Garrison Keillor's Lake Wobegon, where all the women are strong, all the men are good-looking, and all the children are above average. Truly average people— neither grossly underachieving nor outstanding, and existing in great numbers—are the reservoir from which most very good and poor genotypes are randomly reformed through genetic recombination.

Another force also encourages social mobility: environmental regression toward the mean. The lucky and unlucky events that propel parents to high or low social statuses are not recreated in a child. So neither lucky events nor the exact genotypes that produced parental fates are likely to be found in a family's offspring, who must then seek their own fortunes. If husband–wife matching for status-relevant traits were more nearly perfect, of course, the pressure on social mobility to recreate a genetically based social status hierarchy in each generation would be eased. As Romeo and Juliet illustrate, however, love often ignores social convention, and mating systems in Western democracies are not strong engines of social status.

The driving power of effort and merit can be overemphasized, of course. The unshared environmental influences—already acknowledged in the elements of fortune and luck—account for about half the variation in income and one-quarter of the variation in years of education. Moreover, macroeconomic events can devastate the economy. Some years ago, a chief engineer in the aerospace industry was heralded for helping to land men on the moon. His achievements brought him little comfort when, shortly thereafter, an economic recession in the aerospace industry cost him his job; even highly praised engineers are sent pink slips. But in social class variation within the economy at a particular time, a major part of its origin is in the genes.

Social Class and Behavioral Outcomes

The Confusion of Cause and Effect

Even if the variation in an environmental measure is genetic, it is still possible for its association with behavioral outcomes to be environmentally mediated, but it remains unlikely. For the most part, we can expect that the statistical association between social class and any one of these outcomes will be genetically based—a result of shared genes that in a parent may affect income or years of education, and that in a child may affect a particular trait. An edition of the *World Book Encyclopedia* does not appear on a family's book shelf by magic; the parents must want to buy it. Who will so decide? Parents who are bright and intellectually curious, and who wish their children to excel at school. The same genes affecting these parental traits can influence children's IQs. Thus a genetic confound in an environmental measure is not difficult to spot; unfortunately, however, this concept eludes the grasp of many social scientists, who insist on reading causation into the statistical association of social class with children's behaviors.

Abundant data on children's IQs demonstrate this confusion of cause and effect. In biological families, the association between a measure of parental social class (say, income or years of education) or one of rearing environment (say, books in the home) can capitalize on genes shared by parent and child. In adoptive families, by contrast, the opportunity to capitalize on this association has been removed (although selective placement, as noted in Chapter 2, can induce an artificial association between genotypes of the adoptee and adoptive parent). The extent of genetic influence in the association is contained in the difference of the biological parent–child correlation (heredity + rearing) and the adoptive parent–adoptee correlation (rearing alone).

What does the research say? In Leahy's (1935) adoption study, economic class correlated .37 with children's IQs in biological families ($p < .05$), whereas its correlation in adoptive families was only .12. In another early adoption study, family quality correlated about twice as strongly with children's IQs in biological as in adoptive families (about .40 vs. .20, respectively; Burks, 1928). In the Colorado Adoption Project

(Plomin, Loehlin, & DeFries, 1985), the general score on the Home Observation for Measurement of the Environment (HOME; Caldwell & Bradley, 1984)—a widely used assessment of the intellectual qualities of the rearing environment—correlated .44 with infants' IQs in biological families, but only .29 in adoptive families. In one of the Minnesota adoption studies, a combination of mother's education and father's occupation and income correlated .33 with children's IQs in biological families, but only .14 in adoptive families (Scarr & Weinberg, 1978). This last result was published in the prestigious *American Sociological Review*, where it stimulated one round of debate in the same journal in 1980, but has since been mainly ignored by a field unwilling to deal with scientific anomalies. Other studies could be added here, but the trend is already clear: *Environmental* social status variation has been greatly overstated, and *genetic* social class variation has been greatly understated, whenever socialization science has presented data from biological families.

A Case Example: Asian Refugees

Academic achievements of the children of newly arrived Asian refugees may be used to illustrate these principles. Despite coming from illiterate and poor backgrounds in their homelands and arriving in America economically destitute, the refugees' children have performed outstandingly in the inner-city schools of five urban areas—in precisely those schools in poor neighborhoods that are thought to be unable to educate our youth (Caplan, Choy, & Whitmore, 1992). In a randomly chosen sample of 536 school-age refugee Asian children, *one-third* scored above the 90th percentile in mathematics on a standardized test. Their overall test average was at the 54th percentile, but their performance was handicapped on the more language-intensive subtests (the children's parents were non-English-speaking, and English was for many children a second language).

The University of Michigan research team responsible for the study reflexively turned to the families, and to rearing, for an explanation of the ability of these children to thrive academically in an environment thought to be implacably hostile to intellectual pursuits. They identified three possible rearing influences responsible for the "pivotal role of the family in the children's academic success" (p. 36). The first was Asian values, which encouraged a family-based orientation toward achievement, hard work, perseverance, and pride. The second was the tremendous effort devoted to school work: Whole families would gather around the dining room table to spend 3 hours per night on school work (about twice the hours put into school work by the average American child). Third, the siblings taught one another, so that families with more children actually had enhanced levels of academic achievement.

Throughout this book, we have seen a failure of rearing experiences to account for children's traits, and yet this would appear to be a dramatic case of academic achievement, accompanied by patterns of parenting sharply different from those in most poor urban families. Are we now to believe that rearing matters? Are we to accept that the causal influences on these Asian children's achievement were sibling tutors and Asian family values? No, at least not in the sense implied by the Michigan research team. The Michigan researchers imagined that good rearing is like an experimental treatment that can be applied to anyone with equal success: Put other children into an Asian family, with its values and emphasis on achievement, and their test scores should bloom as well. In an experimental treatment, plants given more fertilizer grow larger and produce a more abundant crop than plants given less: Double the fertilizer given to the crop, and its agricultural yield should double. Such experimental results are true when a manipulated variable has produced an outcome, but they are false and profoundly misleading when little *causal* determination lies within rearing environment.

Previous chapters have shown that traits emerge through a process of gene × environment correlation—through Dawkins's (1982) "extended phenotype." In this view, the supportive environments of Asian families *and* a set of genetically based traits lead together to high levels of academic achievement. The Asian children's long attention span, greater self-control, and large working memory capacity constitute a recipe for academic success through self-directed study. Were these traits lacking, the long hours around a dining room table would erupt into family arguments, with jumpy children anxious to break away from the unpleasant duty imposed on them. Even if more average children, lacking the persistence of these Asian boys and girls, could be handcuffed and chained to their books, would not the lesser absorption of academic material make learning less satisfying? In a nutshell, an alternative hypothesis is that these Asian children were indeed different in (genetically based) temperamental and intellectual traits from the other inner-city children with whom they were compared.

Studies of transracially adopted Asian children diminish the argument for the *necessity* of Asian values and family life. One study followed

12 children from Vietnam, 8 from Korea, 3 from Cambodia, and 2 from Thailand, all adopted into American homes prior to 36 months of age (Clark & Hanisee, 1982). About half the babies required hospitalization for malnutrition in the United States prior to their adoptive placements. There was little screening of the babies as adoptable or unadoptable at the time of their placements, and most had had checkered histories in orphanages, foster homes, hospitals, or combinations of these. Like the larger sample of Asian children reared by their natural parents, these adoptees, even as infants, excelled in showing academic ability. Their mean score on the Peabody Picture Vocabulary Test was an IQ of 120, as opposed to national norms of 100. They also excelled on a test of social competence. Two studies of transracially adopted Korean children replicate these results (Frydman & Lynn, 1989; Winick, Meyer, & Harris, 1975). Provided with an environment generally supportive of intellectual work, Asian children seem to find their own ways to thrive.

Indeed, soft-pedaled in the Michigan report was a mention of the Asian children's own satisfaction with studying: ". . . the children experienced intrinsic gratification when they correctly worked a problem through to completion. The pleasure of intellectual growth, based on new knowledge and ideas and combined with increased competence and mastery, was considered highly satisfying" (Caplan et al., 1992, p. 40). Although the Michigan team attributed this intrinsic response to the children's cultural identity, I am convinced that it would be more correctly attributed to their genes and to their reactive and active responses to this genetic endowment. Such gene × environment correlation meant that "no damaging manipulation of their [the children's] lives" (p. 41) was made by their parents and that a "love of learning sustained their academic pursuits" (p. 41). For other children, an educational intervention similar to long, unbroken study periods and difficult mathematical materials, as practiced by these Asian children, would fail miserably. By analogy, putting down a second bag of fertilizer would fail to transform a cherry tomato plant into a beefsteak tomato plant.[3]

The Genetics of Child-Rearing Styles

Acceptance of genetic variation in social class measures is just the peak of a large iceberg, because the same logic applies compellingly to other measures labeled in socialization science as "environmental" (Plomin & Bergeman, 1991; Scarr, 1992).

For decades, socialization science has sought connections between variation in child rearing and behavioral outcomes. Responses to questionnaires on rearing style can be factored mathematically into two broad dimensions: "parental warmth" and "parental control." The former dimension refers to the degree to which parents show their children concern and love; the latter refers to the degree to which they impose on them rules and restrictions. As noted in Chapter 1, the ideal rearing style has been described as a combination of high parental warmth and appropriate parental control (i.e., a degree of control that is tailored to children's maturity and skills)—a rearing style called "authoritative." On the other hand, like social class attainment, rearing styles are no more than parental behaviors; as such, they can be regarded as "phenotypes" of the parents as well as "environments" for children. And as relatively stable parental traits, the rearing practices by which parents raise children can be themselves analyzed for genetic variation.

I first attempted this kind of analysis with adolescent twins' and siblings' self-reports of what kind of parenting they had received (Rowe, 1981, 1983). Perceptions of whether one is loved or controlled, of course, are filtered through each individual's psychology, and so may not exactly match the parents' rearing style as seen by outside observers; on average, one family member's report of rearing explains about 10% of the variation in another's report. Children's reports are one source of information about rearing whose importance cannot be ignored, however, because these perceptions are associated with such developmental outcomes as self-esteem and delinquency.

I found that rearing styles were not innocent of genetic variation. On two different measures of rearing, identical twins reported more similar perceptions of parental love than either DZ twins or nontwin siblings. The traditional twin analysis—greater MZ twin than sibling resemblance—suggests that perceived love is heritable. The results for control were different. As shown in Table 5.2, DZ twins were about as similar as MZ twins in perceptions of parental control (correlations averaging about .45). MZ twins may see more similarity in affection than DZ twins, because their greater behavioral similarity may tend to elicit similar parental treatments. If for reasons of fairness, parents place similar restrictions on both twins (who are, after all, the same age), then the DZ and MZ twins may experience a similar degree of parental control, and this latter dimension of rearing cannot be regarded as heritable when assessed through the eyes of adolescent children.

Another approach lets parents tell us about their rearing styles. In

TABLE 5.2. Twin Correlations for Ratings of Parental
Control and Affection

	Twin correlation	
Measures	MZ	DZ
Control scales		
Control–autonomy of mother[a]	.44	.47
Control–automony of father[a]	.43	.46
Firm–lax control of mother[a]	.55	.46
Firm–lax control of father[a]	.43	.45
Restrictiveness–permissiveness[b]	.44	.45
Warmth/love scales		
Acceptance–rejection of mother[a]	.54	.17
Acceptance–rejection of father[a]	.74	.21
Accepance–rejection[b]	.63	.21

[a]The data are from Rowe (1981) for a sample of 89 twin pairs.
[b]The data are from Rowe (1983) for a sample of 90 twin pairs.

this research design, the subjects are now *adult* twins or siblings who are reporting on how they treat their own children. It may be that adult twins hold in mind an image of how their parents have treated them as children, and that this recollection guides and shapes their rearing practices. If so, we should find some shared childhood rearing influence on adult child rearing, and also little genetic influence. Alternatively, the lessons of the twins' own childhoods may have been long-forgotten casualties of time and maturation, so that rearing may reflect more heritable dispositions.

Although evidence comes from only a few studies, the findings indicate that rearing is like any other behavior—genetically influenced. In Sweden, researchers from the University of Pennsylvania and their Swedish collaborators identified twins who had been raised apart, mainly in the 1920s and 1930s, because of poor economic conditions and epidemic diseases in Sweden (Plomin, McClearn, Pedersen, Nesselroade, & Bergeman, 1989). The separated twins had been placed with different families at an average age of 2.8 years, and about half (48%) had been separated at less than 1 year of age. The separated twins were compared to unseparated twins born during the same historical period. When surveyed by mailed questionnaires, the twins who were now in their 50s and 60s, completed the Family Environment Scale (FES), a widely used measure of child rearing in the family.

Table 5.3 presents the *mean* rearing correlation for the adult twins over the eight scales comprising the FES. The correlations were low, but then the twins were raising different children (who possessed different traits) and had different spouses. One impressive result was that the families of origin lacked an influence on rearing practices, because twins raised together or raised apart in separate adoptive families were equally alike in their rearing styles. Too, with a mean correlation of only .09, the rearing practices of DZ twins were only slightly more alike than those that would be found for randomly paired adults. Genetic influences were confirmed, with the adult MZ twins who had been raised apart proving to be alike in their child-rearing practices. From the MZ twins' correlation, the estimated heritability of child rearing would be .245; from the DZ twins', it would be .18 (i.e., twice .09). In a more complex model-fitting analysis, the twin study team arrived at the following average estimates: heritability, .26; childhood rearing environment, .03; and nonshared environment, .72. Although the degree of genetic influence varied from one scale to another, seven of the eight FES scales showed statistically significant genetic influence. For no scale was the influence of childhood rearing environment statistically significant by a chi-square test. As was not the case for adolescent twins' perceptions of rearing, genetic influence was statistically significant both for control dimensions of rearing (FES organization and control) and for warmth dimensions of rearing (e.g., FES conflict and expressiveness).

In unpublished work, I surveyed a fifth kinship group: 20 pairs of unrelated children reared together. The unrelated children were usually both adopted into the same adoptive family; their average age at placement was under 2 years. Now adults with children 9 years of age

TABLE 5.3. Mean Child-Rearing Correlations for Adult Twins with Families

Group	Rearing r	No. of pairs
Adult MZ twins reared apart	.21	40–50
Adult MZ twins reared together	.28	82–90
Adult DZ twins reared apart	.10	120–129
Adult DZ twins reared together	.09	104–115

Note. Mean correlations averaged over eight subscales in the Family Environment Scales (measuring cohesion, expressiveness, conflict, achievement, culture, activity, organization, and control). The data are from Plomin, McClearn, Pedersen, Nesselroade, & Bergeman (1989).

and under, this group provides another check on the influence of family background on adult rearing correlations. Their child-rearing correlations for both warmth ($r = .00$) and control ($r = .18$) were statistically nonsignificant. Of course, perhaps some effect of childhood environment would emerge in a larger sample of unrelated siblings. But I expect that a larger sample would confirm this discovery—that no two children learn the same things about parenting from their own parents.

Table 5.4 presents correlations of the adults' rearing styles with their self-reports of personality on the Big Five personality traits, discussed in Chapter 3. In particular, the warmth dimension has personality correlates in the domains of extraversion and intellectual openness. The control dimension has such correlates as emotional stability and agreeableness. Of course, in standard personality inventories, some sources of heritable variation in child-rearing styles may be missed. One interesting avenue, which can be pursued in new research, is whether rearing practices contain unique genetic variation, separable from standard traits. The emotional depth we feel in our relationship with our own children suggests that here is a special domain for revealing the inner qualities of human character.

In the association of children's IQ scores and their families' social class, we have already seen causal confounds. But few studies have shown them directly in the more emotional domains of family life. One study to make this demonstration nicely is the Colorado Adoption Project. In the Colorado Adoption Project, as noted in earlier chapters, adoptive families were compared with matched, nonadoptive families. In the former families, the lack of association of parental and child genes meant that heredity would be unable to mediate associations between measures

TABLE 5.4. Correlations between the Parenting Composites and the "Big Five" Self-Descriptions of Personality

Dimensions	Warmth	Control
Extraversion	.35°	.07
Agreeableness	.38°	−.28°
Conscientiousness	.29°	−.15°
Emotional stability	.28°	−.35°
Intellectual openness	.45°	−.14

Note. n = 186. Control dimension includes strictness and negative emotions.
°$p < .05$.

of family environment and children's outcomes. And, as expected, greater correlations between rearing and child outcomes were found in the biological than in the adoptive families. For infants' behavioral problems, the mean environment–behavior correlation was .07 in adoptive families and .23 in biological families; for infants' temperament, the mean correlations were .06 and .20, respectively (Plomin et al., 1985). Primarily, what seems to be a causal association is just the happenstance of similar genes shared by biological parent and child.

The Genetics of Other Environmental Variables

Parental Divorce

Genetic self-selection processes may extend to many other "environmental" variables favored in socialization science. Parental divorce is one important example. Although divorced children suffer worse outcomes for some behavioral traits than children of nondivorced parents, the causality is ambiguous. Divorced and nondivorced parents are not random samples of a population, assigned by some impartial decision maker to two different social statuses; rather, they are people who have elected either to dissolve their marriages or to remain married. Simply put, people who divorce may be different from people who do not.

And once again, an "environmental" variable can reveal genetic variation secreted within its categories. In Minnesota, the divorce status of 1,516 same-sex twin pairs, their parents, and their spouses' parents was studied through a mail survey (McGue & Lykken, 1991). Twin samples in Minnesota are noteworthy for their representativeness of white Americans from northern Europe as such, they are the closest American approximations to the nationally complete data banks of the Scandinavian countries. From the twin and parent–child data, the heritability of divorce can be estimated. The correlations were as follows: for MZ twins, .55; for DZ twins, .16; and for parents and offspring, .17 for the twins and .27 for their spouses. The heritability of divorce was then estimated as 52%. McGue and Lykken found no evidence for a rearing influence on the risk of divorce: The likelihood of divorce did not come from the social example of divorced parents, spouses' parents, or cotwins, according to their mathematical model.

In the case of divorce, the degree of risk can arise from genetic influences brought into the relationship from either the spouses' or

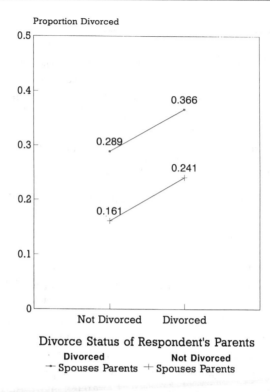

FIGURE 5.3. Parental divorce and the risk of divorce. Adapted from McGue & Lykken (1991). Copyright 1991 by the American Psychological Society. Adapted by permission.

respondents' biological families. As shown in Figure 5.3, divorce risk in this sample increased additively with divorce in (1) neither family of origin of the couple; (2) divorce on the spouse's side alone; (3) divorce on the respondent's side alone; or (4) divorce on both sides. Odds increased even more extremely with information on an MZ twin. In the news, we sometimes read about an MZ twin man taking an MZ twin woman's hand in marriage. The risk for a hypothetical marriage of an MZ twin man to an MZ twin woman with no family history of divorce (5.3%) was 15 times smaller than that for the same type of marriage in which the married MZ twins' biological parents, and both their cotwins, were divorced (77.5%). Given these circumstances, a minister might do well to stop the marriage!

Adolescent Peer Groups

The choice of friends is also a selective process: The Republican avoids the Democrat; the drinker, the teetotaler; the daredevil, the sissy; and the selfish, the altruistic. In light of this self-selection process, friends should be more genetically alike than randomly paired individuals (Rushton, 1988), and peer group choice should show genetic variation.

The Sibling Inventory of Differential Experience (SIDE) nicely demonstrates the component of genetic variation in adolescents' peer group choices (Baker & Daniels, 1990). The inventory requests from a sibling respondent a relative judgment of peer group popularity, achievement, and delinquency. That is, the respondent indicates whether his or her peer group has more of the characteristic than that of his or her sibling, and the sibling makes the same judgment in reverse. Absolute differences on these scales are scored as follows: A score of 2 means that the siblings' peer groups are very different; a score of 1, that they are somewhat different; and a score of 0, that they are exactly alike.

Figure 5.4 presents the absolute differences on the SIDE for kinship groups that differed in genetic and social relatedness. As shown, the family members' adolescent peer groups became increasingly dissimilar in their achievement, delinquency, and popularity as the siblings became less genetically alike—from MZ twins, to DZ twins and nontwin siblings, to adoptees. A simple interpretation can be offered: Siblings select peers partly on the basis of matching personality traits and social interests. Because both traits and interests are heritable, the more genetically dissimilar siblings select different peer groups, which then reinforce their trait dispositions. In Scarr and McCartney's (1983, p. 433) phrase, "genes direct the course of human experience" to the point that the character of people and the environments they choose to inhabit are inseparable.

Differential Treatment within Families

As discussed several times in this book, the evidence against shared environmental effects does not apply to parents' differential treatments of children. Instead, an explanation in terms of shared environments applies to parent–child resemblance. If parents resemble children in psychopathology, personality, or intellect, then it is natural to attribute this

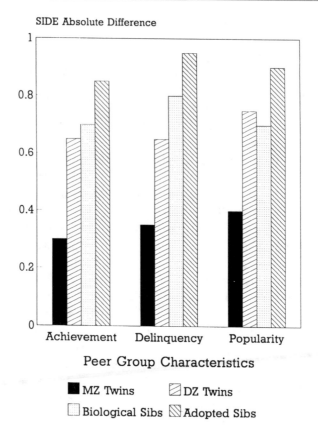

SIDE Absolute Difference

■ MZ Twins   ▨ DZ Twins
▢ Biological Sibs   ◫ Adopted Sibs

FIGURE 5.4. Peer group dissimilarity and biological relatedness. Adapted from Baker & Daniels (1990). Copyright 1990 by the American Psychological Association. Adapted by permission.

resemblance to the causal influence of experiences shared by parents, or in the case of sibling resemblance, the siblings' common experiences. But this book's thesis has been that the correct causal attribution for these resemblances is genetic inheritance, not shared family environment. Nonetheless, behavior genetic models also estimate another environmental term—the nonshared environment that differs among siblings (or between parent and child) and operates to make them different in their behavioral traits. Could parenting practices contribute to family members' behavioral dissimilarities? Are parenting influences more important than low estimates of shared family effects would suggest?

For example, variations in emotional climate among families (with the exception of severe abuse or neglect) are discounted as causal influences by this book's accumulated evidence. But what about variations in the microemotional climate within families as seen from the vantage point of each child? Children may be exquisitely sensitive to unevenness of parental treatments, as when one sibling is favored over another.

In their book *Separate Lives* (1990), the husband-and-wife team of Dunn and Plomin cite the enormous personality differences between two brothers: the gifted novelist Henry James, and the famous psychologist William James. Henry was aloof, quiet, and unsociable, but he was his mother's favorite child. William had an easy gregariousness; he was energetic and vibrant. Although William's traits would seem more likely to be a result of maternal favoritism than Henry's, sometimes true causal influences work in ways different from what common sense would dictate.

Given the possibility of subtle within-family parenting effects, behavior geneticists have called for increased research on the differential treatments of siblings (Rowe & Plomin, 1981; Plomin & Daniels, 1987). A behavior geneticist writing with two environmentally oriented social scientists commented:

> Although differences between siblings in normal and pathological outcomes are beginning to be delineated, we know far less about environmental differences between them. The genetic data suggest that only environmental variables that are significantly different between siblings are likely to be important in developmental differences. (Reiss, Plomin, & Hetherington, 1991, p. 285)

Of course, "environmental differences between siblings" include far more than unequal parental treatments. Isolating what particular non-shared environmental influences are responsible for an observed behavioral difference is a daunting task, all the more so because such influences can be almost anything under the sun. Nonshared environmental influences range from intrauterine environments to attending different colleges. To show that parental treatments are effective non-shared environmental influences, several tests must be passed: (1) The differential treatment must be associated with sibling differences in normal or pathological traits; and (2) the direction of causality must be from parental treatments to the observed behavioral difference between the siblings, rather than vice versa. Genetic influences may reverse the directionality of effects in the second pathway, if nonshared genetic effects produce different phenotypes in siblings, which are then reacted to differently by parents.

I agree with encouraging work aimed at identifying various non-shared environmental influences, including parental favoritism toward one child versus another. Without a large existing body of evidence, any conclusion about the strength of specific nonshared influences must be regarded as tentative. Nonetheless, I am doubtful that new discoveries about nonshared parental treatments will upset this book's thesis that family influences on children's developmental outcomes are limited.

One reason for caution is a distinction between components of variance and developmental processes. As discussed in Chapter 2, components of variance are the results of calculations made for estimating and testing models of environmental and genetic inheritance. One way to understand these components is to say that variance is apportioned to differences among family means (i.e., the shared or between-family component) and to siblings' differences from their respective family means (i.e., the nonshared or within-family component). Let us suppose that in the Smith family John scores 90 on an IQ test and his sister Mary scores 100. The family mean (the average of John's and Mary's IQs) is 95. This mean represents the "shared" component of IQ—an IQ level common to the siblings. The nonshared component of IQ is the 10-point difference between them—John is 5 IQ points below the family mean; Mary is 5 IQ points above it. Thus mathematically, a shared component (the siblings' overall mean of 95) can be distinguished from a nonshared component (the siblings' 10-point IQ difference). As noted in Chapter 2, a larger shared component would means greater family-tied genetic or environmental effects.

Most developmental processes, however, do not map exactly onto this convenient mathematical distinction. Development proceeds, regardless of how variation in trait scores is later apportioned. Suppose, for example, that the book's thesis had proved wrong—that the majority of IQ variation was correctly attributed to intellectual stimulation in families. Over her childhood, Mary's exposure to intellectual stimulation would lead to her IQ level—an IQ of 100. Furthermore, Mary must have received somewhat more intellectual stimulation than her brother John; hence her higher IQ score. If intellectual stimulation by Mary's parents has been responsible for the development of Mary's IQ, then its effects will necessarily appear both in the shared component (the family mean IQ) and in the nonshared component (the siblings' IQ difference). "Intellectual stimulation" does not recognize this distinction of "shared" versus "nonshared" variation. This distinction arises only after development has occurred, when a researcher decides to use statistical procedures by which IQ variation is apportioned to that which is shared by siblings and to that which makes them different.

A special developmental process that makes siblings different could conceivably have a mainly nonshared influence. Let us suppose that Mary is the first-born child and John is the second-born. Let us imagine further that parents typically put most of their intellectual stimulation into a first-born child and less into a second-born child. To complete the picture, all parents use *exactly* the same amount of intellectual stimulation (there are no differences among families), but the first-born child always receives twice the intellectual stimulation of the second-born child. Under these restrictive conditions, the environmental influence would operate entirely within families—as a nonshared influence making siblings different. I do not see why we should expect to find developmental processes with such restrictive effects. In general, developmental processes are seamless; they are not isolated from other processes just to make siblings different from one another.

Consider, for example, that a large scientific literature on birth order has not produced an explanation for sibling differences in behavior. Variation in IQ, in particular, has been attributed in both textbooks and in the popular press to birth order differences. I think that under the scrutiny of carefully collected data, most birth order theories of IQ variation simply collapse (Schooler, 1972). True, only children have higher mean IQs than last-born children in large American families—but this effect may be easily explained as one of selection, because parents with high IQs also often restrict their family sizes more (since the baby-boom generation) than parents with low IQs. When birth orders are compared within families, mean IQ differences are rarely found, and children of different birth orders are equally *similar* to one another in their IQs (Rodgers, 1984; Rodgers & Rowe, 1985).

As in the example above of Henry and William James, another hypothesis of purely nonshared effects is parental favoritism. If this effect arises as one sibling senses how much he or she is favored relative to another sibling, then favoritism would truly create differences mainly between siblings, without any reference to a family's overall level relative to a population. In other words, both siblings may be terribly mistreated (compared to how children in general are treated), but a better-treated sibling may still feel well psychologically, if he or she has received the more favorable treatment of two siblings.

Although this argument is logically consistent, I am again doubt-ful—merely because children make social comparisons not only to their own brothers or sisters, but also to children in other families, and (through media portrayals) even to children in other social classes and countries. Eventually, I believe that two children with little parental affection or interest would come to know their status relative to other children, making parental treatment a shared influence (relative to the general population) instead of a purely nonshared influence (relative to a sibling).

Despite these cautions, it is certainly possible that "nonshared" parenting effects exist, and they may be stronger than I have anticipated. The best way to assess the strength of nonshared parental treatments is through empirical studies designed for this purpose.

In a study of 5- to 11-year-old children in the National Longitudi-nal Study of Youth (NLSY), my colleagues and I evaluated nonshared environmental influences on childhood problem behaviors (Rodgers, Rowe, & Li, in press). The NLSY data source is a representative sample of American families stratified to contain more poor families than there are in the general population. To vary genetic resemblance, four types of related child pairs were identified from over 7,000 children in the NLSY: twin pairs, full-sibling pairs, half-sibling pairs, and cousins. The statistical analyses used a regression equation technique to control sta-tistically for both genetic and environmental *shared* influences. With this technique, the nonshared effect of specific differences in parental treat-ments could be estimated. The twin, sibling, half-sibling, or cousin who was spanked more, read to less, and had a poorer quality of home envi-ronment (as rated on the HOME; Caldwell & Bradley, 1984)—*relative to the child with whom he or she was being compared*—tended to have a greater number of problem behaviors. For some variables, the within-family treatment differences seemed to be attributable to nonshared genetic influences; in other cases, they seemed to be "pure" nonshared environmental effects.

However, one caveat is in order. The full regression equations accounted for some 10–24% of variance in problem behavior. The non-shared variable contributed 1% or even less to the variance explained. Given our large sample sizes, this was often a highly reliable addition statistically; however, in absolute terms, only a small part of the total variance in problem behavior was explained. If measurement error and nonshared genetic influences are excluded, other *nonparental*, nonshared environmental influences must explain the remainder of nonshared differences in problem behavior. If other research programs yield results like ours, this book's thesis that family environments—and child-rearing styles in particular—are limited in the extent of their influence on developmental outcomes will not require modification in light of nonshared parental treatments.

Finding the Thresholds

In this book, I have argued that variation in most rearing experiences does not matter for most developmental outcomes. Yet, as readers have surely noticed, some adoption and twin studies fail to include great numbers of the most seriously disadvantaged children. For instance, most parents in the Texas Adoption Project (described in earlier chapters) had at least a high school education. Such a range covers about 60–80% of the current American population, depending on ethnic group and geographic location, because today a majority of teenagers complete at least 12 years of education. Twin studies are typically more representative than adoption ones, but even in twin studies, parents who physically abuse or who severely neglect their children are rare. Because genetic variation in environmental measures does not preclude their *environmental* effects on children, one should not extrapolate my conclusions about rearing influences to environmental extremes, any more than one should be assured that equipment able to work in Maine's winters can be entrusted with human lives and safety in Antarctica.

Of great concern to Americans are the very poor—the lowest 10% of the population in terms of income and education levels, the families on welfare, the families who are disproportionately black and living in America's inner cities. It is in this group that the rates of child abuse and neglect are greatest, as are the rates of births to teenagers and to single women of all ages. Moreover, among the urban poor, a wave of violence among teenagers has made homicide a leading cause of death. Are we to think that rearing variation makes no difference here?

Unquestionably, these children's lives would be improved if they were not placed in the physical danger and psychological stress of neglectful or abusing parents and neighborhood violence. At some intensity, poor rearing must affect children's development—leaving emotional and physical scars, and actually leaving some children dead. But whether poor rearing is generally the culprit behind the problems of the nation's most disadvantaged children is unclear.

In rearing explanations, one weakness is that the psychological processes invoked to explain extreme outcomes are often identical to those used to explain more normal ones. But why should psychological processes hold only in the extremes? If mothers who hate their children damage them, shouldn't mothers who are just cold create more minor harm? If physical abuse leaves scars, shouldn't overly strict rearing also misdirect personality development?

Thus, we must explain unexpected rearing effects as threshold ones: Previously impotent factors may acquire power once they reach a high level of intensity, but not before. Threshold principles hold in many domains. In the mathematics of catastrophe theory, equations are well behaved up to a certain point, when suddenly a smooth trend breaks apart and predicted values fall sharply, like a stream thundering into a waterfall. A metal bar under stress may fail all at once, snapping in two, rather than bending slowly. In our diets, trace amounts of many vitamins are required for health; let their quantities fall below a threshold, and physical illness and death may result. A person's resentments and hatreds may be held within for years before they explode as murderous revenge. Rearing may have such threshold properties: At some intensity of abuse, neglect, poverty, and poor nutrition, the feelings that bind most people to others may fail to develop, and so unsocialized children become threats to others as well as to themselves.

But threshold principles may be insufficient. To explain the plight of the most disadvantaged Americans, we may need to admit genetic influences into our explanatory framework. After all, if genes account for half the variation in income over a wide range of American families, is it realistic to believe that only the poorest ones lack those genetic disadvantages affecting lower class individuals in general?

With the evidence reviewed above of genetic variation in "environmental" measures, we must, at least be cautious about expecting family environmental change to offer panaceas for children's behavior problems. Consider, for instance, average developmental outcomes for children adopted as infants. Although most adoptive children fare very well, their behavioral outcomes have been, on average, worse than those of nonadoptive comparison children.[4] In childhood, adoptees are statistically overrepresented in clinic referrals for externalizing behavior disorders. Adoptees' rates of delinquency are also higher than those of comparison nonadoptees. Finally, adoptive children have no less serious psychopathology than other children. Worse outcomes, despite materially and socially advantaged upbringings, bode ill for the idea that even a massive redistribution of economic wealth would produce problem-free children or crime-free communities. Although social conditions would be improved for these children raised in relatively economically advantaged situations, their behavior problems would persist.

A nagging fear of a hereditary basis to racial and social class differences is but one reason why socialization science has gone astray, and perhaps not the main one. In seeking an understanding of behavioral traits, we look too closely to ourselves, to the history of just a single ontogeny. By analogy, one might seek the source of the Nile at the Aswan Dam, forgetting entirely the more than 3,500 miles of river further upstream, reaching into the African continent into what the colonial explorers named the Mountains of the Moon and Lake Victoria. The fallacy is in believing that what forms human nature is a 14-year period of rearing, rather than a heavier weight of cultural history, and ultimately human evolutionary roots. In broader terms, cultural traditions can be passed in many ways other than exposure to idealized nuclear families. The adolescents who signed up enthusiastically for Nazi youth groups before World War II did not have souls bent and torn by poor rearing in early childhood; indeed, their families were stolidly middle-class and emotionally supportive. If a nation's youth can be changed by a few years of great cultural change, why emphasize childhood? And more deeply still, what genes has nature selected for us? In the next chapter, I apply ideas from evolutionary biology to behavioral sex differences. In the last chapter, these themes reappear as I discuss alternative routes by which traits may move from one generation to the next.

Notes

[1]Some scholars may ask, "Why look for genetic bases of racial differences at all?" As in other applications presented in this book, the best answer is that genetic influences must be considered if we are to estimate environmental ones accurately. Clearly, studies of racial differences must be carried out with great sensitivity to their potential for social harm (Loehlin, 1992). If a result supports a genetic basis of racial differences, care should be taken neither to exaggerate its strength nor to overgeneralize it to other traits where it may not apply. The issue of genetic differences in racially linked behavioral traits is further discussed by Loehlin, Lindzey, and Spuhler (1975) and by Mackenzie (1984). Turkheimer (1991) discusses reasons for keeping mean differences and individual differences within a single explanatory framework. Transethnic adoption studies include studies of American black children adopted by white adoptive parents and Japa-

nese children adopted by Chinese adoptive parents (Weinberg, Scarr, & Waldman, 1992; Tseng, Ebata, Miguchi, Egawa, & McLaughlin, 1990).

[2]Consider that in Table 4.1, the correlation for parent and child reared apart (.24) is the same as that for biological siblings reared apart (.24). If different genes were to influence IQ in adulthood versus childhood, then the parent–child (far apart in age) would be much weaker than the sibling association (close in age).

[3]The observation that immigrant Asian children are outscoring their American compatriots raises the reasonable possibility that some racial differences in IQ may be attributable to different genes. But evidence on immigrants is not strong. Immigrant people may fail to represent a random draw of their original populations; for example, the Southeast Asians who manage to reach American shores may be more ambitious, determined, and intelligent than those who choose not to migrate or fail in their efforts to do so. If the children of some immigrants are genetically smarter than other Americans, we still cannot be sure that this generalization would hold for their home populations.

[4]Two studies have reported on representative samples of infant adoptees, but are unpublished (Sharma & Benson, 1992; Warren, 1992). A recent book by Brodzinsky and Schechter (1990) also discusses outcomes of adoption.

References

Baker, L. A., & Daniels, D. (1990). Nonshared environmental influences and personality differences in adult twins. *Journal of Personality and Social Psychology, 58,* 103–110.

Brodzinsky, D. M., & Schechter, M. D. (1990). *The psychology of adoption.* New York: Oxford University Press.

Burks, B. S. (1928). The relative influence of nature and nurture on mental development: A comparative study of foster parent–foster child resemblance and true parent–true child resemblance. *27th Yearbook of the National Society for the Study of Education* (Part 1, pp. 219–316).

Caldwell, B. M., & Bradley, R. H. (1984). *Home Observation for Measurement of the Environment* (HOME). Little Rock: University of Arkansas Press.

Caplan, N., Choy, M. H., & Whitmore, J. K. (1992). Indochinese refugee families and academic achievement. *Scientific American, 267,* 36–42.

Clark, E. A., & Hanisee, J. (1982). Intellectual and adaptive performance of Asian children in adoptive American settings. *Developmental Psychology, 18,* 595–599.

Dawkins, R. (1982). *The extended phenotype: The gene as the unit of selection.* Oxford: Oxford University Press.

Degler, C. N. (1991). *In search of human nature: The decline and revival of Darwinism in American social thought.* New York: Oxford University Press.

Dunn, J., & Plomin, R. (1990). *Separate lives: Why siblings are so different.* New York: Basic Books.

Frydman, M., & Lynn, R. (1989). The intelligence of Korean children adopted in Belgium. *Personality and Individual Differences, 12,* 1323–1325.

Herrnstein, R. J. (1973). *I.Q. in the meritocracy.* Boston: Little, Brown.

Jencks, C. (1972). *Inequality: A reassessment of the effect of family and schooling in America.* New York: Basic Books.

Johnson, R. C., Ahern, F. M., & Cole, R. E. (1980). Secular change in degree of assortative mating for ability. *Behavior Genetics, 10,* 1–8.

Kari, S. A., & Avise, J. C. (1992). Balancing selection at allozyme loci in oysters: Implications from nuclear RFLPs. *Science, 256,* 100–102.

Leahy, A. M. (1935). Nature–nurture and intelligence. *Genetic Psychology Monographs, 17,* 237–308.

Loehlin, J. C. (1992). Should we do research on race differences in intelligence? *Intelligence, 16,* 1–4.

Loehlin, J. C., & DeFries, J. C. (1987). Genotype–environment correlation and IQ. *Behavior Genetics, 17,* 263–277.

Loehlin, J. C., Lindzey, G., & Spuhler, J. N. (1975). *Race differences in intelligence.* San Francisco: W. H. Freeman.

Mascie-Taylor, C. G. N., & Gibson, J. B. (1978). Social mobility and IQ components. *Journal of Biosocial Science, 10,* 263–276.

Mackenzie, B. (1984). Explaining race differences in IQ: The logic, the methodology, and the evidence. *American Psychologist, 39,* 1214–1233.

McGue, M., & Lykken, D. T. (1991). Genetic influence on risk of divorce. *Psychological Science, 3,* 368–373.

Neubauer, P. B., & Neubauer, A. (1990). *Nature's thumbprint: The new genetics of personality.* Reading, MA: Addison-Wesley.

Plomin, R., & Bergeman, C. S. (1991). The nature of nurture: Genetic influences on "environmental" measures. *Behavioral and Brain Sciences, 14,* 373–427.

Plomin, R., & Daniels, D. (1987). Why are children in the same family so different from one another? *Behavioral and Brain Sciences, 10,* 1–16.

Plomin, R., Loehlin, J. C., & DeFries, J. C. (1985). Genetic and environmental components of "environmental" influences. *Developmental Psychology, 21,* 391–402.

Plomin, R., McClearn, G. E., Pedersen, N. L., Nesselroade, J. R., & Bergeman, C. S. (1989). Genetic influence on adults' ratings of their current family environment. *Journal of Marriage and the Family, 51,* 791–803.

Reiss, D., Plomin, R., & Hetherington, E. M. (1991). Genetics and psychiatry: An unheralded window on the environment. *American Journal of Psychiatry, 148,* 283–291.

Robertson, I. (1981). *Sociology* (2nd ed.). New York: Worth.

Rodgers, J. L. (1984). Confluence effects: Not here, not now! *Developmental Psychology, 20,* 321–331.

Rodgers, J. L., & Rowe, D. C. (1985). Does contiguity breed similarity?: A within-family analysis of nonshared sources of IQ differences between siblings. *Developmental Psychology, 21,* 743–746.

Rodgers, J. L., Rowe, D. C., & Li, C. (in press). Beyond nature vs. nurture: DF analysis of nonshared influences on problem behaviors. *Developmental Psychology.*

Rowe, D. C. (1981). Environmental and genetic influences on dimensions of perceived parenting: A twin study. *Developmental Psychology, 17,* 203–208.

Rowe, D. C. (1983). A biometrical analysis of perceptions of family environment: A study of twin and singleton sibling kinships. *Child Development, 54,* 416–423.

Rowe, D. C., & Plomin, R. (1981). The importance of nonshared (E_1) environmental influences in behavioral development. *Developmental Psychology, 17,* 517–531.

Rushton, J. P. (1988). Genetic similarity in male friendships. *Ethology and Sociobiology, 10,* 361–373.

Scarr, S. (1992). Developmental theories for the 1990s: Development and individual differences. *Child Development, 63,* 1–19.

Scarr, S., & McCartney, K. (1983). How people make their own environments: A theory of genotype → environment effects. *Child Development, 54,* 424–435.

Scarr, S., & Weinberg, R. A. (1978). The influence of "family background" on intellectual attainment. *American Sociological Review, 43,* 674–692.

Schooler, C. (1972). Birth order effects: Not here, not now! *Psychological Bulletin, 78,* 161–175.

Sharma, A. R., & Benson, P. L. (1992, March). *A comparison of adopted and nonadopted adolescents on psychological at-risk indicators.* Paper presented at the meeting of the *Society for Research on Adolescence,* Washington, DC.

Stark, R. (1985). *Sociology.* Belmont, CA: Wadsworth.

Tambs, K., Sundet, J. M., Magnus, P., & Berg, K. (1989). Genetic and environmental contributions to the covariance between occupational status, educational attainment, and IQ: A study of twins. *Behavior Genetics, 19,* 209–222.

Taubman, P. (1976). The determinants of earnings: Genetics, family and other environments: A study of white male twins. *American Economic Review, 66,* 858–870.

Teasdale, T. W. (1979). Social class correlations among adoptees and their biological and adoptive parents. *Behavior Genetics, 9,* 103–114.

Teasdale, T. W., & Owen, D. R. (1981). Social class correlations among separately adopted siblings and unrelated individuals adopted together. *Behavior Genetics, 11,* 577–588.

Tseng, W., Ebata, K., Miguchi, M., Egawa, M., & McLaughlin, D. G. (1990). Transethnic adoption and personality traits: A lesson from Japanese orphans returned from China to Japan. *American Journal of Psychiatry, 147,* 330–335.

Turkheimer, E. (1991). Individual and group differences in adoption studies of IQ. *Psychological Bulletin, 110,* 392–405.

Waller, J. H. (1971). Achievement and social mobility: Relationships among IQ score, education, and occupation in two generations. *Social Biology, 18,* 252–259.

Warren, S. B. (1992, March). *Types and prevalence of behavior problems among adopted and nonadopted adolescents: An epidemiological study.* Paper presented at the meeting of the *Society for Research on Adolescence,* Washington, DC.

Weinberg, R. A., Scarr, S., & Waldman, I. D. (1992). The Minnesota transracial adoption study: A follow-up of IQ test performance at adolescence. *Intelligence, 16,* 117–135.

Winick, M., Meyer, K. K., & Harris, R. C. (1975). Malnutrition and environmental enrichment by early adoption. *Science, 190,* 1173–1175.

CHAPTER 6

GENDER DIFFERENCES

I n at least some respects, families rear boys and girls differently, with an expectation that the sexes will be different. This observation is widely accepted in socialization science, but sharp disagreement exists over the attribution of causality. The most widespread view today is that differential rearing *causes* behavioral gender differences. Yet this book has drawn attention to other misattributions of causality. In a contrary view, boys and girls may be reared differently because they *are* different, not because rearing has made them so. Ideally, to demonstrate causal influence, an experiment would be first performed: Typical rearing pressures on sons and daughters would be sex-reversed, with an expectation of reversal in sex-typed behaviors. Few parents, though, would allow their sons to be raised as daughters, or vice versa. And ethical considerations prohibit the approval of intentional experimentation on sex-reversed rearing.

Anecdotally, though, voluntary efforts to change gender-linked behaviors through sex-reversed rearing pressures have demonstrated little success, as reported in occasional newspaper stories. Here we can read about one family's efforts (Churchman, 1984):

> As I write this, my son—the one with the gray plastic knight's helmet and the purple soccer suit—is playing at rescuing his sister, the self-styled base-ball-playing princess. This is what comes, you see, of raising children in a nonsexist manner: absolutely nothing. (p. 9)

Churchman first describes her attempts with her daughter:

> We purchased at least $25 worth of Legos for our daughter, who spent her early years watching Mom and Dad build with them. Occasionally we could get her to pick up one or two bumpy blocks and fit them together. But

then, when she got to a more sophisticated age, she gave them to her brother . . . (p. 9)

Her son proved no more malleable:

> Then there was the suggestion I made to our male offspring that he might like to read to his sweet stuffed animals, "like a good daddy." He shot me one of his "get real" looks and said, logically, "They're only stuffed animals, Mom, they can't really see." (p. 9)

Churchman ends her account by describing how her son played with a non-English-speaking Laotian refugee. The boys found a universal basis for friendship by pushing trucks around in the backyard, saying, "Vrroom! Vrrooom!"

Churchman's personal experiment failed. But the public, and many social scientists, remain convinced that the differential rearing of boys and girls determines gender differences in behavior. A reason for this cultural belief may be that gender differences are highly visible. More often then women, for example, men get into a car, gun the engine, and make the tires squeal. The statistics on auto crashes confirm that men are worse drivers, or at least that they have more accidents than women. Rates of all sorts of crimes are substantially greater in males than in females (Wilson & Herrnstein, 1985). In broad personality domains, men score higher on traits such as dominance, activity, and competitiveness; women score higher on traits reflecting emotionality and kindness (Spence & Helmreich, 1978). Men retreat to play poker in the evenings; women gather to discuss their families or the latest self-help book. True, all these statements can be seen as in part "stereotypical," because male and female trait distributions overlap. Nonetheless, one would not misidentify biological sex too often if one guessed that a reader of hard-core pornography was male; that a reader of romance novels was female; that a player of a high-stakes game of chance was male; and that a person attending to the needs of an infant was female.

Studies of Sex-Linked Personality Traits

The earlier chapters have documented a general lack of family environmental influence on development. This pattern holds across the "Big Five" personality trait dimensions; it also holds for IQ, at least in families from the working class to the professional class.

Although most twin studies focus on general traits, two small ones looked at sex-linked personality traits in particular. My study of MZ and DZ twins investigated Janet Spence's masculinity and femininity trait dimensions (Rowe, 1982). The first dimension consists of stereotypically masculine traits; the second is made up of stereotypically feminine ones. As would be expected from their construction, the male trait mean was greater for masculinity in the twin sample, whereas the female trait mean was greater for femininity. Because the sample size was small (31 MZ pairs and 28 DZ pairs), my study lacked enough statistical power to detect all variance components that might exist. Nonetheless, genetic influence was found in masculinity, and a possible influence of rearing was found in femininity; of course, this last result was unexpected.

In a study conceptually replicating my work, Mitchell, Baker, and Jacklin (1989) administered childhood scales for masculinity and femininity to twins. They found results very compatible with this book's thesis. In childhood, genetic variation explained 20–48% of the individual differences in these trait dimensions; unshared environment, about half to 80% of the variation; and shared environment, none at all. Mitchell and her colleagues failed to replicate any shared rearing influence on femininity. Their data, mine on masculinity, and other studies reviewed by Mitchell et al. suggest together that sex-linked personality traits do not behave any differently from other traits. Indeed, it is hard how to imagine how they could, given that masculinity and femininity overlap conceptually with standard Big Five trait dimensions such as extraversion and agreeableness, respectively.

I believe that family experiences shared by brothers and sisters may *not* influence the development of their sex-typed traits. After all, they live in the same households, as siblings. Parents model behaviors that both brothers and sisters can see, and brothers and sisters feel the same home emotional climate in many other ways. They attend the same neighborhood schools. They are both rich or poor, fawned over or ignored. True, the treatment of siblings is never exactly alike; however, opposite-sex siblings reared together receive more similar "treatment" than do boys and girls raised in different families. Now, from behavior genetic data, we have established that variation in shared rearing influences makes little difference for personality outcomes *within* sex. If a boy exposed to a more competitive, aggressive father is not, as a result, more competitive and aggressive than a boy exposed to a milquetoast father, how can rearing variations produce any *mean* sex difference at all?

Behavioral development is seamless; whatever the causes, they should influence both within- and between-group variation, as apportioned in the analysis of variance (Turkheimer, 1991). In this case, personality variation can be apportioned to two sources—within-gender and between-gender. But in terms of development, socialization science posits the *same developmental processes* in both cases: That is, the boy (girl) who has been exposed to more of a sex-biased treatment should be more sex-stereotypical in behavior than the boy (girl) who has been exposed to less of a sex-biased treatment. This is the familiar *within-gender hypothesis*. From the accumulation of many within-gender effects, the *average* sex difference would be expected to emerge (because boys, on the whole, receive more or less of the parental treatments than girls). But insofar as personality development is concerned, variation in family environments is not influential. Therefore, this developmental process with which we are concerned—that of differences in family environments—can explain neither individual differences nor the average sex difference. That is, the sum of many "null" effects is not a mean sex difference.

We could take a different tack, and say that treatments for males and females were exactly alike—denying for a moment any differential treatments we might observe. Perhaps similar treatments would be experienced differently by males and females. But is this not just another way of saying that males and females are different? Could not the different perceptions of "similar" experiences be attributed to biological differences inherent in males and females? Could not biologically based sex differences evoke observably different treatments?

Studies of Differential Treatments

Are the genders treated differently? Do these treatments influence them? Differential treatments of boys and girls are sometimes readily seen. Most parents buy dolls and kitchens for their daughters, but trucks and trains for their sons. Haircuts and dress styles are selected to be culturally sex-appropriate. And in at least some treatments, differences start early: Boys are more likely to be swaddled in blue, girls in pink. Ask the parents of a newborn what their son or daughter will be like, and they will more likely than not answer in gender-typed adjectives: A boy will be strong and hardy, whereas a girl will be pretty and sweet.

As in the previous chapters, the fundamental issue is not one of association, but rather one of causation. As we just mentioned, parents may treat children differently in response to different preferences already inside the children. Toy manufacturers, like all companies with products to sell, may want to tailor their products to potential consumers—in this case, to the different tastes of boys and girls. Parents may give gender-stereotypical responses about their infant's potential, not because those expectations causally shape the next generation, but because their knowledge of the current generation allows them to anticipate what the next one will become.

Although we tend to think that the sexes are treated differently, cultural beliefs about differential socialization may be misleading. For instance, a substantial sex difference has been found in the upper ranges of mathematical ability (Benbow, 1988). For many years, a research project at Johns Hopkins University has tested 12-year-old children in an effort to identify the mathematically gifted ones. Seventh- and eighth-graders take the SAT mathematics test normally reserved for high school students heading to college. Of the students in this project studied by Benbow, more boys than girls were mathematically gifted in their test performance: About 4 boys scored over 600 for every girl, and about 12 boys scored over 700 for every girl. Because all these precocious children did very well in mathematics, sex difference explanations based on environmental variation may fail. For instance, the girls took as many math courses as the boys; they had somewhat better grades; they were not math-anxious; they received no less parental encouragement of their talents than the boys; and in at least one such group, more girls than boys wanted to do college work in mathematics. So where was the treatment difference "causing" the sex difference?

More unexpectedly, such small average sex differences in socialization may hold in many populations for many dimensions of parenting. Lytton and Romney (1991) reviewed 172 different studies of the differential socialization of males and females. The studies varied in sample size, in the use of direct observations versus self-reports, in location (North America vs. other parts of the world), in scientific quality, and in year of publication. Lytton and Romney used these scorable qualities in their meta-analysis, a quantitative review of study outcomes. Their conclusion was that, for the most part, boys and girls are raised similarly—there was no great divide in the treatment of the two sexes.

To see the basis for their conclusion, consider the effects presented in Table 6.1. This table translates Lytton and Romney's (1991) differential treatment effects by major socialization areas (see their Table 4) into IQ-type units. Treatment of females has been set to a mean of 100 "treat-

TABLE 6.1. Gender "Treatment Quotients" by Major
Socialization Area for North American Studies

Area	Boys' mean	Girls' mean	No. of studies
Interaction	99.6	100	74
Encouragement of achievement	100.3	100	22
Warmth	99.0	100	63
Encouragement of dependency	98.5	100	16
Restrictiveness	101.2	100	40
Discipline	101.2	100	53
Encouragement of sex-typed activities	106.5	100°	20
Clarity/reasoning	99.3	100	13

Note. Conversion from standard scores to IQ-type metric assumes a female
mean of 100 and a standard deviation of 15. Data are from Lytton &
Romney (1991).
°Difference statistically significant.

ment points"; the mean of males is higher or lower, depending on
whether they received more or less of the same treatment than females.
Amazingly, in only one area (parental encouragement of sex-typed activities in play and household chores) was the treatment of the genders
differential at conventional levels of statistical significance: In the IQ-
type units, the males' mean in this area was 106.5 to the females' 100.
In most other treatment areas, the sexes' means were less than 1 "treatment quotient" point apart.

Lytton and Romney's (1991) statistical control variables left this conclusion unaltered. No tendency existed for studies published more
recently to produce smaller treatment differences. Results for unpublished studies were not unlike those for published ones. Studies from
outside North America added one possible gender difference: Males
received harsher physical punishment than females. By a head count of
studies, a trend existed for females to receive more encouragement of
dependency, and males more disciplinary strictness. But Lytton and
Romney's conclusions refute the widely accepted belief that treatment
differences between males and females are large or pervasive. A possible explanation is that people generalize from sex-typed play preferences (where sex differences are most visible and treatment differences

the largest) to other patterns of child rearing (where real treatment differences are often absent or quite weak).

Occasional case histories have been cited to show extraordinary treatment effects; however, these effects often fade in clarity when examined more closely. In social science, many college textbooks tell a story about MZ twin boys. At birth, one twin boy's penis was severely damaged during circumcision, and his doctors and parents made a decision to reconstruct his genitals surgically to female form. Hormonal therapy was then provided to feminize his body. "Her" parents then raised this genetic boy consistently with her assigned sex as a girl. Textbooks declare this "experiment" a resounding success in showing that sex of rearing determines sex-typed behaviors.

A follow-up report when the twins reached early adolescence, though, was not so sanguine (Diamond, 1982). At the time of the follow-up, the "girl" was in therapy for psychiatric problems that included sex role uncertainty. Her career ambition was to be a mechanic. She refused to draw a picture of a female, saying that it was easier to draw a man. Her masculine traits produced some unkind words from peers, who had nicknamed her "cave woman." Given the confusion and emotional distress she experienced, little support can be proffered for the idea that arbitrary sex role reassignment—even when aided with powerful steroid hormones—can change biologically based gender dispositions.

The Biological Basis of Sex Differences

Is a biological explanation of gender differences in behavior more compelling than an environmental one? Scientifically, experimental manipulation gives the strongest proof of causation. Can the relative gender typing of boys and girls be manipulated through biological means? The answer to this question, for us and other species, is "yes."

In many mammals, biological differentiation requires two phases. The first phase takes place during fetal development in humans, or shortly after birth in laboratory mice and rats. In these periods, the sex hormones biologically organize the brain into female or male patterns. During this organizational phase, brain tissue is actually differentiated in different ways in human males and females (Lacoste-Utamsing & Holloway, 1982; Swaab & Fliers, 1985). For example, the corpus callosum and the cell nuclei within the preoptic area of the brain grow to different sizes; the hypothalamus (brain tissue that controls the pituitary and the secretion of hormones) also develops a different inner organization in men and women. The second phase takes place at puberty. Brain organization has been completed, but increasing sex hormone levels now activate sexual dimorphism in physical development and can trigger sex-typed behaviors, especially in the sexual domain (Udry, 1988).

Animal Studies

In mammals such as rats, mice, and monkeys, no researcher has attempted to change sex role behavior through manipulation of rearing circumstances; the idea would be seen as ludicrous, because it is understood that in most mammals these behaviors possess a strongly biological basis. Biological manipulations, in contrast, have successfully altered physical and behavioral forms of sex-typed behaviors in nonhuman animals. In a classic series of experiments on rabbits, Jost removed male gonadal tissue from genetically male (XY) fetuses (see Jost, 1979, for a summary). Without the organizing influence of secreted male hormones, these rabbits developed into physically and behaviorally "female" rabbits. Thus, the basic developmental plan of both male (XY) and female (XX) mammals is female, unless genes on the Y chromosome cause gonadal tissue to form, followed by the secretion of male hormones. Jost found further that if genetically male (XY) rabbits that had been "feminized" as described above were exposed to externally administered female hormones at puberty, they displayed species-typical female social behaviors, including sexual interest in male partners and female-typical sexual positions.

The reverse experiment also worked. Jost found that if genetically female (XX) fetuses or newborns were exposed to male hormones at the proper time during fetal or early postfetal development, they were "masculinized." Furthermore, when exposed to externally administered male hormones at the time of puberty, these females displayed species-typical male behaviors, including fighting, sexual interest in females, and male-typical positions for sexual intercourse. Given the ability to manipulate the amount and duration of hormone injections during pregnancy, the kind of gender reversal produced can be finely tuned. Genetically female (XX) monkeys can be influenced to be aggressive in their play, but not to mount male playmates; or to mount monkeys about the same age, but not their mothers (Moir & Jessel, 1991).

Reviewing both the animal and human literature on hormone

effects, Ellis and Ashley (1987) concluded that hormone exposure during the second and third months of human pregnancy is responsible for the differentiation of sexual orientation, whereas other male- and female-typical behavior patterns may be differentiated later, from the fourth to sixth months. Neural differentiation is complex and has a long time course. Its duration may explain how hormones can produce gender reversals in some behavior patterns, but not in others: A hormonal effect is not "all or none," but rather allows for gradations and subtleties.

Human Studies

On rats, mice, and monkeys, those animals that bear the major experimental burden for the biological and behavioral sciences, hormone effects have been dramatic; however, caution is called for in generalizing from other animals to humans. In humans, of course, these classic animal experiments cannot be replicated without flagrantly violating our ethical codes. But nature, in the form of rare genetic disorders, and medicine, in the form of misapplied drugs, have provided experiment-like contexts for the evaluation of hormone effects in humans. On the whole, people display the same susceptibility to having sex-typed behaviors reorganized through hormones as do other animals; therefore, gender differences may have a pervasive biological basis in humans as well as in other animals (Ellis & Ashley, 1987; Moir & Jessel, 1991; Reinisch, Rosenblum, & Sanders, 1987).

Consider the one child-rearing area in which males and females are clearly treated differently: the encouragement of sex-typed behaviors. Do these treatments cause these gender differences? Or do the gender differences result from biologically based tastes and preferences of young boys and girls? The latter view can be tested if behavior is changed through hormonal manipulations, when genetic sex remains unchanged.

For this purpose, nature's manipulation is a rare genetic disorder, adrenal hyperplasia, which leads to the kidney's adrenal glands to secrete excessive testosterone. The syndrome prenatally masculinizes the developing brain of a female (XX) fetus, whereas the excessive testosterone does not clearly change the development of a male (XY) fetus. Newborn girls may also suffer some degree of abnormality in their genitals as a result of exposure, but its severity differs greatly among them. Usually these genital abnormalities can be surgically corrected shortly after birth, and prescribed drugs can block any further masculinization.

Berenbaum and Hines (1992) studied a series of girls affected with this disorder. Except for one girl raised for the first month as a boy, the girls (n = 25) had been diagnosed early (mostly in the neonatal period) and raised as girls. To learn about their "tastes," the researchers gave them choices in a short play session in which male-typed toys (a helicopter, two cars, a fire engine, blocks, and Lincoln Logs), female-typed toys (three dolls, kitchen supplies, a toy telephone, and crayons and paper), and gender-neutral toys (books, board games) were equally available. They scored the amount of time the girls played with each type of toy. The girls with adrenal hyperplasia were compared with a control group consisting of their sisters and female cousins.

As expected, affected girls played more with the male-typed toys and less with the female-typed toys; play with gender-neutral toys was about equal in the two "experimental" groups. Because play with one type of toy excludes play with another, I reproduce in Figure 6.1 only playing time with male-typed toys. As shown in Figure 6.1, the mean playing time for the affected (CAH) girls was about twice (about 6 minutes) that of the unaffected sisters and cousins (about 3 minutes). In terms of IQ-type units, the mean playing time would be 100 in the control group and about 113 in the affected group. In these units, this difference was greater than that between girls and boys for sex-typed socialization (as given earlier, 100 vs. 106.5). Neither the degree of abnormality in the genitals at birth, nor the age at diagnosis, influenced toy choice. Of course, these results do not prove that a unitary brain mechanism for toy preference exists (although it may), because the hormone exposures might have changed activity level, motor skills, or temperamental traits in gender-linked areas.

In another rare genetic disorder, a hormonal abnormality changed the genital area at birth, instead of influencing brain organization (Imperato-McGinley, Guerrero, Gautier, & Peterson, 1975; Imperato-McGinley, Peterson, Gautier, & Sturla, 1979). Born in rural villages in the Dominican Republic, the affected male (XY) babies lacked external testes, which were still undescended inside their bodies, and had clitoral-like penises hidden in labial-like folds. To uninformed observers, they looked like newborn girls; so convincing were the external genitalia that they were raised as such, although genetically they were male.

The cause of the disorder was later discovered to be an absence of one form of testosterone, which is responsible for the growth of male genitalia. A chemically different form of testosterone, though, still masculinized the affected boys' brains before birth. During puberty, more

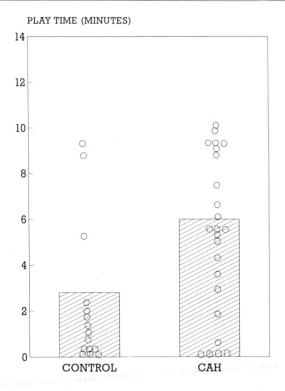

FIGURE 6.1. Play time with male-typed toys in control girls and hormone-exposed congenital androgenital syndrome (CAH) girls. Adapted from Berenbaum & Hines (1992). Copyright 1992 by the American Psychological Society. Adapted by permission.

hormone was secreted; each boy's body reacted by growing a penis and allowing the testes to descend. This sudden and shocking completion of reproductive development led to a local nickname for the disorder, translatable as "penis at 12 years."

What were the results of 12–14 years of raising boys with neuronally male brains as females? Although the scientific reports were less complete than social scientists would desire—the field work was done by medical doctors intent on solving the puzzle of the inherited metabolic errors—it was clear that once the affected boys reached puberty, almost all of them rapidly and easily shifted from female to male identities, adopting male clothing, marrying, and working as farmers, miners, or woodsmen in rural villages.[1] Although the affected men thus were successful "normal" males, their hormonal abnormality had some persistent physical effects (scanty or absent beard and a lack of balding).

A recessive gene was found to cause the "penis at 12 years" syndrome. Suppose it were common, rather than rare. Then we could raise all children as girls—and still have them turn out all right in adolescence, with boys adopting male gender roles. So much for the power of socialization. Therefore, let us look in the brain for the basis of sex differences. Unlike behavior, the brain's composition is invisible to outside inspection, and only a few studies have used dissection to compare male and female brains. One important finding—undoubtedly, one of many that will emerge as sex differences in the brain are further explored—is related to sexual orientation (LeVay, 1991).

LeVay looked within human brains for structural differentiation in areas sensitive to sex hormones in other animals. He tested particular cell groups called nuclei (clusters of nerve cell bodies) that were reported to be larger in men than in women, and that were located in the hypothalamus, a brain structure associated with male-typical sexual behavior in primates. His brain samples, acquired from routine autopsies, included the brains of 19 homosexual men, 16 heterosexual men, and 6 heterosexual women. One hypothalamic cell nucleus was larger in the heterosexual men than in either the women or the homosexual men; thus, this group of cells no larger than a pinprick was sexually dimorphic, and in males it could be used to distinguish sexual orientation.

The studies just described belong to a larger literature showing consistent hormonal influences on sex-typed behaviors in humans (Becker, Breedlove, & Crews, 1992; Moir & Jessel, 1991; Reinisch et al., 1987). No one study is as perfect in its experimental controls as are the studies of nonhuman primates, rats, and mice; together, however, they place the cause of behavioral sex differences in the biology of the brain. In the socialization studies summarized earlier in this chapter, differential treatments were far weaker than folklore commonly supposes, and where they were strong, the evidence of the directionality of the influence was itself the weakest. Perhaps the socialization effects have been underestimated by poor questionnaires, or by wrongly constructed observational measures. Nonetheless, the burden of proof now falls on environmentally oriented socialization scientists to show that treatments can causally induce sex differences.

The Evolutionary Perspective

Primarily, this book is about individual differences rather than about group differences. But the case of sex differences must be simultaneously viewed from both perspectives: Males and females are self-evident groups, but within each biologically defined sex, people differ in the degree of "masculinity" and "femininity" they show in the behaviors relevant to average sex differences. Thus, it is useful to ask about the origins of sex differences. For this purpose, the chapter now takes a brief foray into evolutionary theory—a picture on the broad canvas of evolutionary millennia, rather than the historical time of a few generations. As I indicate in Chapter 7, an evolutionary understanding is integral to answering fundamental questions about the transmission of behavioral variation from one generation to the next.

Sexual Selection Theory

Sexual selection theory is an evolutionary explanation for the origin of biologically based gender differences. According to Darwin, two struggles have shaped the evolution of a species: that of natural selection, as adaptations have evolved in response to forces in the natural environment and to the inevitable competition of other species, including predators; and that of sexual selection, as adaptations have evolved from within-species competition to find mates and to protect and succor the young. In this latter arena of selection in most species, the sexes have entered into the selective process with asymmetries of biological function that dispose them toward different evolutionary solutions.

Females can be severely limited in the number of offspring they can bear and care for, and they must carry the biological burdens of pregnancy and giving milk. In contrast, males produce vast numbers of sperm, and in many species they contribute far less than females do to the care and protection of the young. The strength of this asymmetry varies among mammalian species. In some species, almost no parental care is provided by the male parent. In such species, rates of male reproduction are limited mainly by the access to mating opportunities; it pays males (in the evolutionary currency of increased reproductive success) to seek as many such opportunities as possible. Although the male-versus-male competition need not always involve aggression (e.g., a male may find more mates by reaching them faster than by fighting more against other males), his genetic traits will persist by whichever means he succeeds in securing mates, whereas the genetic traits of other males will die out. The number of successful matings is thus, to borrow Richard Dawkins's (1987) metaphor of evolution, like a "sieve"—selecting some traits for survival and increase, and straining out others for extinction. In many species, females hurt their reproductive chances if they seek additional mates once they are fertilized successfully by one. This thesis is true even if males contribute little or nothing to rearing, because females' pursuit of mating opportunities may distract them from nurturing offspring. Thus competitive pressures that apply to males do not always apply to females, and vice versa.

One result of intramale competition for a greater number of mates, and of intrafemale competition for the best mate, is an evolution of sexually dimorphic traits. In species in which males and females have such different life histories, greater muscular strength and body size often (but not always) aid males in the competition for mating opportunities. A stronger, larger male will sire more offspring than a smaller, weaker one. For example, an antelope carrying a larger head of antlers wins more fights than do weakly armed opponents.

Physical and behavioral dimorphisms coevolve. That is, when weapons for sexual competition against other males grow larger, so must the willingness to use them—the desire to be aggressive and to maintain a dominant status, even at the risk of one's own death. Or, if the competition is a "scramble" search for mates rather than a physical fight, better location abilities and a desire to run in open areas (where the risk of predation is greater) must increase along with fleetness of foot. So strong sexual selection pressures appear in the skeleton, which shows the adaptive specializations for gaining mates in males, and the adaptive specializations for pregnancy and lactation in females; they also appear in the brain, which must guide the use of these specializations. This logical connection seems neglected in many theories of human gender differences that ignore physical differences but trumpet psychological ones.

The intensity of sexual selection varies among species. The crucial variable in determining this intensity is the degree of "parental investment"—the total time, energy, and effort devoted to caring for offspring. In species such as deer or elephant seals, a strong asymmetry in parental investment exists, because males invest virtually nothing in parenting the young. On the other hand, competition can be more relaxed in species in which males make heavy parental investments. If offspring cannot survive without a biparental investment in their care and protection, then no reproductive advantage accrues to a male to seek additional mates during a breeding season; rather, it pays to bond stably with a female partner in a sharing of parenting. Many bird species seem to approach this ideal (or at least come more closely to it than deer or elephant seals), because chicks cannot survive without the provision of food and shelter by both adults.

Humans probably lie somewhere in the middle of the range of sexual selection intensities. A human skeleton exhibits its past history of sexual selection. For instance, a randomly chosen man has about a 92% chance of being taller than a randomly chosen female—in statistical jargon, a large "effect size" (McGraw & Wong, 1992). Presumably, greater strength, size, and weight at one time helped men in intrasexual competition—either by helping them in direct combat with other men, or by improving some other outcome that led indirectly to superior competition. But the absolute physical height difference between men and women is only about 8%, far less than the enormous weight and size gaps separating males and females in some primates that have been under stronger sexual selection pressure. Among baboons, for example, adult males weigh twice what females do. An evolutionary interpretation is that human males, who must offer some investment in offspring, are constrained in the time and energy they can devote to mating competition. Gender dimorphisms have evolved in humans, but not as ruthlessly as they might have if males had not been selected to nurture.

Although socialization science can offer environmental explanations of behavioral dimorphisms, it is strangely silent concerning these gender differences in height, weight, strength, and other visible traits. For most students of animal behavior, the presence of such purely physical differences is a reliable guide to the existence of related behavioral differences. As the husband-and-wife team of Martin Daly and Margo Wilson (1988) has noted, "Armed with the theory of sexual selection . . . and with no more knowledge of *Homo sapiens* than that provided by a few skeletons, a biologist from outer space would guess right about every aspect of male–female relations" (p. 155).

Examples of Gender-Dimorphic Traits

Behavioral sex differences fit well into the expectations of evolutionary biology. Daly and Wilson (1988) have identified one powerful example: murder. Murder is the ultimate solution to intrasexual competition—removing one's competition entirely by taking another person's life. But it is costly, because of the risk of retribution either by the victim's relatives or by the state. It is also costly because in direct confrontations, who is the victim and who is the victor may partly depend on chance. But the psychological disposition to murder can persist evolutionarily if males who murder, or threaten murder, obtain more mates than those who do not. Note the emphasis on male intrasexual competition. If one female were to kill another, her victory would do little to enhance her reproductive chances; even if she were to gain the affection of her victim's mate, the availability of two males would not raise her birth rate (which is physically limited) nearly as much as one male's marriage to two females would raise his reproductive rate.

According to this argument, adult males should kill one another with some frequency, but the murder of one adult female by another should be extremely rare. From a variety of the world's societies, Daly and Wilson (1988) examined differences in murder rates of (1) adult males killing other adult males and (2) adult females killing other adult females. Because murder statistics were not collected with this exact comparison in mind, the numbers of female perpetrator–female victim murders were biased against the main hypothesis, as women killing female children were sometimes counted. Nonetheless, as shown in Table 6.2, nearly all same-sex murders involved one man killing another. Among the LaLuyia of Kenya, 95% of same-sex murders were male against male; among Chicagoans, 96%; among the Munda of India, 100%; and so on.

Other strong gender dimorphisms appear in the area of sexual behavior, dating, and marriage. To pick an illustrative example, Kenrick and Keefe (1992) investigated preferences for the age of a potential spouse. According to a sociobiological perspective, men should prefer younger mates (who are still capable of reproduction), whereas females should prefer older mates (who are in a stronger position to provide for them economically). Although these general expectations do not translate into precise age range predictions, they suggest that a male preference for younger mates should exist unless a man is himself young. In the latter case, a slightly older spouse should have about the same reproductive potential as one slightly younger. In contrast, women gain little reproductively from preferring younger mates.

Kenrick and Keefe (1992) used one unalloyed source to compare mate preferences: advertisements in urban "singles" newspapers. Because such ads are not placed to advance science, they permit a "naturalistic observation" of mating preferences, and Figures 6.2 and 6.3 show the oldest and youngest ages of preferred partners plotted against the advertisers' own ages. For instance, in Figure 6.2, a 40-year-old "single white male" advertising for a 30-year-old "single white female" would be plot-

TABLE 6.2. Same-Sex Homicides in Various Societies

Location	Proportion of total killings where males killed males
Canada	94%
Miami	96%
Chicago	96%
Detroit	96%
Tzeltal Mayans (Mexico)	100%
Belo Horizonte (Brazil)	97%
New South Wales (Australia)	94%
Oxford (England, 1296–1398)	99%
Iceland	100%
Munda (India)	100%
!Kung San (Botswana)	100%
Tiv (Nigeria)	97%
BaSoga (Uganda)	98%
LaLuyia (Kenya)	95%

Note. Adapted from Daly & Wilson (1988). Copyright 1988 by Aldine de Gruyter. Adapted by permission. (For additional examples, see original table.)

ted midway between the two lines—as 40 years on the x axis and –10 years on the y axis. That is, she is 10 years younger than he.

The plots conform closely to sociobiological expectations. Men in their 20s advertised for mates from 5 years younger to 5 years older than themselves; they did not prefer only younger women. As men aged, their preferences became increasingly discrepant from their own ages, with men in their 30s preferring 25-year-old partners, men in their 40s preferring 33-year-old partners, and men in their 50s preferring 40-year-old partners. Marriages embody these preferences in the United States and elsewhere, as men of a given age typically marry women younger than themselves in years about midway between the preference curves shown in Figure 6.2. Women's preferences remained relatively constant over the lifespan (see Figure 6.3): They preferred men from a few years younger than themselves to about 10 years older. The idea that women are constrained by their economic limitations to prefer older men was unsupported, because even well-to-do women placed singles advertisements for older men. Fantasy and mundane prospects are blended in unknown proportions in singles advertisements. Yet they capture a certain reality about marriage markets: A worldwide marriage pattern *is* one of older men marrying younger women, and in many societies in which polygyny is legal, one older man may marry *several* younger women.

Not all sexual dimorphisms are as overt as murder or spousal age (Buss, 1989). In social meetings, for instance, males may interpret females' friendliness as promiscuous and seductive, but women do not make similar attributions about men (Abbey, 1982). Differently disposed, men and women have vast differences in rates of some behaviors; they also must suffer from the frequent sexual miscommunications of everyday life.

Gender Dimorphisms and Individual Differences

The consideration of sociobiology has added to this book's main theme of individual variability. As shown in the last several examples, the great-

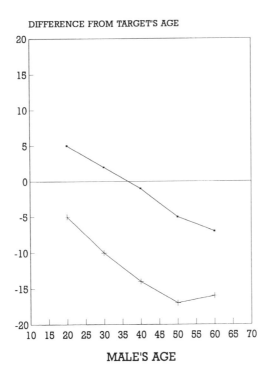

FIGURE 6.2. Males' preference for partners' age in singles advertisements. Upper curve, oldest age preferred; lower curve, youngest age preferred. Adapted from Kendrick & Keefe (1992). Copyright 1992 by Cambridge University Press. Adapted by permission.

DIFFERENCE FROM TARGET'S AGE

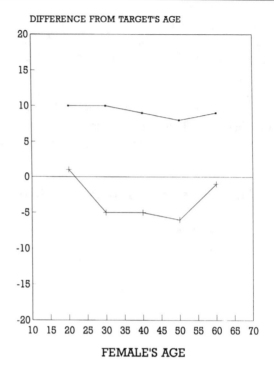

FEMALE'S AGE

FIGURE 6.3. Females' preference for partners' age in singles advertisements. Upper curve, oldest age preferred; lower curve, youngest age preferred. Adapted from Kendrick & Keefe (1992). Copyright 1992 by Cambridge University Press. Adapted by permission.

est insights are produced whenever gender differences are most magnified. The gender gap can be so great as to suggest qualitative rather than quantitative differences between the sexes, as in the case of murder. And to some extent, the two sexes can be viewed as qualitatively different biological adaptations: A genetic "switch" (in humans, the sex-determining X or Y chromosome) puts a fetus onto one of these two developmental pathways.

On the other hand, personality trait distributions may overlap in men and women. A well-known law of normally distributed traits is that moderate mean differences may translate into huge differences at the extremes. Suppose that just the top 16% of males are overtly violent. If one standard deviation separated the male and female dispositional means, only 2.3% of females would score as high as these males (i.e., just 1 female for every 7 males). If only the top 2.3% of males are overtly violent, then just 0.13% of females would score as high (i.e., 1 female for every 18 males). Thus, in populations of limited size, few females may possess enough "aggressiveness" disposition to commit overtly violent acts. For sex differences in other traits, the size of the male–female mean difference may be a smaller one (e.g., spatial rotation, ideational fluency; Kimura, 1992), but this principle will still apply: Gender differences will grow greater at trait extremes.

Thus, rather than viewing sex differences as "all or none," we may conclude that biology may just shift the distributional means for men and women. Consider one kinship group especially suited for evaluating sex differences: brother–sister sibling pairs.

Opposite-sex siblings can show whether the *same* genes influence variation in male and female phenotypes. That is, the sibling correlation indicates the degree to which different or identical genetic loci affect trait expression in both sexes. When different genes produce similar phenotypes in males and females, they will obey Mendel's genetic law of independent assortment. This law is that traits of different genetic determination must be unassociated within individuals or across family members. Interracial marriages provide a visual proof of this law: For instance, in a child of a Caucasian man and a Japanese woman, light brown hair may be delightfully combined with dark Asian eyes. Because different physical features are determined by different genetic loci, any combination of them can occur in an interracial child. Given a heritability of .70 for some trait, but different sets of genetic influences in males and females, then brothers may correlate .35; sisters may also correlate .35; but a brother and sister may not correlate at all ($r = 0$). However, if the genes are the *same* in males and females, then the mixed-sex pairs should correlate .35 as well.

A pattern of separate genetic influences is not what is usually seen, though. Sibling correlations, rather than being lower in mixed-sex siblings, are usually about equal to those in same-sex pairs. Eaves, Eysenck, and Martin (1989) have tested broad personality traits for "sex limitation." Their study included the "Big Three" traits of psychoticism, neuroticism, and extraversion, and also a "lie scale" trait dimension. Using English data from same-sex and mixed-sex twin pairs, they conclude:

> The data provide no evidence that the four aspects of personality [including the lie scale] are better explained by a model in which different genes and environmental effects contribute to variation in males and females. The

values of r_{AMF} [the genetic correlation across the genders] are instructive. They all exceed 0.70, confirming a high degree of commonality between genetic effects on the two sexes. (p. 99)

Their larger Swedish and Australian samples necessitated one qualification to this conclusion. For neuroticism, the genetic correlation across genders was significantly less than unity (r_g = .58). In criminality, in which sex differences are especially large, some genes may also be sex-specific (shared-genetic-causes r = .61; Cloninger, Christiansen, Reich, & Gottesman, 1978).[2] Nonetheless, even with these exceptions, most loci affecting trait variation appear to be the same in males and females.

If, in general, many identical genes influence traits in males and females, their expression may remain unequal because average phenotypes do differ in mixed-sex siblings. Thus I would argue that the same set of genes receive a somewhat different level of expression in men and women. Consider as a concrete example that steroid hormones, when injected externally, build up women's muscle tissue less then men's. As a chemical messenger, steroid hormones activate DNA synthesis, but this chemical message is not as well received in a female's muscle cells as in a male's. In these same genetic pathways, allelic variation may also contribute to individual differences in strength. Genes that act earlier in development may be especially important, because it is at this time that the sensitivity of the nervous system to later, sex-specific environmental and biological influences is set. Thus, different biological influences can explain mean and individual differences in a unitary system: The former may arise from sex-linked, hormonal modulation of gene expression, and the latter from allelic variation in these same biological pathways.

Biological Sex Differences and Cultural Transmission

The view proposed here is that sex differences should be little influenced by variations in family environments. But I certainly believe that cultural systems and biological sex differences interact. Moir and Jessel (1991), in discussing this interaction, choose to focus on how biological sex differences may limit the malleability of behavioral sex differences. Consider that men and women may differ in the drive to succeed in toughly competitive, hierarchical professions. Some women, in fact, may prefer to stay at home with their children rather than to scale a career ladder. Some feminists decry these women's lack of drive and initiative; die-hard environmentalists attribute it entirely to limitations imposed by social constructions. But from a biological view, the choice of family versus career may reflect inherent biological sex differences that are stronger in some women and weaker (if not absent) in others. Those women who have a strong desire to succeed in careers may not understand or sympathize with women who lack this desire (and vice versa). Women who do not want to compete, though, do not see themselves as handicapped by their choice. Consider that people who do not want to be athletes cannot be said to be handicapped by their own indifference to winning (Moir & Jessel, 1991).

But the existence of different distributional curves can be viewed from a slightly different angle. The women who want to compete *are* handicapped by societies that do not permit them to be educated, or to enter worlds of business and commerce. Not long ago in Saudi Arabia, women spontaneously revolted against patriarchal authority by driving their husbands' cars. Because women were not permitted to drive in Saudi society, what women in the industrialized countries of the West may take for granted was for them real defiance. The response of Saudi authorities was unfriendly to the women's revolt: A restriction of women's driving was reaffirmed. Any woman near the masculine tail of the "masculinity" distribution will find her biological proclivities thwarted in a society that so restricts her social roles.

Societies have dealt with the unequal distributions of male and female "preferences" in different ways. Some have treated sex differences categorically—ignoring any distributional overlap of men and women, and restricting sharply the social alternatives available to both sexes. In other societies, legal restrictions on men and women have been fewer; women with the relevant inclinations have had the possibility of exploring predominantly male roles, and vice versa. Ironically, biological determination may be greater under the latter arrangement than under the former. When men and women are allowed to explore social roles over a wide social range, they may pick ones better suited to their *individual* biological dispositions; that is, only when there is freedom of choice can men and women make choices truly diagnostic of their biological proclivities. If people can find greater happiness in "niche picking" (Scarr & McCartney, 1983)—a position that is intuitively plausible, but for which empirical support is lacking—then permitting "biological determinism" to flourish may be evaluated more positively than social engineering programs of either the radical left or the radical right.

Notes

[1]One of 18 affected XY males raised as girls failed to shift to a male gender identity. She was reported to live alone and to work as a domestic. She was not sexually involved with other men at the time of the latest report, but she had "married" a man who had left her after 1 year (Imperato-McGinley et al., 1979).

[2]A sex difference in the expression of traits may support a threshold model. For criminality and antisocial personality, women may need a greater number of genetic factors contributing to risk than men before they express criminality or antisocial personality traits outwardly. Thus, the biological relatives of such affected women (high dose) would be at greater risk of developing criminality or antisocial personality traits than those of affected men (moderate dose). The data presented by Cloninger et al. (1978) were generally consistent with this threshold idea.

References

Abbey, A. (1982). Sex differences in attributions for friendly behavior: Do males misperceive females' friendliness? *Journal of Personality and Social Psychology, 42,* 830–838.

Becker, J. B., Breedlove, S. M., & Crews, D. (1992). *Behavioral endocrinology.* Cambridge, MA: MIT Press/Bradford Books.

Benbow, C. P. (1988). Sex differences in mathematical reasoning ability in intellectually talented preadolescents: Their nature, effects, and possible causes. *Behavioral and Brain Sciences, 11,* 169–232.

Berenbaum, S. A., & Hines, M. (1992). Early androgens are related to childhood sex-typed toy preferences. *Psychological Science, 3,* 203–206.

Buss, D. M. (1989). Sex differences in human mate preferences: Evolutionary hypotheses tested in 37 cultures. *Behavioral and Brain Sciences, 12,* 1–49.

Churchman, D. (1984, January 15). Mother's attempts come to naught in the end. *Norman* (Oklahoma) *Transcript,* p. 9A.

Cloninger, C. R., Christiansen, K. O., Reich, T., & Gottesman, I. I. (1978). Implications of sex differences in the prevalences of antisocial personality, alcoholism, and criminality for familial transmission. *Archives of General Psychiatry, 35,* 941–951.

Daly, M., & Wilson, M. (1988). *Homicide.* New York: Aldine de Gruyter.

Dawkins, R. (1987). *The blind watchmaker: Why the evidence of evolution reveals a universe without design*. New York: Norton.

Diamond, M. (1982). Sexual identity: Monozygotic twins reared in discordant sex roles and a BBC followup. *Archives of Sexual Behavior, 11*, 181–186.

Eaves, L. J., Eysenck, H. J., & Martin, N. G. (1989). *Genes, culture and personality: An empirical approach*. London: Academic Press.

Ellis, L., & Ashley, A. M. (1987). Neurohormonal functioning and sexual orientation: A theory of homosexuality–heterosexuality. *Psychological Bulletin, 101*, 233–250.

Imperato-McGinley, J., Guerrero, L., Gautier, T., & Peterson, R. E. (1974). Steroid 5 alpha-reductase deficiency in man: An inherited form of male pseudohermaphrodism. *Science, 186*, 1213–1215.

Imperato-McGinley, J., Peterson, R. E., Gautier, T., & Sturla, E. (1979). Androgens and the evolution of male gender identity among male pseudohermaphrodites with 5 alpha-reductase deficiency. *New England Journal of Medicine, 300*(22), 1233–1237.

Jost, A. (1979). Basic sexual trends in the development of vertebrates. In *Sex, hormones, and behavior* (Ciba Foundation Symposium No. 62, pp. 5–18). Amsterdam: Excerpta Medica.

Kenrick, D. T., & Keefe, R. C. (1992). Age preferences in mates reflect sex differences in human reproductive strategies. *Behavioral and Brain Sciences, 15*, 75–133.

Kimura, D. (1992). Sex differences in the brain. *Scientific American*, 119–125.

Lacoste-Utamsing, C. de, & Holloway, R. L. (1982). Sexual dimorphism in the human corpus callosum. *Science, 216*, 1431–1432.

LeVay, S. (1991). A difference in hypothalamic structure between heterosexual and homosexual men. *Science, 253*, 1034–1037.

Lytton, H., & Romney, D. M. (1991). Parents' differential socialization of boys and girls: A meta-analysis. *Psychological Bulletin, 109*, 267–296.

McGraw, K. O., & Wong, S. P. (1992). A common language effect size statistic. *Psychological Bulletin, 111*, 361–365.

Mitchell, J. E., Baker, L. A., & Jacklin, C. N. (1989). Masculinity and femininity in twin children: Genetic and environmental factors. *Child Development, 60*, 1475–1485.

Moir, A., & Jessel, D. (1991). *Brain sex: The real difference between men and women*. New York: Carol.

Rowe, D. C. (1982). Sources of variability in sex-linked personality attributes: A twin study. *Developmental Psychology, 18*, 431–434.

Reinisch, J. M., Rosenblum, L. A., & Sanders, S. A. (1987). *Masculinity/femininity*. Oxford: Oxford University Press.

Scarr, S., & McCartney, K. (1983). How people make their own environments: A theory of genotype → environment effects. *Child Development, 54*, 424–435.

Spence, J. T., & Helmreich, R. L. (1978). *Masculinity and femininity: Correlates and antecedents*. Austin: University of Texas Press.

Swaab, D. F., & Fliers, E. (1985). A sexually dimorphic nucleus in the human brain. *Science, 228*, 1112–1115.

Turkheimer, E. (1991). Individual and group differences in adoption studies of IQ. *Psychological Bulletin, 110*, 392–405.

Udry, J. (1988). Biological predispositions and social control in adolescent sexual behavior. *American Sociological Review, 53*, 709–722.

Wilson, J. Q., & Herrnstein, R. J. (1985). *Crime and human nature*. New York: Simon and Schuster.

CHAPTER 7

WHY FAMILIES HAVE
LITTLE INFLUENCE

mo spat out the sand clinging to her sweet potato, put it into the sea, and rubbed it vigorously with her free hand. She ate the cleaned potato, enjoying its salty taste. Nearby, Nimby watched—and thrust her potato into the sea. She didn't get all the sand off, but it still tasted better than ever before. The two young playmates' example taught others; soon their age-mates, both male and female, had caught on to the potato-washing routine. Imo's mother also learned, and soon was teaching potato washing to Imo's younger siblings. Imo's father, though he enjoyed a reputation for toughness and leadership, was too stubborn to try the new trick.

The potato-washing clan members were not humans, of course. They were rhesus monkeys inhabiting the unpopulated Japanese island of Koshima, where curious researchers had provisioned the band with fresh sweet potatoes by leaving them on a beach. Although my rendition has taken some literary license, it holds true to the basic events (Kummer, 1971). Imo was the name assigned to the brilliant monkey who first came up with the idea of washing the potatoes, and later discovered that sand and grain could be separated by throwing them onto water. Her potato-washing innovation was copied first by other juvenile males and females, and then by older females (about 18% initially), who passed it on to their offspring. Adult males failed to pick it up, partly because they had less contact with feeding juveniles, but perhaps also because they resisted novelty in general. After a few years, potato washing was an established tradition among the Koshima monkeys, and the episode had moved into the lore of the social sciences.

But one lesson of the Koshima monkeys has been all but ignored in socialization science: Cultural transmission occurs *outside* the family

193

and *inside* the family with equal facility. Indeed, the direction of influence is "wrong" for these monkeys. The innovation was originated by a preadolescent female, who taught other juveniles, who then taught their mothers, who then raised their offspring in this new tradition. In the Koshima case history, parent-to-child transmission did occur; however, it was only one of several transmission pathways, and (at least initially) far from the most important.

This chapter discusses the following question: "Why does variation in family environments have so little influence on children's personality development?" To answer this question, the chapter works backward from this conclusion to the conditions that must be responsible for it— and moves a large intellectual distance, from individuals to the sweep of evolutionary and cultural history. The chapter takes several tacks. First, it suggests that human learning mechanisms are general with respect to informational source, and that a disposition to tie learning exclusively to a family source is unlikely to have evolved in humans; second, it explores methods of describing the cultural transmission of traits; third, it considers some of the forces maintaining genetic variability; and fourth, it considers the dual role of culture and genetics in the maintenance of human traits. The last topic leads necessarily to a high level of abstraction—probably one too high to be immediately applicable to solving such social problems as street crime, school dropouts, or poverty. But this level of abstraction is needed as an intellectual inspiration for middle-level developmental theories that may supply the practical and theoretical means to solve pressing social problems.

The Generality of Learning

A Thought Experiment

In physics, central insights sometimes come from "thought experiments." With all due respect to Albert Einstein, who practiced thought experiments more brilliantly than anyone else, let us carry family effects to a logical extreme. In our thought experiment, what is learned in a family context is weighted more heavily by the learner than what is learned from any other person. Concepts acquired by direct parental teaching, behaviors modeled by imitating parents, and emotional states induced by family life stay with children throughout their adult lives. Such effects are so robust that children never change the ideas, habits, or feeling states acquired during early socialization. A situation like that depicted in George Bernard Shaw's *Pygmalion* is impossible: A young woman cannot give up her Cockney accent, her poor table manners, or her habits of thought, because what her working-class parents have taught her is fixed in her forever. Our thought experiment assumes that a tendency to learn from parents is a "hard-wired" instinct—in other words, that a "learn from parents only" gene has gone to fixation (i.e., 100%) in the human population, whereas its defeated "rival," the "learn from any source" gene, has gone extinct.[1]

Our primate ancestors probably did not possess a hard-wired disposition to learn just from their parents. My evidence, though indirect, is persuasive: No current monkey or ape species seems to be so tightly restricted in its learning capacities. Thus, for humans to possess such a powerful and inflexible disposition, the rare "learn from parents only" gene must have arisen by mutation in our evolutionary line, and then spread through the human population because it increased the inclusive fitness of its bearers. (The term "inclusive fitness" refers to whether the gene's bearers and their immediate relatives leave more offspring than others. Immediate relatives count [hence: "inclusive"], because they are more likely than unrelated persons to carry the same gene as a known bearer.)

Some features of parent–child transmission are certainly attractive. Family traditions are well preserved. And if parents make some innovation in a cultural tradition, then their children quickly and reliably reproduce it. If it is reproductively beneficial, the innovation may slowly spread through the population much as a gene would, because its bearers should enjoy larger family sizes than others, contributing more members to future populations.

A problem with a "learn from parents only" gene, though, is that its bearers will ignore innovations introduced by anyone other than their own parents. Thus if children learn from their parents to make arrows *without* dipping the heads in poison, they will continue to do so, even after others in the population discover poisoned arrowheads and teach this technique to their own children. In contrast, the bearer of the "learn from any source" gene will try the innovation and rapidly adopt it. Those individuals who carry the rare mutation for "learn from parents only" will fail to take advantage of many successful innovations. Furthermore, their innovations will stay in lines of parent–child descent, with children in each line able to adopt only the few innovations their own parents have managed to make. They will also miss innovations made by uniting ideas from several unrelated adults. In general, their cultural learning will have properties of genetic change: It will be slow, depending on how many children innovative parents leave behind.

If a "learn from any source" gene is to thrive in human evolution, our thought experiment must assume some ability on the part of people to select those innovations that contribute most to reproductive success; otherwise, sticking with a family tradition may be better than trying an innovation of dubious value. Certainly, evaluating some innovations does not require great genius. A blow gun dart that flies straight is immediately better than one that doesn't. Small and large improvements in game-stalking practices, farming practices, and other areas important to survival and reproduction can be recognized for what they are—improvements. I do not claim that people consciously know the value of all cultural practices—(e.g., the benefits of cod liver oil for obtaining Vitamin D were probably not consciously understood by Eskimos); nevertheless, the value of many innovations is recognizable.

Benefits were probably seen even before people became as knowledgeable as they are today. In the "great leap forward" period, 40,000 years ago in western Europe, an explosive wave of cultural innovation occurred: Cro-Magnon people discovered art, musical instruments, tools with different and specific functions (e.g., needles, awls, spear points set in shafts, mortars, fishhooks, and rope), and trade, all in one historical moment (Diamond, 1992). I believe that the value of many of these cultural innovations must have been immediately perceived. Indeed, if rhesus monkeys, who are intellectually no match for our evolutionary ancestors, acquire a simple but useful innovation such as potato washing, it is no great leap to infer that the bearers of a gene for "learn only from parents" should be outreproduced by the bearers of one for "learn from any source," whenever the latter have any sense at all about which innovations are best kept and which are best dropped.

Models of Cultural Transmission

Formal models can give some indication that *cultural* transmission from parent to child alone is unlikely. Carey (1991) tried to create a mathematical model of parent–child cultural transmission that would be similar to standard behavior genetic models, in which parental phenotypes directly affect children's environments. In his model, maternal and paternal cultural inheritance would be blended; that is, a child's environment would lie midway between the mother's and father's traits. For instance, a child exposed to a painfully shy father and a moderately shy mother would be regarded as having an environment midway between the parents' shyness levels. But Carey's cultural model produced some anomalous results. When parent-to-child cultural transmission was the only kind allowed, the regression coefficient linking parental traits to children's environments had to be exactly .50 for meaningful results to be obtained; no other values would do. Such an odd and unexpected restriction implies a logical flaw in his model. As Carey observed, this flaw may have been the failure to recognize multiple avenues of cultural transmission:

> It is indisputable from observation of human behavior that members of *Homo sapiens* are not constrained to imitate the behavior of only mother and father. Other conspecifics are also imitated. Perhaps a generalized mechanism for imitation evolved instead of a specific one for imitating one's parents. (1991, p. 442)

Figure 7.1 presents quick schematic diagrams illustrating various models of cultural transmission (Cavalli-Sforza & Feldman, 1981). In the top diagram (A), "vertical" transmission from parent to child is presented; here, cultural inheritance mimics genetic inheritance, and vice versa. The next diagram (B) shows "horizontal" transmission among age-mates. Childhood games like hopscotch pass along purely in this way, from one generation of children to another, without intervening assistance from adults. The third diagram (C) illustrates one form of "oblique" transmission, in which an unrelated person in the adult generation is a source of knowledge for a child. Rock stars and movie idols are clearly oblique transmitters to the next (not much younger) generation. The fourth diagram (D) represents oblique teaching influence, in which a single teacher transmits cultural knowledge to many individuals. This pattern applies formally to the media of television, radio, books, and newspapers, as well as to the typical educational model employed in most schools. Finally, the fifth diagram (E) illustrates a reversal in the vertical flow of culture— from child back to mother, father, and an unrelated adult. As in the case of the Koshima monkeys, the young may be the innovators and the old may be the imitators.

Sex role learning provides a direct illustration of the potential of multiple models to influence behavior. Of course, for most such behaviors, human instincts also guide children into the right channels. But what if a behavior appears that is so novel that children are unsure whether

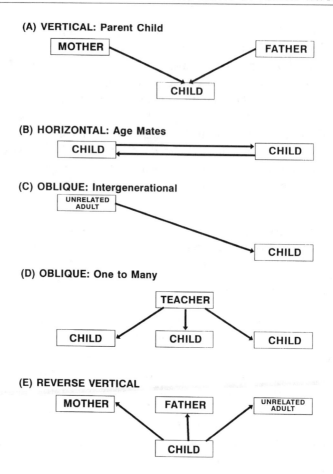

FIGURE 7.1. Trait transmission models.

it is male- or female-typed? How will they know what to do? As Chapter 6 has shown, some theories of sex role development emphasize socialization influences in the family, but children's acquisition of sex-appropriate behavior is robust. When parents avoid stereotypic behavior in their daily lives, children often display sex-typed behaviors anyway.

A fair rule—one unlikely to lead youngsters badly astray in most circumstances—is to imitate what *most* same-sex individuals do. This majority rule implies attention to what is typical for one's sex, and inattention to the potentially misleading influence of a few odd, sex-reversed parents or teachers, whose guidance may well lead away from cultural norms and away from average biological proclivities.

David Perry and Kay Bussey (1979), working in the tradition of the famous social learning theorist Alfred Bandura, created a choice experiment to test the influence of multiple models. They employed eight adult assistants—four females and four males—to make arbitrary choices between pairs of small items that were not obviously sex-typed. The adult might face a choice between an apple and a banana (as far as I know, fruits remain psychologically sex-neutral, although adult imaginations and botanical theories may not be so restrained). But for the young children in the control condition at least, no preference was shown for one choice over the other. The other experimental conditions were designed to create preferences. In one, the same-sex majority ruled (the four men made one choice, whereas the four women made the other), giving the children a clear direction as to a sex-typed social standard. In another condition, the adults were divided: Six adults made a sex-typed choice, but two, one male and one female, broke ranks with their sex and chose oppositely.

Adult examples were earnestly copied when they were consistent with the children's own sex. Table 7.1 shows the number of male-typed choices made by the children (out of 16 opportunities). When same-sex majorities ruled, the young boys made an average of 14 male-typed choices; the young girls made just 3 (i.e., they made 13 female-typed choices). As within-sex consensus began to break down (in the condition where three same-sex adults made the "right" choice and one the "wrong" choice), less imitation was shown (boys 12, girls 6). Finally, in the control condition, in which the children lacked any models, the preferences were about evenly split: The boys made the male-typed choice 9 of 16 times, the girls 8 of 16 times (a nonsignificant difference). Ironi-

TABLE 7.1. Children's Following of the Majority Rule in Making Choices

Child	Consistent same-sex adult models	Inconsistent adult models	No adult models
Boy	14	12	9
Girl	3	6	8

Note. Average number of male-typed choices out of 16 choice opportunities. Adapted from Perry & Bussey (1979). Copyright 1979 by the American Psychological Association. Adapted by permission.

cally, Perry and Bussey included in their article's title that "imitation is alive and well" in the origin of sex differences. And so it is. But without much fanfare, the two social learning theorists placed parent-centered conceptions of sex role learning in an early grave, as they recognized: "We would expect that children who initially adopt responses by . . . imitating a same-sex parent would ultimately drop the responses . . . if they eventually realize that no other same-sex individuals perform the responses but that many opposite-sex persons do" (1979, p. 1709).

From the current perspective, as children have more potential adult or child models, the weight on parental example becomes progressively diminished. Parents may seem pretty important to a 3-year-old child, who has seen few other adults or children. But to a 16-year-old, the weight on the parental example should be no more than $1/n$, where n is the total number of adult or child models relevant to a particular trait. Like any other source of information, parents make a contribution—though one of no greater *a priori* strength than any other (except that the parent–child emotional bond may pull a child's attention initially), and on many occasions one of even less strength, because acceptance will be biased by "majority rules" and by the functional value of particular knowledge and behaviors. As many newly arrived immigrants have discovered, children may learn the folkways of a new country better than those of an old: For finding mates and employment, the folkways of the new country will work, whereas those of the old country will often fail miserably.

The Transmission of Emotions?

Thus far, the examples of cultural transmission have dealt with the transmission of knowledge or the imitation of specific behaviors. Yet theories of family influence may focus more on the emotional aftereffects of familial socialization—on scars believed to have been inflicted by parents' emotional neglect or cruelty, whether conscious or unwitting. "Ah," say the proponents of familial influences, "you can't deny the powerful legacy of a family's love or denial."

If only the world would follow our emotional intuitions! One problem—perhaps not self-evident to northern Europeans, for whom nuclear families are typical ones—is that worldwide family patterns are as varied as pre-European-contact societies. In much of Africa, as described by anthropologist Patricia Draper (1989), the family "unit" consists of a mother and female relatives. Men play a less direct emotional role in the lives of their children than fathers do in the lives of northern European children. Indeed, biological fathers and mothers are often both physically absent, as children are cared for by kin (primarily older women who are no longer in their reproductive years). Nor are attachments to female relatives simple: As a child is shuttled from the mother to the other female kin and back, multiple attachments and sources of emotional bonding form. Furthermore, even when children are living with their biological mothers, older siblings often adopt the role of child minders. Polygyny, a common form of marriage in Africa, places a father at some psychological and structural distance from a mother and her children; he often sleeps in a separate hut, either alone or with his adolescent sons. A notion of a dense family crucible in a child's emotional life—with a child's attachments confined to a biological mother and father—is no more true, in general, of humans than the idea that the Neanderthals got their news on television.

I may have drawn contrasts between the northern European pattern and the African pattern too sharply. Although the nuclear family is held up as an "ideal" of family organization, more diverse forms are usually the reality in Western industrialized societies. Given recent high divorce rates, children often possess nonbiological relatives from new marriages—stepsiblings and stepparents. And northern European children possess uncles and aunts and grandparents, a larger family circle in which emotional attachments can form. Finally, even when no biological relatives are available, the many ways in which children can cope with unloving parents should not be underestimated. To argue a moment from anecdote, an acquaintance of mine had emotionally cold and distant parents, but found succor in the nearby Italian family of a friend. As a child, he became so close to the members of this other family that they habitually set a place for him at the table. And now, as an adult, his visits home mean visits both to his biological parents and to his "adoptive" ones.

But emphasizing the emotional complexity of "families" skirts the issue of "Why does variation in families have so little influence on emotional development?" An evolutionary reason is that genes that did not permit recovery from early emotional trauma—whether inflicted by parents or by others—would have been excluded from the population by the sieve of natural selection, whereas genes that permitted recovery from early emotional trauma would have been favored. No organism can afford to be as brittle as an egg, cracked and unrepairable after life's first hardship. As said in the vernacular, "Life's a bitch, and then we die"; trauma, pain, and difficult trials can be avoided only by the extremely lucky, or by those who die very young. In reviewing her behavior genetic studies, Sandra Scarr (1992) has expressed this evolutionary perspective:

> Fortunately, evolution has not left development of the human species, nor any other, at the easy mercy of variations in their environments. We are robust and able to adapt to wide-ranging circumstances—a lesson that seems lost on some ethnocentric developmentalists. If we were so vulnerable as to be led off the normal developmental track by slight variations in our parenting, we should not long have survived. (pp. 15–16)

The converse message of this statement, though, is less encouraging. For when children seem to be following less desirable developmental paths (e.g., children who pick on classmates aggressively or who are extremely anxious), the traits may be heritable developmental outcomes that stubbornly resist familial actions attempting to change them. As Scarr (1992) has bluntly reminded social scientists,

> . . . for children whose development is on a predictable but undesirable trajectory and whose parents are providing a supportive environment, interventions have only temporary and limited effects. . . . Should we be surprised? Feeding a well-nourished but short child more and more will not give him the stature of a basketball player. Feeding a [child with a] below-average intellect more and more information will not make her brilliant. Exposing a shy child to socially demanding events will not make him feel less shy. (pp. 16–17)

Fundamentally, the lesson is that desirable and undesirable traits alike are maintained in human populations neither by parental intention nor by parental blunders; etiology is more complex and multifaceted than such a simplistic and overly optimistic picture would suggest. As Chapter 5 has indicated, the typical environmental explanations of social pathology—social class, child-rearing styles, and others—take their explanatory power from genetic variation underlying behavioral variation in modern industrialized societies. If we are to understand the maintenance of traits, we must learn more about the sources of this genetic variation. Before turning to this task, let us consider an example of how socialization science can examine various models of cultural transmission.

The Diffusion of Cigarette Smoking:
Examining Models of Cultural Transmission

Cigarette smoking is an interesting behavior for contrasting different models of cultural transmission. Cigarettes are an old cultural innovation, discovered first by Native Americans and then spread around the rest of the world (Ferrence, 1989). Manufactured, rolled cigarettes were used in the United States in the 1800s, but smoking did not become popular among adult males until after World War I and among adult females until after World War II. Smoking was first popular among the better-educated segments of the population, and then diffused to less well-educated groups. However, in a complete reversal of smoking patterns for people born early in this century (before 1910), smoking in younger groups is much more common today among the poorly educated than among the well educated.

Cigarettes (by virtue of containing a physiologically addicting substance, nicotine) manage to promote themselves, but smoking also has cultural meaning to young adults, who are certainly unaddicted during the early stages of experimentation with cigarettes. These cultural meanings, as well as physiological pleasure, give cigarettes their "functional value" that maintains them in the population. But each new generation is naive to cigarettes. From age 10 to about age 20 years, individuals either become regular smokers, experiment with cigarettes and then quit, or avoid them altogether. Almost no one—not even a middle-aged man in a full-blown midlife crisis—begins smoking later in life. Although he may buy a red Porsche, he doesn't try Camel cigarettes for the first time.

As we have seen for personality and intellectual traits, socialization scientists most often refer to social influences in the family as the cause of the intergenerational transmission of smoking behavior. And as usual, they use only weak and ambiguous evidence: the well-replicated association of smoking in a biological parent with smoking in a biological child. Rates of smoking in the offspring of smokers can be two to four times those in the offspring of nonsmokers.

But this interpretation foolishly neglects to consider the genetic component of parent–child similarity. Table 7.2 summarizes reports of two twin studies, an adoptive study, and a family study. In all these studies, the offspring of smokers were adults at the time they were surveyed. Smoking's heritability averaged 43%, whereas smoking's rearing environmental variation was close to zero. In other words, effects of rearing variation (e.g., parents' lighting up or not, or having cigarettes in the

TABLE 7.2. Rearing Effects for Cigarette Smoking?

Type	Heritability (h^2)	Shared rearing variation (c^2)	Citation
Family	42%	N/A	Eysenck (1980)
Twin	36%	<0%	Carmelli, Swan, Robinette, & Fabsitz (1990)
Twin	50%	<0%	Swan, Carmelli, Rosenman, Fabsitz, & Christian (1990)
Adoptive	N/A	<0%	Eysenck (1980)
Mean	43%	0%	

Note. In Eysenck (1980, p. 242), the biological parent–child correlation was .21 (n = 533 pairs); the adoptive parent–adoptee correlation was –.02. In Carmelli et al. (1990, p. 70, Table 3): adjusted cigarettes, MZ twin r = .32, DZ twin = .14 (n = 2,390 MZ twin pairs and n = 2,570 DZ twin pairs). In Swan et al. (1990, p. 45, Table 3): adjusted smoking, MZ twin r = .42 and DZ twin r = .17 (n = 176 MZ twin pairs and n = 184 DZ twin pairs). N/A, not applicable.

home or not) were nil by the time the children had reached adulthood. In Eysenck's (1980) report on adoptees, the smoking correlation of *biologically unrelated* parent–child pairs was essentially zero (r = –.02). Parental smoking may influence a child's risk through genetic inheritance: The role of parents is a passive one—providing a set of genes at loci relevant to smoking risk, but not socially influencing their offspring.

Socially, learning to smoke is primarily a peer group process: Age-mates provide cigarettes, smoking opportunities, and words of encouragement. As established in many studies, nearly all adolescents first acquire smoking by experimenting with cigarettes with their friends and acquaintances—usually other adolescents close in age to themselves. After the smoking habit has been established, however, the presence of others is no longer as crucial for maintaining it; some evidence suggests that adults smoke with a goal of keeping a consistent blood level of the psychoactive substance, nicotine. In the cultural transmission models of Figure 7.1, note that smoking habits correspond most closely to horizontal transmission among age-mates (model B), not to vertical parent-–child transmission (model A).

With my colleague Joseph Rodgers, I recently modeled mathematically the horizontal "contagion" of various adolescent-onset behaviors, including alcohol use, smoking, and sexual intercourse (Rowe & Rodgers, 1991a, 1991b). Our models share the basic structure of mathematical models of the spread of cultural innovations or that of infectious disease organisms (see Cavalli-Sforza & Feldman, 1981). For this reason, we sometimes call them "epidemic" models, in an analogy with epidemic disease. People who have not adopted a new behavior are the "susceptibles" in a population; those who have adopted it are the "carriers." But such analogies are not intended to be taken literally; we certainly do not mean to make a moral judgment about smoking or any other behavior by means of this analogy. The analogy is an aid to understanding, because concepts such as the (population) mixing of "carriers" and "susceptibles" puts the emphasis on horizontal transmission, and away from the vertical transmission models so dominant in socialization science.

Consider the horizontal spread of smoking in adolescent groups (Rowe, Chassin, Presson, Edwards, & Sherman, 1992). Our smoking model assumes that four smoking stages exist: (1) "nonsmoker," (2) "trier" (defined as smoking no more than once per week), (3) "regular smoker," and (4) "former smoker." As shown in Figure 7.2, transitions exist between these stages: A child may move from nonsmoker to trier, from trier to regular smoker, and back and forth between former smoker and smoker, as smokers can both quit and (unfortunately) relapse. In a transition from nonsmoker to trier, we assume that social contacts are involved. If John is a nonsmoker, for example, he must meet a cigarette-using friend or acquaintance before starting to smoke himself.

This assumption is fairly noncontroversial: According to my research, nearly 90% of American adolescents initiate smoking in a small group of one to three friends and acquaintances. Of course, not everyone obeys a mathematical model—but because the exceptions may be relatively rare, they are omitted here. We may also assume that the transition from trier to regular smoker does not involve any kind of social contact. According to this model, kids get "hooked" as a result of suffi-

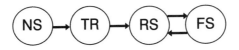

NON SMOKERS
TRIERS
REGULAR SMOKERS
FORMER SMOKERS

FIGURE 7.2. Smoking stages.

cient smoking experience, not because of repeated social pressures to do so. This assumption may be more controversial, but it works well in our mathematical model (Rowe et al., 1992).

To give readers a feel for the model, the proportion of new triers is assumed to depend on social contacts with smokers. Mathematically, what the model says is this:

$$(1) \quad \text{New } P_{\text{TR}_{a+1}} = TP_{S_a} \cdot P_{\text{NS}_a}$$

where T is a rate constant, $P_{\text{TR}_{a+1}}$ is the proportion of new triers at age a plus 1 year, P_{S_a} is the proportion of smokers (including both triers and regular smokers) at age a years, and P_{NS_a} is the proportion of nonsmokers at age a years. If few smokers exist in a population at a given time, clearly smoking rates can increase only slowly. As new smokers are added to this population, contacts between smokers and nonsmokers become more common, and the rate of spread increases still further.

The rate of spread also depends on the constant, T. When T takes on a larger value, spread is more rapid. In equation (1), T represents a population average; of course, some individuals have greater T values than others, either because they are more susceptible or because they have more contact opportunities.

What determines the rate constant? One influence is the probability that a person will try cigarettes, when she is given the chance. Given the prevalence of smoking, T is probably greater for poor adolescents than rich ones, reflecting different expectations and values surrounding smoking. At the individual level, T may vary with heritable personality traits; for instance, individuals who are genetically more impulsive probably have greater T values than ones who are not. T can also depend on the degree of social mixing: The more encounters between smokers and nonsmokers, under circumstances where experimentation with cigarettes is possible, the greater the value of T for a particular population. In a sense, a dissection of T uncovers the many causes of smoking, and hence the conceptual complexity of this single number.

The transition from trier to regular smoker requires a different mathematical representation:

$$(2) \quad \text{New } P_{\text{RS}_{a+1}} = jP_{\text{TR}_a}$$

where j is a rate constant, $P_{\text{RS}_{a+1}}$ is the proportion of regular smokers at the next age, and P_{TR_a} is the proportion of triers at the prior age. Here, a constant proportion of triers become regular smokers at any age. For example, if $j = .2$ and $P_{TR} = .6$, then the proportion of those becoming regular smokers would be .12.

Difference equations can be used to represent our model for the children of smoking and nonsmoking parents.[2] There are four equations for the children of smoking parents, and four for those of nonsmoking parents. We used these equations to fit data on smoking collected by Laurie Chassin and Clark Presson, and their colleagues, in the college town of Bloomington, Indiana (Rowe et al., 1992). The sample size was about 5,000 students in grades 6–12. The model was fitted to proportions—that is, the proportion of nonsmokers, triers, regular smokers, and former smokers in each grade (this was done separately for the children of smoking and nonsmoking parents). Sixth-grade proportions were fed into the model equations, which then returned *predicted* ones for grades 7–11. On the assumption that social contacts predominate within sex, males and females were fitted separately.

For simplicity, predictions of former smokers have been omitted from Table 7.3, which shows the predicted proportions of nonsmokers, triers, and regular smokers in grades 7–12 separately for the daughters of smoking and nonsmoking parents. About half our sample had at least one smoking parent, so the two sets of population growth curves represent about equal numbers of children. As shown, the children of smoking parents were about twice as likely to smoke as those of nonsmoking parents. Although the increase rates appear fairly similar for the two kinds of children, a mathematical analysis revealed that the *rate constants* were greater for the children of smoking parents than for those of nonsmoking parents. In the nonsmoker-to-trier transition, they were .52 and .32, respectively; in the trier-to-regular smoker transition, they were .14 and .10, respectively.

Thus, vertical "influence" (parent to child) is described in our model as greater susceptibility to peer influence. Furthermore, the familial role is interpreted here as a genetic one, attributable to children's inheritance of different personality traits. The values of both rate constants may be changed by familial background traits—one reflected in the social influence of age-mates, the other in the development of long-term psychological dependence on smoking. The literature on smoking allows one to postulate what these heritable traits may be. For example, sensation seeking and extraversion have been statistically linked with smoking behavior; they may influence the nonsmoker-to-trier transition. The other transition, from trier to regular smoker, may depend in part on other

TABLE 7.3. Predicted Smoking for Female Children of Smokers and Nonsmokers

School grade	Nonsmokers	Triers	Regular smokers
	Smoking parents		
7	.62	.31	.04
8	.55	.34	.07
9	.46	.38	.11
10	.36	.41	.15
11	.28	.45	.18
12	.20	.46	.22
	Nonsmoking parents		
7	.74	.12	.00
8	.68	.17	.01
9	.61	.23	.03
10	.54	.30	.05
11	.45	.36	.07
12	.37	.41	.10

Note. Epidemic model fit, $\chi^2 = 16.6$, $df = 25$, $p > .05$. A small chi-square value indicates a good fit. Parameter values: smoking parents, $T_1 = .52$, $j_1 = .14$; nonsmoking parents, $T_2 = .32$, $j_2 = .10$. Relapse rate $v = .05$; quitting rate $u = .18$.

heritable traits, including the body's own physiological adaptation to nicotine.

Like the monkey Imo's potato-washing innovation, smoking behavior cascades through society via horizontal transmission. Heritable trait variation is relevant to the flow of these social innovations through society, but variation in how children are reared may have little relevance. Rather, the time scale for social influences on smoking is shorter than a biological generation. Changes in price, in availability, and in social knowledge of cigarette's harmfulness to health diffuse quickly through society via the pathways of Figure 7.1, altering cigarette usage patterns. The genes underlying susceptibility to cigarettes change much more slowly, at the pace of biological rather than cultural evolution. And finally, cultural and biological evolutionary pathways may interact—a "coevolution" of changing cultural innovations and changing gene frequencies. That is, a cultural innovation may reduce its adopters' average number of surviving children (and hence lower their biological fitness), or it may increase reproductive rates and survivorship.

At first glance, one might think that the health risks of smoking make it biologically maladaptive. But smoking's harmfulness to fitness is probably weaker than is commonly supposed, because its ill-health effects may be delayed beyond the reproductive years. In addition, one social meaning of smoking is the early initiation of adult roles and behaviors, including sexuality. Teenage smokers may adopt a general lifestyle that leads to earlier and more frequent childbearing. Thus, contrary to common belief, smoking may be biologically adaptive (though undesirable) for young adults, at least over the short term, in the current cultural climate of the United States.

In summary, smoking must be understood in terms of a "diffusion–exposure" model of the spread of cigarette use and its attendant beliefs and attitudes. An "initial use" theory must explain the beginning of experimentation with cigarettes; an "amount–persistence" theory must explain why some adolescents who experiment with cigarettes eventually cease smoking, whereas others become addicted (see Carey, 1992, for another mathematical approach to these ideas). Most broadly, effects of cultural innovations will be played out against long-term population changes in gene frequencies—a biological concomitant to cultural change.

Forces Maintaining Genetic Variability

Why Are Some People "Bad"?

This broader evolutionary view reveals a limiting myopia in socialization scientists' understanding of how "bad" behavioral dispositions persist. No modern theory of human evolution can possibly postulate a simple human nature, lacking self-interest as well as social interest in others, lacking antisocial tendencies as well as prosocial ones, or lacking motives that conflict as much as ones that complement.

A complete analysis of human nature, of course, falls outside this book's scope. But some discussion of the evolutionary forces maintaining genetic variability is necessary if socialization science is to move from family-based theories of trait maintenance and transmission to more powerful and general coevolutionary ones.

Socialization scientists' error has been to ignore completely the role of differential reproductive rates in maintaining behavioral variation. If genetic variation determines trait variability, then the crucial question is that of which genes are put into the next generation. The answer in turn depends on the relative reproductive rates of the genes' bearers, and on the survivorship of the bearers' offspring. Given the moral neutrality of the guiding hand of evolution, "bad" traits can evolve as easily as "good" ones. Indeed, typical animal behavior patterns contain many examples of biologically evolved traits considered morally reprehensible in human societies—from "forced extrapartner copulation" in mallard ducks (something loosely akin to human rape) to the killing of unrelated infants by male troop leaders among rhesus monkeys.

To take a less extreme trait as an example, Marten deVries (1984) investigated infant temperament among the Masai, a nomadic, Nilo-Hamitic people living in central Kenya; he classified babies as either "easy" or "difficult" in temperament. The 10 easiest and 10 most difficult babies were chosen for further study. deVries then left Kenya for about a year before returning to continue his field work. During the interim, a devastating drought caused a heavy loss of cattle (the main food resource for the Masai), and child mortality rates increased sharply. On his return, deVries managed to relocate 13 of the 20 originally studied families; he discovered that five of seven babies classified as "easy" in temperament had died, whereas only one of six difficult ones had met the same fate ($p < .07$). deVries speculated that the "difficult" babies might have outsurvived the "easy" ones because, under a condition of resource scarcity, their noisy demands brought them the additional amount of parental care and food that their quieter age-mates never received. In the entire Masai sample, the correlation of difficult temperament with larger body size endorsed deVries's "squeaky wheel" hypothesis.[3] Thus, traits that parents of young infants may regard with some dismay and apprehension may, under certain conditions, be evolutionarily favored.

The capacity of "bad" traits to evolve is even more apparent when one considers how reproductive success can be balanced evolutionarily against the dark force of mortality itself. Young males of many species are more violent and more willing to take high-stakes risks than older, established males or females. Of course, males deciding not to fight for social status and mating opportunities could do so, eating jungle fruits and surviving into admirable dotage; however, their behavioral tendencies would lack any genetic representation in the next generation. The same conditions may apply to adolescents and young adults in human societies. If the more aggressive, risk-taking adolescents had an 80% survival chance, but fathered (on average) 3.0 children, their reproductive success would surely exceed that of more cautious males with a 95%

survivorship and, on average, 2.3 biological children. Evolutionary processes can easily maintain trait prevalences, though they may upset moral sensibilities. In both U.S. cities and suburbs, adolescents may unconsciously use high-risk behaviors to increase their reproductive chances, as violent behavior and teenage fatherhood do occur together in adolescent males.

Hawks and Doves

Game-theoretic ideas give us powerful metaphors for real evolutionary processes, ones probably operating daily in our societies to produce behavioral variability. The game metaphor of "Hawks and Doves" describes the ability of evolution to maintain mixed traits or mixed motives in a population (Dawkins, 1989; Maynard-Smith, 1982). For a human analogy, imagine two adolescent boys confronting each other over a girl they both like. The boy taking the "Hawk" strategy will fight. In contrast, a boy adopting a "Dove" strategy will make a few threats, but if a real fight then ensues, he will flee quickly from the scene. For simplicity, we may assume that boys act either as Hawks or as Doves for their entire lives. But the model works just as well if every adolescent boy has both motivational systems, but spends part of his day as a Hawk and part as a Dove. Thus a population may be composed of two-thirds Hawks and one-third Doves, or of people who behave as Hawks two-thirds of the time and as Doves one-third of the time.

For both Hawks and Doves, payoffs must be in some currency that ultimately counts as greater or lesser reproductive success. Fighting may cause injuries that reduce average success in mating and fathering children. When Hawks meet, both may get hurt. When Doves meet, they may posture and threaten, but ultimately both may leave with some social prestige intact. Suppose that winning a fight enhances social prestige. When a Hawk meets a Dove, the outcome is foreordained: The Hawk wins the fight and enhances his social status, while the Dove leaves defeated. These ideas can be translated into a set of numerical "payoffs" for both the Hawk and the Dove lifestyles:

   −.3 to the Hawk meeting another Hawk
    .6 to the Hawk meeting a Dove
    0 to the Dove meeting a Hawk
    .2 to the Dove meeting another Dove

In this interpretation, these payoff numbers represent real gains or losses of social prestige that ultimately increase or decrease fitness. For convenience, the units are treated as though they were scaled to reproductive rates—so that, for instance, the −.3 means that fighting Hawks suffer, *on average*, the loss of one-third of a child. (Clearly, no Hawk loses exactly one-third of a child—some have one child fewer than they would if they had never fought, some none fewer, some two fewer, etc.) The units can be rescaled relative to average reproductive rates in the full population: If the average reproductive success is 2.0 among all adolescent boys, then a Hawk's encounter with another Hawk reduces it to 1.7. His encounter with a Dove increases it to 2.6.

Overall social prestige and reproductive success thus depend on a whole history of social contests. Under such conditions, a Hawk's payoff will depend on how often his contests are with another Hawk (in which he may be injured), and how often with another Dove (in which he surely wins). If the population were divided into "p" Hawks (a proportion between 0 and 1) and "q" Doves, and if encounters with a Hawk or Dove partner take place essentially by chance (unlikely in the real world, but a useful simplification for demonstrating general principles), then p proportion of the time a Hawk encounters another Hawk, and q proportion of the time a Hawk encounters another Dove. Weighting the *payoff per encounter* by the relative frequencies of encounters yields a payoff for each life history. Living as a Hawk leads to this equation:

$$(3) \quad \text{Hawk payoff} = -.3p + .6q$$

Because a Dove will also encounter other Hawks and Doves at the same relative rates, the equation is the same except for the payoffs:

$$(4) \quad \text{Dove payoff} = 0p + .2q$$

Using these two equations, and substituting different values for p and q (where $q = 1 - p$), one can derive the payoffs for the two life histories according to different population compositions. Table 7.4 presents results for equations (3) and (4) for proportions from one-seventh Hawks to six-sevenths Hawks. When Hawks are rare relative to Doves, they do better reproductively; that is, they average 2.47 children, whereas the Doves average just 2.17 children. In contrast, when the Doves are relatively rare, they do better reproductively than Hawks, averaging 2.03 children versus Hawks' 1.83. When the population composition is four-

TABLE 7.4. Reproductive Payoffs in Hawk and Dove Contests

Population composition		Average lifetime births	
Hawks	Doves	Hawks	Doves
1/7	6/7	2.47	2.17
2/7	5/7	2.34	2.14
3/7	4/7	2.21	2.11
4/7	3/7	2.09	2.09
5/7	2/7	1.96	2.06
6/7	1/7	1.83	2.03

sevenths Hawks and three-sevenths Doves, the two life histories do equally well reproductively (payoff = 2.09 in each case; see Table 7.4).

Therefore, over generations, differential reproductive rates always take population compositions to this one equilibrium. The dynamic nature of this process can be modeled with a computer program a few lines long.[4] As shown in Figure 7.3, a population starting with 95% Hawks and 5% Doves reaches equilibrium in about 30 generations. One starting with the opposite composition (95% Doves and 5% Hawks) takes a little longer, reaching equilibrium after about 60 generations. After about 80 generations the population composition would be completely stable, except if perturbed.

This process is called "frequency-dependent selection." Rare behavior patterns enjoy increased reproductive success while they are rare, but reduced success as they become more common. With several such behavior patterns, an equilibrium point may exist at which all behaviors possess equal reproductive success. Unless research investigators can long outlive their subjects, verifying frequency-dependent selection in human populations will be extremely difficult, if not impossible. True, the assessment of *current* selection is possible in modern societies, and this evidence could be used to strengthen the case for a selective process. But long-term selection would be extremely difficult to study, given the weaknesses of historical data, as well as the many ambiguities that must accompany reconstruction of the Pleistosine period in which humans evolved.

Nevertheless, the idea of such a selective process maintaining genetic variability in a context as rich and as diverse as human societies is intuitively appealing. Consider that street criminals offer a rough parallel to our game-theoretic Hawks, and law-abiding people to our Doves.

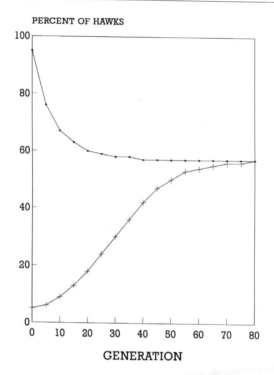

PERCENT OF HAWKS

GENERATION

FIGURE 7.3. Approach to equilibrium in the Hawks and Doves game.

Like Hawks and Doves, people at extremes of criminality or law obedience fail to switch to the other life history, or at least switches are quite uncommon (Loeber, 1991). The tendency toward crime is also heritable (Rowe & Osgood, 1984). And in sharp distinction from the case for schizophrenia or severe mental retardation, criminals have children at reasonable rates, often having them earlier in life than noncriminals (Robins, 1966). These empirical observations—a heritable and relatively stable life history, and a lack of reproductive loss—meet the requirements for real-life contests between Hawks and Doves. For the full process to hold, one must further imagine that criminals do better reproductively when they are rare (perhaps when society is less vigilant), and do more poorly when they are common (when society may be more vigilant, and when their mutual encounters would extract their own reproductive cost).

Evolutionary biology is now receiving some recognition in the environmentalist strongholds of the social sciences. Two sociologists, Lawrence Cohen and Richard Machalek (1988), also applied the concept of frequency-dependent selection to crime. They argued that a population of cooperating and productive individuals, in which exploitative individuals were rare, would invite "invasion by opportunistic alternative strategists" (p. 481). Hence, populations composed of both productive noncriminals and exploitative criminals should be the rule rather than the exception, and in this way, "crime can be said to be 'normal' in populations" (p. 481). Cohen and Machalek saw that criminal strategies can be understood in the same dynamic way as Hawk-versus-Dove contests: as a competition of behavioral alternatives, with success at least partly dependent on the rarity or commonness of the different strategies themselves.

Nonetheless, the form of these ideas offered by Cohen and Machalek (1988) de-emphasized heritable traits. The relevance of birth rates to passing criminal dispositions from one generation to the next was not mentioned. Indeed, Cohen and Machalek described most criminal acts not as results of "genetic selection," but rather as the results of "strategies employed by motivated persons, often cognitively aware that their behavior violates normative rules" (p. 477). They further imagined a situation in which two populations would have nearly identical traits of "age, gender, IQ, arousal levels, ethnicity, body type, values, and so forth" (p. 496). In such perfectly matched populations, different behavioral strategies could still spread and find their own equilibriums, but through cultural rather than genetic transmission.

The theory of frequency-dependent selection recognizes that genetic and cultural systems are *dual* modes of transmission, each operating with some independence of the other. One may find nongenetic reasons why criminal and noncriminal strategies may have different frequencies in two populations. For example, a novel form of criminal behavior (e.g., "computer viruses") may be introduced in one population and not but not another. This partial independence, though, fails to excuse ignoring biology in criminal behavior, as there is ample evidence of its importance. In reality, individuals do differ in heritable traits that make criminal strategies more or less attractive. Understanding criminality demands that the ideas of cultural and genetic transmission be considered simultaneously. In summary, although frequency-dependent selection is difficult to prove, the Hawks–Doves metaphor is appealing because it can account for the maintenance of antisocial behavioral tendencies without a return to false theories about variation in child rearing.

Evolution operates in many ways, not all of which are frequency-dependent. The existence of environmental "niches" that can be better occupied by one genotype than by another is another general process that maintains variability. As discussed in Chapter 5, in human societies people of very different levels of measured intelligence occupy different social niches. They can earn enough income to support families, despite their disparate economic activities. Thus, the existence of different occupational roles tends to encourage continuing genetic variation in IQ; conversely, genetic variation in IQ tends to create occupational niches, which are filled by people of different levels of ability.

Further Sources of Variation

Social competition is not the only source of genetic variation. First, new DNA mutations in each generation may create variability. Second, biological pathogens exert selective pressure on all complex organisms. Tooby (1982), in particular, argues that the bulk of genetic variability in human populations may arise from pathogen-driven selection; this position may be extreme, but it is not without merit.

Biological pathogens—those awful germs that make us sick—are a major selective force because they weed out genotypes that succumb to them, while surviving genotypes manage to reproduce. One of the few documented cases of heterozygote advantage, sickle cell anemia, arises from the selective pressure of malarial disease on human populations (Durham, 1991). In the case of sickle cell anemia, individuals with one abnormal gene (s) and one normal gene (S) are less susceptible to malaria than those with two normal genes (SS). In the former individuals, red blood cells infected with the malarial organism become misshapen, and they are then destroyed by natural processes in the body. In normal individuals, infected cells are not removed, so that the risk of severe malarial disease (which may cause death) is greater. But the protection conferred by the sickling gene carries a heavy price: Individuals born with it in a double dose, genotype ss, will die (without medical intervention) in infancy or in early childhood. Other cases of genetic variation may also hold evidence of natural selection wrought by disease, although these instances are less well documented. In the well-known ABO blood group, the O gene may confer protection against smallpox; hence its greater frequency in European populations, in which the disease was once rampant (Diamond, 1990). Other blood group genes may tell similar stories for other illnesses.

Tooby and Cosmides (1990) speculate that this pathogen-driven genetic variation may also influence psychological traits—not by design, of course. Protective gene products work inside the cell to ward off disease organisms. Cumulatively, though, this genetic variation may affect the nervous system, and hence behavior. Thus viruses and bacteria may unwittingly create the genetic variation leading to psychological differences.

The Effects of Genetic Variation

According to Tooby and Cosmides (1990), psychological adaptations are more likely to be maintained by genes that are fixed (i.e., the same in everyone) than by those that vary. The reasoning behind their assertion is subtle: Genotypes get broken apart and reassembled in the process of sexual reproduction. In other words, the genotype of a parent is not the same as that of any child. But complex adaptations must require the cooperation and coordination of many genes scattered about the chromosomes to create, through interdependent steps, a finely tuned neurological system. If such a finely honed system existed in one parent, it would be taken apart when one random half of genes were passed to a child—because the exact combination of genes that had existed in a parent would not exist in a child, unless the genes were *already identical* in both parents.

The implication of this analysis is that most genetic variation fails to create new, complex adaptations, or new kinds of human psychology. Rather, it may modify universal psychological tendencies set by those genes humans share as a species. True, in the case of human gender differences (as discussed in Chapter 6), a genetic "switch" does exist on the Y chromosome that determines two different psychologies—male and female—but we have not found any corresponding bimodalities in psychological traits within the sexes.[5] Therefore, I agree with Tooby and Cosmides that genetic variation in the personality realm may change just response and perceptual thresholds under particular conditions, and that genetic variation in the intellectual realm may change just the *quantitative* capacity to assimilate and manipulate information mentally. In neither case does genetic variation change the underlying adaptive plan. That is, most humans react emotionally in broadly the same way to similar circumstances, even though the range of differences in emotional attachment between criminals and noncriminals may give the appearance of qualitatively different human psychologies. Similarly, the mental processes used in reasoning are similar in most humans, even though the capacities of the very bright and very dull are so disparate as to give an appearance of qualitatively different human psychologies. Overall, much remains to be learned about the sources and functions of genetic variability. But certain points are undisputable: It exists; it is thrown up at the social system in each generation; and we ignore these facts at our peril.

The Need for Theories of Coevolution

The conclusion of this chapter is that a broader socialization science must be based on theories of gene–environment coevolution (Durham, 1991; Boyd & Richerson, 1985; Wilson, 1975; Lumsden & Wilson, 1983). These theories are currently undergoing the processes of discovery, analysis, and refinement, and their final form remains to be seen. In a seminal effort to put forth a theory of coevolution, Durham (1991) has reviewed existing coevolutionary theories and proposed a general model of his own. Like other theories of coevolution, Durham's distinguishes two independent but interacting systems of inheritance: genetic and cultural inheritance. They are independent systems because, though they both carry information from one generation to the next, they operate under different rules and by different mechanisms. The genetic system relies on the biological process of sexual reproduction and on genes—physical stretches of DNA. The cultural system relies on the transfer of information between human minds. The unit here is more difficult to define than a gene, and it certainly cannot be cut out of a molecular biologist's gel. Following Dawkins (1989), Durham proposes the concept of a "meme"—a unit of information resembling a "gene" in that it is transmissible between generations, is potentially variable in human populations, and is able to influence eventual phenotypes. In a cultural system, social innovation has a role corresponding to mutation in a biological system: It introduces new variability in memes. But the cultural system of inheritance also violates restrictions placed by biology on genetic inheritance. As shown in Figure 7.1, memes may move between minds in the same generations, from parent to child, from child to parent, and from teachers to students.

Any theory of coevolution must address two fundamental questions. First, what filters the replication of memes from one generation to the next? Second, what is the relation of biological to cultural fitness?

Durham (1991) has identified a number of mechanisms that influence the likelihood of cultural transmission. One is merely the rate of biological reproduction of subgroups that use a particular meme: Ideas may flourish as their bearers grow more numerous, much as genes may flourish. But ideas also replicate independently of growth in numbers of people; indeed, new innovations may sweep through a population without a change in its genetic composition. In the United States, an example would be the shift in the late 20th century toward regarding working women more favorably (Firebaugh, 1992).

Memes' succcess (replication) depends on their "cultural fitness"— that is, on their attractiveness to people in a particular culture, enabling them to spread there. Although many processes may influence a meme's cultural fitness, Durham has emphasized human choice and decision making. Durham calls this process "selection according *to* consequences," as opposed to the unconscious Darwinian "selection *by* consequences." It is the ability of people to compare different cultural variants, and to decide which ones possess the greatest utility for them.

Of course, in understanding the spread of particular memes, a key must be the criteria by which they are selected. Here, Durham (1991) has distinguished "primary values" from "secondary values." The former have a more direct and stronger biological component than the latter, but both are ultimately tied to biological evolution. Primary values include the instinctive love of parent for child, sexual attraction, and other emotions with a strong biological basis. The secondary values are elaborations of these primary ones through cultural evolution. In U.S. society today, for example, competing belief systems exist about the importance of marriage and the necessity of childbearing within the context of marriage; these are secondary values, each with a particular history of cultural evolution. In summary, theories of selective mechanisms are not well advanced, but uncovering them is essential for understanding cultural transmission.

The second question concerns the relation of cultural and genetic evolution. Genes may hold culture on a leash, but at issue is how short that leash is. At times, the leash may be quite long, because examples can be found in which cultural memes have damaged their bearers' biological fitness. Joined in a communal group, the 19th-century Shakers believed in community dancing and in sharing all material things, and they left us a legacy of elegant furniture (Halsey & Johnston, 1990). The Shakers, however, also eschewed sexual relations—a cultural practice that totally opposed their biological fitness, as they left behind no children.

Because the Shakers also converted few adherents, their opposition to reproduction ultimately led to their own demise.

More recently, some Western companies made the meme of bottle feeding and its associated technology available to Third World countries, and thus inadvertently caused an increase in child mortality over that of breast-fed children. The cultural fitness of the bottle-feeding meme conflicted in societies that adopted it with its lack of biological fitness. Durham (1991) has made the insightful observation that many instances of coevolutionary "opposition"—cases in which a meme hurts biological fitness—may result from memes imposed on one social group by another. This reasoning applies to conquests, which are often followed by the destruction of the defeated society's cultural traditions.

Although other examples of conflicts between culture and genetic evolution can be found, I agree wholeheartedly with Durham that in most instances the two forces for change are mutually supportive. That is, cultural memes chosen within a particular social group more often than not increase their bearers' reproductive success. Durham has called this kind of gene–meme relationship "enhancement," because bearers of memes with greater cultural fitness also possess greater biological fitness. Examples of such memes are cultural values opposing the marriage of close relatives—a practice that is biologically damaging because of the way inbreeding may cause genetic abnormalities. Cultural practices may also favor particular genotypes, as when dairying cultures made a genetic ability to digest milk an advantage (Durham, 1991).

In "neutrality," choice among memes lacks a relation to biological fitness. An example is the arbitrary relationship of a word to an object so signified: Whether one says "boat" or "bateau," for instance, makes little difference for biological fitness. Durham says more about the relation of cultural and genetic evolution, but we need not consider all his ideas here. What we need to remember is that a multiplicity of relationships can exist between genetic inheritance and culture. The leash metaphor may be extended from one leash to many leashes—some tight, others so loose as to be unnoticeable.

The purpose of this book is not to present a full-fledged theory of coevolution. Rather, it is to shake socialization science out of its complacent emphasis on the family as the bearer of culture, and on familial variation as the environmental cause of observed phenotypic diversity. In the light of data reviewed in the previous chapters, both assumptions appear to be false to the core, leading to a theory of social and personality development that is weak and has little ultimate intellectual power.

In this chapter, I have presented reasons for the weakness of the family-based model. I have found it unlikely that any genes could have become fixed in human populations that would restrict learning to parental example; the generality of learning diminishes family influence. Other transmission pathways should be routinely modeled in socialization science, and the "epidemic" model of smoking provides one such example (an extensive developmental literature on "peer influence" does this, although without explicitly using cultural transmission models). Both genetic and cultural avenues of trait maintenance must be considered. A number of biologically selective mechanisms—most notably, frequency-dependent selection—may account for the maintenance of difficult personality dispositions, ones commonly attributed to variation in family environments. Finally, a theory of phenotype development must identify both genetic and cultural components in a theory of gene–environment coevolution. Although the two interact, cultural memes have a transmission history separable from that of genes, and an understanding of human social behavior must adopt this dual perspective.

The diverse paths of cultural transmission also permit different genotypes to find their own environmental "niches." Each individual is potentially a recipient of information from parents, peers, teachers, unrelated adults, and so on, so that the range of information sampled broadens rapidly after early childhood. True, family effects can be stronger when no other opportunity exists for a particular kind of exposure. As mentioned in an earlier chapter, musical performance at the high school level shows some rearing influence. But violin lessons are usually first a parental idea, and schools lack programs to expose all children to classical instruments.

In some closed cultures, opportunities may be limited because all adults agree to impose fairly consistent social norms. For instance, among the Amish, a fairly rigid social structure can be maintained because all families agree to limit the exposure of young people to other alternatives. Nonetheless, even Amish teenagers "sow their wild oats"; in some cases allowance is made for their behavior, but in others the violator must leave. A process of expelling nonconformists may lead to genotypic as well as to cultural selection. For most forms of social behavior, though, the industrialized societies afford so many opportunities for sampling different memes that nongenetic parent–child resemblance is ultimately weak or nonexistent. In a few unfortunate cases, middle-class adoptive parents have been shocked when their adoptees discovered violent subcultures, which were previously unknown to them. The process that I have variously called in this book "gene–environment correlation," "niche picking," or "an extended phenotype" needs much further exploration.

Current socialization science reminds me of a famous *New Yorker* cover showing a map of the United States dominated by Manhattan, with the remainder of the country barely represented. In much the same way that Manhattan crowds everything else out of the consciousness of New Yorkers, families dominate socialization science. Although New Yorkers may be incorrigible in their thought habits, it is time for socialization scientists to adopt a broader basis for their empirical and theoretical work.

Social and Policy Implications

Best-selling novels rarely have unhappy endings; similarly, books about genetics and social science usually close with some kind of sugarcoating about how biological traits are not really determined, or about how a heritable trait is malleable. These endings are not false ones, but in the context of this book's central discoveries they may be misleading, at least in emphasis.

The malleability of heritable traits cannot be doubted. Physical height is a commonly cited example. In the United States, heights have increased over the past century, despite the heritability of height (80% or better). Height gains are real and noticeable to designers of doors and airline seats (although further improvements can be made in these areas). But these historic gains do not mean that well-nourished middle-class children are still growing taller; indeed, groups of children born more recently are no longer putting on extra inches. Had twin or adoption studies recruited families with well-nourished and malnourished children, they would have shown that rearing variation affects height—a result that they do not find today.[6] With adequate nutrition now widespread, a major impediment to attaining one's genetic potential for height has been removed. Genetic variation in height remains, nonetheless, persistently operative.

The nostrums for many social problems involve recommendations that we rear our children differently. Ironically, for such policy recommendations to be at all effective, heritability must be much less important for the traits in question than is the estimate of the shared rearing component of variation. Consider two traits—one with a heritability of 45% and a family rearing influence of 25%; another with a heritability of 10% but no family rearing variation. With the former, we would have a good idea of what social policy choices to adopt. We would advise parents to rear their children as do families with the "best" outcomes, whatever those methods may be (e.g., putting the children into cribs with fancy mobiles, or taking them to museums, or making sure that both parents stay home with them), because in this case 25% of trait variation is open to programmatic manipulation. The latter trait shows only a small amount of genetic variation and much unshared environmental variation—but how do we identify what unshared influences to change with our policy options? They may be anything from embryological development to a bad teacher. Shared rearing variation, not heritability, is a standard for the upper-bound influence of some social policies—those policies that change the environments of the most disadvantaged to be like those of the most advantaged.

This book concludes, however, that variation in shared rearing experiences is a weak source of trait variation. As with malnutrition, everything possible should be done to combat child abuse, child neglect, and other parenting wrongs. And as with height, doing away with the greatest harms may make some improvement in trait distributions. Many problem youths, though, come from the range of normal parenting variation, from families that are working- or middle-class and that are not extremely poor—in other words, from that range of diminished or nonexistent family influence. Changes in parenting styles may make only a small dent in the sum total of our social problems. Too, if social scientists come to accept these conclusions, the idea that the way academics raise children would really be best for everyone must be abandoned as well. If environmental interventions are to succeed, they must be truly novel ones, representing kinds of treatments that will be new to most populations.

These remarks will certainly call out Lewontin, Rose, and Kamin's (1984) "fire brigade":

> Critics of biological determinism are like members of a fire brigade, constantly being called out in the middle of the night to put out the latest conflagration, always responding to immediate emergencies, but never with the leisure to draw up plans for a truly fireproof building. Now it is IQ and race, now criminal genes, now the biological inferiority of women, now the genetic fixity of human nature. All of these deterministic fires need to be doused with the cold water of reason before the entire intellectual neighborhood is in flames. (p. 265)

But in this case, I hope that the fire brigade arrives late. It is time to rethink socialization science critically. The best policy recommendation is not for us to throw out all deterministic notions, or to throw up our hands; it is to try to understand how things really work and what levers for change may exist in them. Theories that do not seek components, that do not simplify and seek abstract principles, and that do not look for determinants and causes are unlikely to leave socialization science more advanced than it is today. When Lewontin et al. (1984) start to propose scientific directions rather than criticize, their prose loses its power and immediacy, and confuses individual differences with universal developmental processes:

> . . . we would insist on the unitary ontological nature of a material world in which it is impossible to partition out the "causes" of the twitching muscle of the frog into x percent social (or holistic) and y percent biological (or reductionist). The biological and the social are neither separable, nor antithetical, nor alternatives, but complementary. All causes of the behavior of organisms, in the temporal sense to which we should restrict the term *cause*, are simultaneously both social and biological, as they are all amenable to analysis at many levels. (p. 282)

But there is much to discover in our genes, as there is much to discover in better models of cultural transmission. Let us hope that in the next generation social scientists keep after the causes of behavior, whatever they may be, and are ready to let discovery guide policy, whatever it may be. The lessons of the monkey Imo and her cousins should not be lost on socialization science.

Notes

[1]Evolutionary models typically work first with selection at a single locus, where gene A is a rival to gene a. This approach is convenient because it simplifies both mathematical and conceptual treatments of evolution. It is assumed that the selective pressure at the hypothesized loci would apply to other loci; hence many genes would finally produce either the "learn from parents only" or "learn from any source" trait, as distributed in a real population.

[2]A difference equation represents the state of a system at later age in terms of its state at the prior age. For more quantitatively minded readers, the equations used in this analysis are given below.

Children of smoking parents:

(1) $P'_{NS_{a+1}} = P'_{NS_a} - (T_1 \times M \times P'_{NS_a})$

(2) $P'_{TR_{a+1}} = P'_{TR_a} + (T_1 \times M \times P'_{NS_a}) - j_1 P'_{TR_a}$

(3) $P'_{RS_{a+1}} = P'_{RS_a} + j_1 P'_{TR_a} - u P'_{RS_a} + v P'_{FS_a}$

(4) $P'_{FS_{a+1}} = .54 - P'_{NS_{a+1}} - P'_{TR_{a+1}} - P'_{RS_{a+1}}$

Children of nonsmoking parents

(5) $P_{NS_{a+1}} = P_{NS_a} - (T_2 \times M \times P_{NS_a})$

(6) $P_{TR_{a+1}} = P_{TR_a} + (T_2 \times M \times P_{NS_a}) - j_2 P_{TR_a}$

(7) $P_{RS_{a+1}} = P_{RS_a} + j_2 P_{TR_a} - u P_{RS_a} + v P_{FS_a}$

(8) $P_{FS_{a+1}} = .46 - P_{NS_{a+1}} - P_{TR_{a+1}} - P_{RS_{a+1}}$

where $M = P'_{TR_a} + P_{TR_a} + P'_{RS_a} + P_{RS_a}$
u = the quitting rate
v = the relapse rate.

[3]A *within-family* correlation of body size and temperament in the Masai would be stronger evidence for the hypothesis. A within-family correlation would show that a child with the more difficult temperament was also heavier than his or her sibling.

[4]The basic computer program has these lines of code:

```
10 dim p(1000)
20 'created May 14, 1992'
30 'hawk.bas'
40 'basic program for evolution of Hawks and Doves'
50 input "starting proportion of hawks";p(i)
60 for i = 1 to 1000
70 t = i + 1
80 b = -.3°p(i) + .6°(1 - p(i)) + 2.0
90 c =.2°(1 - p(i)) + 2.0
100 rb = b/(b + c)
110 rc = c/(b + c)
120 'recursive equation based on differential birth rates'
130 p(t) = p(i) + rb°p(i) - rc°p(i)
140 ct = ct + 1
145 if t > 20 goto 210
150 if t <= 5 then goto 160 else goto 165
160 if ct = 4 then goto 170 else goto 200
165 if ct = 5 goto 170 else goto 200
170 print "generation = ", t, "Hawks = ", p(t)
180 ct = 0
200 next
210 print "stop"
```

[5]Genes predisposing toward homosexual orientation may be an exception (Bailey & Pillard, 1991).

[6]In a sample of black South Africans, where over 20% of the children (68 of 300) had been hospitalized for kwashiorkor, strong correlations existed between parental education and family crowding on the one hand, and both physical and cognitive outcomes in 5- and 6-year-old children on the other. For instance, parental education correlated .48 with height, .41 with head circumference, and .51 with vocabulary (Goduka, Poole, & Aotaki-Phenice, 1992).

References

Bailey, J. M., & Pillard, R. C. (1991). A genetic study of male sexual orientation. *Archives of General Psychiatry, 48*, 1089–1096.

Boyd, R., & Richerson, P. J. (1985). *Culture and the evolutionary process.* Chicago: University of Chicago Press.

Carey, G. (1991). Evolution and path models in human behavioral genetics. *Behavior Genetics, 21*, 433–444.

Carey, G. (1992). Simulated twin data on substance use. *Behavior Genetics, 22*, 193–196.

Carmelli, D., Swan, G. E., Robinette, D., & Fabsitz, R. R. (1990). Heritability of substance use in the NAS-NRC twin registry. *Acta Geneticae Medicae et Gemellologiae, 39*, 91–98.

Cavalli-Sforza, L. L., & Feldman, M. W. (1981). *Cultural transmission and evolution: A quantitative approach.* Princeton, NJ: Princeton University Press.

Cohen, L. E., & Machalek, R. (1988). A general theory of expropriative crime: An evolutionary ecological approach. *American Journal of Sociology, 94*, 465–501.

Dawkins, R. (1989). *The selfish gene* (2nd ed.). Oxford: Oxford University Press.

deVries, M. W. (1984). Temperament and infant mortality among the Masai of East Africa. *American Journal of Psychiatry, 141*, 1189–1194.

Diamond, J. (1990). A pox upon our genes. *Natural History, 2*, 26–30.

Diamond, J. (1992). *The third chimpanzee: The evolution and future of the human animal.* New York: HarperCollins.

Draper, P. (1989). African marriage systems: Perspectives from evolutionary ecology. *Ethology and Sociobiology, 10*, 145–169.

Durham, W. H. (1991). *Coevolution: Genes, culture, and human diversity.* Stanford, CA: Stanford University Press.

Eysenck, H. J. (1980). *The causes and effects of smoking.* London: M. T. Smith.

Ferrence, R. G. (1989). *Deadly fashion: The rise and fall of cigarette smoking in North America.* New York: Garland.

Firebaugh, G. (1992). Where does social change come from? Estimating the relative contributions of individual change and population turnover. *Population Research and Policy Review, 11*, 1–20.

Goduka, I. N., Poole, D. A., & Aotaki-Phenice, L. (1992). A comparative study of black South African children from three different contexts. *Child Development, 63*, 509–525.

Halseyk, W. D., & Johnson, B. (1990). *Collier's encyclopedia* (vol. 20). New York: Macmillan.

Kummer, H. (1971). *Primate societies: Group techniques of ecological adaptation*. Chicago: Aldine.

Lewis, A. M. (1992). APA, mental health community react to Goodwin's resignation. *Psychological Science Agenda, 5,* 1.

Lewontin, R. C., Rose, S., & Kamin, L. J. (1984). *Not in our genes: Biology, ideology, and human nature*. New York: Pantheon.

Loeber, R. (1991). Antisocial behavior: More enduring than changeable? *Journal of the American Academy of Child and Adolescent Psychiatry, 30,* 393–397.

Lumsden, C. J., & Wilson, E. O. (1983). *Promethean fire: Reflections on the origin of mind*. Cambridge, MA: Harvard University Press.

Maynard-Smith, J. (1982). *Evolution and the theory of games*. Cambridge, England: Cambridge University Press.

Perry, D. G., & Bussey, K. (1979). The social learning theory of sex differences: Imitation is alive and well. *Journal of Personality and Social Psychology, 37,* 1699–1712.

Robins, L. N. (1966). *Deviant children grown up: A sociological and psychiatric study of sociopathic personality*. Baltimore: Williams & Wilkins.

Rowe, D. C., Chassin, L., Presson, C. C., Edwards, D., & Sherman, S. J. (1992). An "epidemic" model of adolescent cigarette smoking. *Journal of Applied Social Psychology, 22,* 261–285.

Rowe, D. C., & Osgood, D. W. (1984). Sociological theories of delinquency and heredity: A reconsideration. *American Sociological Review, 49,* 526–540.

Rowe, D. C., & Rodgers, J. L. (1991a). An "epidemic" model of adolescent sexual intercourse: Applications to national survey data. *Journal of Biosocial Science, 23,* 211–219.

Rowe, D. C., & Rodgers, J. L. (1991b). Adolescent smoking and drinking: Are they "epidemics"? *Journal of Studies on Alcohol, 52,* 110–117.

Scarr, S. (1992). Developmental theories for the 1990s: Development and individual differences. *Developmental Psychology, 63,* 1–19.

Swan, G. E., Carmelli, D., Rosenman, R. H., Fabsitz, R. H., & Christian, J. C. (1990). Smoking and alcohol consumption in adult male twins: Genetic heritability and shared environmental influences. *Journal of Substance Abuse, 2,* 39–50.

Tooby, J. (1982). Pathogens, polymorphism, and the evolution of sex. *Journal of Theoretical Biology, 97,* 557–576.

Tooby, J., & Cosmides, L. (1990). On the universality of human nature and the uniqueness of the individual: The role of genetics and adaptation. *Journal of Personality, 58,* 17–67.

Wilson, E. O. (1975). *Sociobiology: The new synthesis*. Cambridge, MA: Belknap Press.

INDEX